The Making of the

The Making of the 20th Century

Series Editor: GEOFFREY WARNER

David Armstrong, Lorna Lloyd and John Redmond, *From Versailles to Maastricht: International Organisation in the Twentieth Century*
S. R. Ashton, *In Search of Détente:
The Politics of East–West Relations Since 1945*
V. R. Berghahn, *Germany and the Approach of War in 1914* (second edition)
Raymond F. Betts, *France and Decolonisation 1900–1960*
John Darwin, *Britain and Decolonisation:
The Retreat from Empire in the Post-War World*
John F. V. Keiger, *France and the Origins of the First World War*
Dominic Lieven, *Russia and the Origins of the First World War*
Sally Marks, *The Illusion of Peace: International Relations in Europe 1918–1933*
Philip Morgan, *Italian Fascism 1919–1945*
A. J. Nicholls, *Weimar and the Rise of Hitler* (third edition)
R. A. C. Parker, *Chamberlain and Appeasement: British Policy
and the Coming of the Second World War*
Geoffrey Roberts, *The Soviet Union and the Origins of the Second World War*
Alan Sharp, *The Versailles Settlement: Peacemaking in Paris, 1919*
Zara Steiner, *Britain and the Origins of the First World War*
Samuel R. Williamson, *Austria-Hungary and the Origins of the First World War*

FORTHCOMING TITLES

Saki Dockrill, *Japan and the Origins of the Second World War*
J. E. Spence, *South Africa in International Society*
Glyn Stone, *Great Powers and the Iberian Peninsular 1931–1941*
Jonathan Wright, *Germany and the Origins of the Second World War*
R. Young, *France and the Origins of the Second World War*

From Versailles to Maastricht
International Organisation in the Twentieth Century

David Armstrong, Lorna Lloyd and John Redmond

Chapters 1 and 2 were first published in David Armstrong's
The Rise of the International Organisation: A Short History, published
by Macmillan in 1982.

First published 1996 by
MACMILLAN PRESS LTD
Houndmills, Basingstoke, Hampshire RG21 6XS
and London
Companies and representatives
throughout the world

ISBN 0–333–62034–8 hardcover
ISBN 0–333–62035–6 paperback

A catalogue record for this book is available
from the British Library

10   9   8   7   6   5   4   3   2   1
05 04 03 02 01 00 99 98 97 96

Printed in Hong Kong

Contents

Preface

This book is a completely revised, expanded and updated version of David Armstrong's *The Rise of the International Organisation: A Short History* (Macmillan, 1982). That book was used as a basic framework by the authors, but the three chapters on the United Nations contributed by Lorna Lloyd and the three chapters on the European Union by John Redmond represent not just a threefold expansion of the original two chapters (one on each organisation) in Armstrong's book but a complete rewriting of those chapters. John Redmond was also primarily responsible for the section in chapter 9 on ASEAN, while David Armstrong contributed the remainder of the book. The result, we hope, is a historical overview of the most important international organisations of the twentieth century that provides enough factual detail and analytical depth for it to be of value not just to students of the subject but to the general reader seeking to understand one of the most significant and interesting developments of twentieth-century international relations.

The Rise of the International Organisation appeared at a time of general loss of faith in international organisations, particularly the United Nations and the European Community. The one seemed to have become less and less relevant to the resolution of international issues which were certainly no less serious. The other appeared becalmed in the all too familiar waters of conflicting national interests and the jealous guardianship by states of their sovereignty. The contrast with the situation thirteen years later is remarkable. The states of the European Union (whose name change is itself a highly significant symbolic act), having already achieved a greater degree of integration than most would have thought likely in 1992, are contemplating an extraordinary series of further moves towards possible federalism over the next five years. The United Nations was given a new lease of life by the end of the Cold War, and, although still facing serious difficulties (not least of finance), certainly has a more secure and substantial role in international affairs than

vii

seemed possible at the start of the 1980s. Part of the purpose of this book is to explain how and why such dramatic changes were able to occur.

The book is based in part upon courses taught by the three authors at the Universities of Birmingham and Keele, and we should like to take this opportunity to thank past and present students for their many helpful comments. We also wish to thank our colleagues at those universities and elsewhere for freely dispensing of their time and expertise, although we naturally accept full responsibility for any errors of fact and judgement. Thanks are also due to Geoffrey Warner, General Editor of the Macmillan series on The Making of the Twentieth Century, to Lord Beloff and most of all to Maggie Armstrong, Alan James and Carol Redmond.

Abbreviations

ACP	African, Caribbean and Pacific
AEC	African Economic Community (1991–)
ALADI	Latin American Integration Association, formerly LAFTA (1990–)
ASEAN	Association of South East Asian Nations (1967–)
CACM	Central American Common Market (1960–)
CAP	Common Agricultural Policy
CARICOM	Caribbean Community formerly CARIFTA (1975–)
CARIFTA	Caribbean Free Trade Area (1968–75)
CFP	Common Fisheries Policy
CFSP	Common Foreign and Security Policy
CSCE	Conference on Security and Cooperation in Europe (1975–94)
DOMREP	Mission of the Representative of the Secretary-General in the Dominican Republic (1965–6)
EAEC	(Euratom) The European Atomic Energy Agency
EAI	Enterprise for the Americas Initiative
ECCM	Eastern Caribbean Common Market (1968–)
ECOWAS	Economic Community of West African States (1975–)
ECOSOC	United Nations Economic and Social Council (1945–)
ECSC	European Coal and Steel Community (1951–)
ECU	European Currency Unit
EDC	European Defence Community (1952)
EEA	European Economic Area
EEC	European Economic Community (1957–)
EFTA	European Free Trade Association (1959–)
EMS	European Monetary System
EMU	European Monetary Union

EPC	European Political Cooperation
ERDF	European Regional Development Fund
ERM	Exchange Rate Mechanism
EU	European Union
FAO	Food and Agriculture Organisation (1945–)
GATT	General Agreement on Tariffs and Trade (1947–)
IAEA	International Atomic Energy Agency (1957–)
IBRD	International Bank for Reconstruction and Development (World Bank) (1946/7–)
ICAO	International Civil Aviation Organisation (1947–)
ICJ	International Court of Justice (1945–)
IDA	International Development Association (1960–)
IFAD	International Fund for Agricultural Development (1977–)
IGC	Inter-Governmental Conference
ILO	International Labour Organisation (1920–)
IMF	International Monetary Fund (1944–)
IMO	International Maritime Organisation (1958–)
IPDC	International Programme for the Development of Communication
ISA	International Seabed Authority
ITO	International Trade Organisation
ITU	International Telecommunication Union (1865–)
LAFTA	Latin American Free Trade Association (1960–90)
MINSURO	UN Mission for the Referendum in Western Sahara (1991–)
NAFTA	North American Free Trade Area (1992–)
NGO	Non-Governmental Organisation
NIEO	New International Economic Order
NWICO	New World Information and Communications Order
OAS	Organisation of American States (1948–)
OAU	Organisation of African Unity (1963–)
ODECA	Organisation of Central American States (1951–)
OECD	Organisation of Economic Cooperation and Development
OEEC	Organisation for European Economic Cooperation
ONUC	*Opération des Nations Unies au Congo* (UN operation in the Congo) (1960–4)
ONUCA	UN Observer Group in Central America (1989–92)

ONUMOZ	UN Operation in Mozambique (1992–)
ONUSAL	UN Observer Mission in El Salvador (1991–)
OPEC	Organisation of Petroleum Exporting Countries
OSCE	Organisation for Security and Cooperation in Europe (1995–)
PCIJ	Permanent Court of International Justice (1922–46)
P5	Permanent members of the Security Council
PRC	People's Republic of China
TEU	Treaty of European Union
SEA	Single European Act
SEM	Single European Market
SMP	Single Market Programme
UNAMIC	UN Advance Mission in Cambodia (1991–2)
UNAMIR	UN Assistance Mission for Rwanda (1993–)
UNASOG	UN Aouzou Strip Observer Group
UNAVEM I	First UN Angola Verification Mission (1989–91)
UNAVEM II	Second UN Angola Verification Mission (1991–)
UNCDF	UN Capital Development Fund
UNCLOS	United Nations Conference on the Law of the Sea
UNCTAD	United Nations Conference on Trade and Development (1964–)
UNDOF	UN Disengagement Observer Force (in Syria) (1974–)
UNDP	UN Development Programme
UNEP	UN Environment Programme
UNESCO	UN Educational, Scientific and Cultural Organisation (1945–)
UNEF I	First UN Emergency Force (in Egypt) (1956–67)
UNEF II	Second UN Emergency Force (between Israel and Egypt) (1973–9)
UNFICYP	UN Peacekeeping Force in Cyprus (1964–)
UNFPA	UN Fund for Population Activities
UNGOMAP	UN Good Offices Mission in Afghanistan and Pakistan (1988–90)
UNHCR	UN High Commissioner for Refugees
UNICEF	UN Children's Fund
UNIDO	UN Industrial Development Organisation (1966–) (Became specialised agency 1986)
UNIFIL	UN Interim Force in Lebanon (1978–)

UNIIMOG	UN Iran–Iraq Military Observer Group (1988–91)
UNIKOM	UN Iraq–Kuwait Observation Mission (1991–)
UNIPOM	UN India–Pakistan Observation Mission (1965–6)
UNITAR	UN Institute for Training and Research (1966–)
UNMIH	UN Mission in Haiti (1993–)
UNMOGIP	UN Military Observer Group in India and Pakistan (1949–)
UNOGIL	UN Observation Group in Lebanon (1958)
UNOMIG	UN Observer Mission in Georgia (1993–)
UNOMUR	UN Observer Mission in Uganda Rwanda (1993–)
UNOSOM I	First UN Operation in Somalia (1992–3)
UNOSOM II	Second UN Operation in Somalia (1993–)
UNPREDEP	UN Preventive Deployment Force
UNPROFOR	UN Protection Force in the former Yugoslavia (1992–)
UNSCOB	UN Special Committee on the Balkans (1947–52)
UNSF	UN Security Force in West New Guinea (West Irian) (1962–3)
UNTAC	UN Transitional Authority in Cambodia (1991–2)
UNTAG	UN Transition Assistance Group (in Namibia) (1989–90)
UNTEA	UN Temporary Executive Authority (in West New Guinea/West Irian) (1962–3)
UNTSO	UN Truce Supervision Organisation (in Palestine) (1948–)
UNYOM	UN Yemen Observation Mission (1963–4)
UPU	Universal Postal Union (1874–)
WEU	Western European Union
WFC	World Food Council
WFP	World Food Programme
WHO	World Health Organisation (1948–)
WIPO	World Intellectual Property Organisation (1970–) (Became specialised agency 1974)
WMO	World Meteorological Organisation (1950–) (Successor to International Meteorological Organisation, formed 1873)
WTO	World Trade Organisation

Introduction

During 1995 two new international organisations came into being: the Organisation on Security and Cooperation in Europe (OSCE, formerly the Conference on Security and Cooperation in Europe: CSCE) and the World Trade Organisation (formerly the General Agreement on Tariffs and Trade: GATT). Hence, 50 years after the creation of the United Nations, states still saw advantages in the further creation and development of international institutions. This is despite the fact that most of the major organisations have been as much targets of criticism, and even derision, as praise.

In the case of the United Nations, such criticism was heard almost from its inception in 1946, sometimes in remarkably similar terms to attacks on the UN 30 or 40 years later. For example, in 1949 George Kennan wrote a characteristically perceptive memorandum considering the UN from the perspective of traditional diplomacy.[1] He began by pointing to the lack of recognition given to inequalities of size between states in the General Assembly and the dubious validity of some states' claim to equal sovereign status, concluding that the Assembly merely represented 'a fortuitous collection of social entities which happen at this stage in human history to enjoy a wide degree of acceptance as independent states'. He went on to express doubts about the role of the Assembly as a 'new theatre of diplomatic operations':

> Whereas in traditional diplomatic practice, the opinions of interested states were consulted and given recognition in slow, deliberate processes which left plenty of time for reflection and plenty of room for flexibility in the preparation of decisions, here decisions, when they come, are instantaneous and final and represent the voting attitudes taken at the crucial moment by the countries concerned. Everything is staked, for better or worse, on that particular moment. Such measures of precaution as may be taken in advance to assure a favourable outcome on a particular

1

issue must proceed through a highly complex system of contact with the delegates of dozens of other countries, most of them far removed, administratively and geographically, from their home office.[2]

He singled out for special criticism the general declaratory resolutions that were already becoming popular in the General Assembly:

There is present in the United Nations milieu an illusion that the postures assumed by the Assembly in relation to various bodies of verbiage . . . are somehow the decisive events in world affairs. This turns the work of the Assembly, which should be addressed to real things, into a sort of parliamentary shadow boxing: a competition in the striking of attitudes in which the stance is taken for the deed, and the realities are inferred rather than experienced.[3]

These sentiments, it should be noted, were being expressed long before the arrival in the UN of large numbers of Third World states, the usual culprits to be nominated whenever charges are raised about the UN's alleged departure from 'reality'. The essential problem for the UN, and to a lesser extent other international organisations, is less their own lack of correspondence with 'reality' than the flight of fancy that often seems to grip observers of such institutions. Because they are invariably based on constitutional documents containing ambitious declarations of idealistic principles as their preamble, the UN and other organisations are often judged against the standards set by those principles rather than the more pragmatic criteria that are normally applied to domestic politics. Thus, for example, widespread violations of the criminal code inside states are not generally thought of as signifying the essential worthlessness of domestic laws, courts, police forces and the other paraphernalia of any legal system. Yet the relatively infrequent violations of international law are often seen in the public mind as denoting the meaninglessness of international law as such. The failure of international society to deal with crises in Bosnia or Somalia is similarly seen as evidence of the fundamental weakness of the European Union or the UN, as if a forceful act of will by the organisations would suffice to resolve the tragic conflicts in those states. The more difficult questions, such as which countries' soldiers are to risk their lives in these crises, how many would be needed, how long would they have to stay, and who is to pay for them, amongst other issues, are seldom addressed. Some of the strongest criticisms of the UN have been voiced in Washington, a city with one of the highest murder rates in the world, notwithstanding the existence of a powerful well-armed police force, operating in its own sovereign territory, with the full backing of the lawful authorities of that territory, and the overwhelming majority of public opinion on its side: conditions that would never apply in any international intervention into any internal conflict.

The central fact about international society is that, in most important respects, we still live in a world that is shaped, constrained and impelled by the various ramifications of state sovereignty. Nor does this does simply mean that international organisations can do little to limit the damage caused by wilful states. It should not be forgotten that they themselves are the creatures and instruments of states. They exist because states find them useful, and utility is not always a matter of serving some idealistic or even merely functional purpose: it may also consist of more cynical political ends. For example, states pressed by their publics to 'do something about' some intractable international situation, can pass the buck by referring the matter to the United Nations. Other political purposes have always been in evidence. Although the UN was sold to the American public in idealistic terms, American officials were privately beginning to see it as an important part of US strategy against the Soviet Union from an early stage in the developing Cold War atmosphere. Even before the first General Assembly opened in London on 10 January 1946, a State Department memorandum had hinted at the possibility of using the UN in this way.[4] The bluntest and perhaps most cynical statement of the policy of employing the UN as part of a first, diplomatic phase of resisting Soviet expansion came in a State Department memorandum on 1 April 1946:

The Charter of the United Nations affords the best and most unassailable means through which the US can implement its opposition to Soviet physical expansion. It not only offers the basis upon which the greatest degrees of popular support can be obtained in the US but it will also ensure the support and even assistance of other members of the United Nations. If, as may occur, the United Nations breaks down under the test of opposition to Soviet aggression it will have served the purpose of clarifying the issues before American and world opinion and thus make easier whatever step may be required by the US and other like minded nations in the face of a new threat of world aggression.[5]

Not all of the purposes performed on behalf of states by international organisations are as coldly calculating as this. The Concert of Europe (in reality more an informal consultative arrangement than an international organisation in the sense employed here) was set up in 1814 because states accepted that the traditional *laissez-faire* system of the balance of power was inadequate to provide the international stability they all desired without some degree of management by the great powers. Ever since that time, international order has been seen to depend, at least in part, upon the existence of institutions charged with upholding order. In less controversial or intractable areas than peace and security or economic integration, large numbers of international organisations have been created by states simply because that appeared to be the most effective way of regulating some everyday international activity, such as postal services or telecommunications.

International organisations may also have an impact upon states' conduct of their affairs in ways that states themselves might not have foreseen or intended when they established the organisations. It is important to avoid exaggerating the significance of this factor, if only because in the study of international organisations a degree of scepticism may in the long run provide a sounder perspective, even for those anxious to see progress in international affairs, than an overly optimistic idealisation of their role. Nonetheless, with the proviso that the impact of norms, rules and institutions upon the behaviour and motivation of states is amongst the most complex areas in the theory and analysis of international relations, it is possible to make some tentative generalisations about the influence of international organisations in this context.

First, international organisations affect the habitual conduct of states. For example, their existence needs to be taken account of in the bureaucratic routines through which the modern state transacts its business. At a more substantive level, organisations help to prompt states to seek cooperative or multilateral solutions to their problems. The great growth of UN sponsored international conferences on subjects as diverse as terrorism, arms control, drugs, human rights, the law of the sea and the environment all bear witness to this. Such international habits also form part of the vast array of structures, processes and 'best practices' into which new states are socialised on their entry into international society. Although nothing *forces* states to observe international 'good habits', their general acceptance means that departure from them becomes increasingly the exception, and something that needs special justification.

Secondly, international organisations, particularly the UN, play a key role in the processes through which international society collectively legitimates both international actors and certain kinds of international acts. Membership of the UN is a keenly sought objective of new states, but the UN is also seen as conferring a kind of international legitimacy on certain non-state actors to whom it grants various rights of access. The most notable case in this respect is the Palestine Liberation Organisation, but numerous non-governmental organisations (NGOs) cherish the legitimacy that is accorded them by virtue of Article 71 of the UN Charter, granting them consultant status with the UN Economic and Social Council. Another indication of legitimacy came in 1977, when a committee of the International Court of Justice suggested that NGOs should be enabled to ask the court for advisory opinions relating to human rights and also to submit memoranda to the Court.[6] Finally, since the end of the Cold War made the UN Security Council less of an arena of confrontation between the superpowers, it is notable that the United States has been increasingly concerned to win Security Council backing for what in essence have been unilateral American acts. For example, the United States sought Security Council support for its intervention in Haiti in 1994, unlike the not dissimilar case of its intervention in Panama in 1989. Hence, even the most powerful state in the world saw some value in UN legitimation of its policies, which in turn strengthened the underlying principle that the UN actually had the capacity to confer such legitimation.

Finally, the UN and other organisations have played a role in establishing, upholding and developing the limited normative basis that underpins international affairs. Until relatively recently, the only norms that really counted in international relations were those that defined and defended state sovereignty, including such principles as non-intervention in states' internal affairs. The UN Charter confirmed sovereignty and its attendant rights as the cornerstones of international society. But the Charter paid much more attention than its predecessor, the Covenant of the League of Nations, to other norms, such as human rights, economic and social development and decolonisation. All of these, strictly speaking, belonged to the domestic jurisdiction of states, which had traditionally been excluded from what was regarded as the rightful concern of the international community. In recent years, especially since the end of the Cold War, international organisations have laid increasing stress on norms relating to the internal governance of states, such as human rights and democracy. Of course, affirming normative principles and making them play an active part in international relations are two quite separate things, but constant repetition of such principles in international organisations is not without effect. For example, denunciation of South African apartheid in many UN organs helped to establish the principle that racism was internationally unacceptable and, over time, to wear down resistance to change in South Africa itself.

1 The Origins of the League of Nations

The creation of the League of Nations was an extraordinary event. Not only had there been nothing like it before, but there was very little in the system of international relations which existed in 1914 or in the previous history of diplomacy to suggest its possibility. The guiding principle of all states in their relations with each other was the protection of their national sovereignty, and any development that might interfere with this, even in a very small way, had always been resisted. International cooperation in the most important area of peace and security had, perhaps inevitably, been limited and temporary, but even in much less contentious matters, such as setting up an efficient international postal system, or deciding upon rules to govern the laying down of marine cables, or regulating the spread of epidemic diseases by international sanitary conventions, progress had taken many years. In each case this was because one or more states had opposed change in the belief that its sovereignty might be infringed or that it might lose some narrow national advantage. Even so derisory an issue as an attempt to determine internationally agreed safety standards in the manufacture of matches had been vigorously resisted by Britain on the latter grounds. Yet a few years after this episode Britain was one of the principal founders of the League: a permanent international organisation with wide-ranging responsibilities.

The League, therefore, was not simply the culmination of a long evolutionary process but was also in some respects a radical departure from past practice, owing as much to the immediate circumstances of its creation as to the previous history of international organisation. This chapter is devoted to a detailed discussion of the origins of the League but for the sake of clarity it will be useful first to consider briefly the relative importance of the various factors which contributed something to the League's genesis.

In certain limited respects the League may be seen as the logical outcome of developments in international cooperation in the nineteenth century. After the defeat of Napoleon in 1815 the European powers had formed the habit of consulting regularly with each other in the system known as the Concert of Europe. The Concert system also signified an acceptance of the principle that the great powers had some special responsibility for the management of international affairs and the maintenance of international order. Secondly, the enormous growth in the quantity and range of interaction between states in the nineteenth century created a correspondingly greater need for some regulation of those relations, or in other words for a more developed international legal system. States increasingly resorted to legal or quasi-legal means of resolving their minor disputes and the nineteenth century witnessed a notable growth in the practice of submitting such disputes to arbitration tribunals. In some cases permanent international institutions were established to regulate certain areas of international life. Two of the primary purposes of the League were to give international law a more central role in international relations and to institutionalise the Concert of Europe's principles of great power consultation and collective responsibility for international order, so to that extent there were important antecedents to the League in the nineteenth century. But some more immediate considerations were of at least equal significance.

The first of these was the impact of the 1914–18 war. This gave rise to a widespread discontent with international relations in their present form and to demands for a new collective security system which would outlaw aggression. When the American President, Woodrow Wilson, publicly supported the general principle of reforming the international system in May 1916, he lent credibility to the various unofficial schemes for a League of Nations which meant that the major European states were obliged to take the idea more seriously. The Russian revolution of 1917 provided an additional reason for the European powers to seek to change the international order since this was the most appropriate means of countering the adverse propaganda effects of the Bolshevik demands for an end to the old diplomacy. Draft constitutions for a League of Nations appeared from several official quarters during 1918, with discussions during the peace conference of 1919 based on a joint Anglo-American draft.

But the League also had many important features whose true origin is to be discovered in the period of intensive inter-allied diplomacy just before and during the peace conference: diplomacy that was guided in the main by a variety of short-term considerations. This meant that the League which was eventually decided upon was not in all respects a carefully constructed edifice, built upon past experience and the outcome of orderly deliberations. Winston Churchill wrote of the Paris Peace Conference as a whole: 'Decisions were taken not as the result of systematised study and discussion but only when some individual topic reached a condition of crisis. Throughout there was no considered order of priority, no thought-out plan of descending from the general to the particular'.[1] It could hardly be expected that the meetings of the League of Nations Commission, which drafted the Covenant of the League, alone remained immune from the effects of this atmosphere.

The development of international organisations before 1919

The profound changes in the political, economic and social landscape during the nineteenth and early twentieth centuries were instrumental both in establishing a favourable climate for the proliferation of international organisations and in determining their agenda. This is most obvious in the fields of trade and international communications. The massive increase in production sparked off by the Industrial Revolution led to an equally heavy growth in trade; with the coming of steam this trade was carried on at ever-faster rates on land and sea. As more and more of the globe was penetrated by European imperialism, so a highly complex worldwide economic network emerged. This influenced the growth of international institutions in four distinct ways. Firstly, the greater number of international transactions increased the risk of war arising out of some trivial conflict. This was one factor behind the growing tendency during the nineteenth century for states to accept international arbitration of various types of disputes where, as the standard formula ran, 'neither honour nor vital interests' were involved.[2] Secondly, agreed regulations and common standards had to be determined for such purposes as patenting inventions, classifying goods for customs duties and deciding exchange rates between currencies. What were then termed 'public international unions' were established to deal with such matters, and by the end of the nineteenth century the movement towards international standardisation had begun in less technical and more obviously political fields, such as the protection of workers and children. Thirdly, the traditional insistence by states upon a rigid interpretation of their sovereign rights became an increasingly serious barrier to the efficient conduct of international business. The classic illustration of this concerned the transmission of postal items across frontiers. Before the establishment of the General Postal Union in 1875 and its successor, the Universal Postal Union in 1878, international postal communication was governed by numerous bilateral treaties rather than by a single convention. The objective of each state was to ensure that the balance of financial advantage deriving from these treaties was in its favour, which led to extremely high foreign postage rates being charged by all. As charges were levied at each frontier, the cost of sending a postal item from one country to another varied according to the route taken, with a 1/2 oz letter from the United States to Australia costing anything from 5 cents to $1.02.[3] Fourthly, the economies of the major powers were becoming increasingly interdependent, which provided them with certain mutual interests to set against their many rivalries.[4] The nineteenth century saw the first attempts to translate this interdependence into institutional form through the establishment of international commissions to regulate the trade of specific commodities, such as sugar.[5] Another effect of interdependence was that it helped to internationalise issues – to turn what would once have been purely national questions into matters of general concern. The control of disease was one such area, in which several international unions had been set up by the end of the century. The first of these, in 1838, was the Conseil Supérieur de Santé at Constantinople, whose aim was to prevent the introduction of cholera into Turkey. This was followed by sanitary councils in Tangier, Teheran, Alexandria and elsewhere and eventually by the important Sanitary Convention of 1903 and the establishment of the International Office of Public Hygiene in 1907.[6]

None of these landmarks in the history of international organisation had an untroubled birth, nor did they hint at any prospect of more ambitious undertakings being successful. France, fearing possible financial losses, had delayed the formation of the postal union; Britain had resisted for many years any attempt to sign a sanitary convention on the grounds that this might harm its maritime interests. The sanitary councils had themselves been arenas for the conflicts of great power interests that went on throughout the nineteenth century.

The continuing influence of national rivalries may be illustrated further by two of the most acclaimed events of the turn of the century: the Hague Conferences of 1899 and 1907. These originated from a proposal for a disarmament conference made by Tsar Nicholas II and marked the high point in the history of international arbitration. They were also the most widely attended conferences to date, with delegates from Europe, North and South America and Asia, their popularity being a clear response to the interdependence that many now felt to be a crucial factor in international relations. As the President of the first Conference put it: 'We perceive that there is a community of material and moral interests between nations, which is constantly increasing. . . . If a nation wished to remain isolated it could not . . . It is part of a single organism.'[7] The most important implication of this interdependence was, he felt, that 'when a dispute arises between two or more nations, the others, without being directly involved, are seriously affected'. This in turn meant that further machinery for states to submit their disputes for mediation, conciliation or arbitration needed to be developed.[8]

Although many delegates echoed these sentiments, they found it more difficult to agree upon the concrete obligations their states would have to accept if these principles were to be given substance. The discussions at the Hague Conferences consisted of a curious amalgam of idealistic statements of purpose and careful disavowals by everyone that they were undertaking any binding commitments. Hence the specific achievements of the first Conference were few: a so-called Permanent Court of Arbitration[9] and some provision for the use of International Commissions of Inquiry in certain disputes. The second Conference revised the conventions that had been agreed by the first and added ten new ones. Somewhat ominously these mostly concerned the laws of war. No significant progress was made in the area of disarmament – the original occasion of the Conferences.

The Hague agreements were hailed at the time as a new beginning in international relations but they achieved little, and when the League of Nations was being constructed at the Paris Peace Conference, the Hague experience was generally ignored. Concerned about this, Léon Bourgeois, the French delegate to the Paris

Commission responsible for drafting the Covenant, who had played a notable part at The Hague, made several attempts to link the Covenant to the work of the Hague Conferences. In this he was supported only by the Portuguese delegate, who made a formal declaration regretting that the League of Nations Commission was not attempting to advance the work of the Hague Conferences in arbitration. All such pressure was resisted by the British and Americans, who argued that the League needed to be free from any association with previous ventures.[10] The only concession made in the Covenant to the sensibilities of Léon Bourgeois was what has been described as an 'afterthought' in the form of a reference in Article 13 stating that certain disputes might be suitable for arbitration.[11]

The only nineteenth-century international institution to have a directly important influence on the League of Nations Covenant was the Concert of Europe: the informal arrangement whereby the European powers consulted together at times of crisis. The Concert, originating in the post-Napoleonic settlement, had at first fluctuated between the opposing concepts of the Tsar and Metternich, on the one hand, that the Concert should be a kind of international government with wide powers of intervention in the domestic affairs of states, and Castlereagh and Canning, on the other hand, who upheld 'all correct notions of internal sovereign authority'.[12] Later it settled down into a loose association of major powers with the primary aim of preventing the Eastern Question from getting out of hand and with a general concern to uphold international order when this did not conflict unduly with their separate national interests. In the 40 years up to 1914 the Concert system decreased in significance until its last meeting to consider the Albanian situation in 1913, when, in the opinion of one of the participants, it still had a useful, albeit very modest role to play:

> We had not settled anything, not even all the details of the Albanian boundaries; but we had served a useful purpose. We had been something to which point after point could be referred; we had been a means of keeping all the six powers in direct and friendly contact. The mere fact that we were in existence and that we should have to be broken up before peace was broken, was in itself an appreciable barrier against war. We were a means of gaining time, and the longer we remained in being the more re-

luctance was there for us to disperse. The Governments concerned got used to us and to the habit of making us useful.[13]

Considerations of this kind played a part in the deliberations at the
Paris Peace Conference, while the underlying idea of the Concert –
that the great powers possessed distinctive rights and duties with
regard to the management of international relations – was embodied in the League Council, which was seen, at least by the great
powers, as an institutionalised Concert.

However the League probably owed less to the Concert itself
than it did to the breakdown of the balance of power which had
underpinned the Concert until the emergence of modern Germany. This, together with the rise to world power of a United States
which had long distrusted traditional European diplomacy, and
with the new social pressures that had been building up during the
nineteenth century and which culminated in the Russian Revolution, contributed significantly to the political climate in Paris in
1919.

The League idea and the role of Woodrow Wilson

Schemes to replace the endemic anarchy of international relations
by a system designed to ensure peace, security and order were not
unique to this century, but the unparalleled destruction of the First
World War meant that for the first time they had to be taken seriously by the practitioners as well as the theorists of politics. Not only
was there a popular clamour for some new means of controlling
international violence which democratically elected statesmen
could hardly ignore, but the old international order had been decisively swept away, and its only successors with clear-cut answers to
everything were Lenin's Bolsheviks, who threatened to overthrow
the domestic orders as well. The Western powers at Paris were well
aware of this, and the first problem that faced them was how to
translate into concrete form a bewildering range of ideas as to what
the League should be, while ensuring that the resulting organisation offered a viable reformist alternative to the revolutionary vision
of the Bolsheviks.

The term 'League of Nations' probably originated with Léon
Bourgeois' book, *La Société des Nations*, published in 1908.[14]

Bourgeois was one of a number of leading figures from several countries who, having advocated a new system for the management of international relations before the war, became active in popular movements to that end during it. In the United States these included two former Presidents, Roosevelt and Taft, who called for what would today be termed a collective security system: some arrangement whereby aggressors would incur automatic economic and military sanctions imposed by the whole international community.[15] Taft was one of the sponsors in June 1915 of the League to Enforce Peace, a pressure group with the objective of promoting a League of Nations based on the twin principles of collective security and a greatly enhanced status for international law.[16] Similar groups existed in Britain, France and elsewhere, most of them basing their programmes on an extension of the work of the Hague Conferences in the field of arbitration.[17]

The impact of these groups was strictly limited. They helped to focus public opinion upon the idea of a new international order and they popularised the name 'League of Nations', but the League that was eventually created owed little of substance to their efforts. The first detailed British government draft of a possible League, the Phillmore Report, accepted some of their underlying ideas but dismissed as 'impracticable' their specific provisions.[18] Similar sentiments were more forcefully expressed by such hardened realists as Lloyd George and Clemenceau. More significantly, President Woodrow Wilson, regarded by many as the 'father' of the League, refused to associate himself with any of the unofficial schemes, privately referring to the members of organisations like the League to Enforce Peace as 'woolgatherers'.[19]

Wilson's role in the genesis of the League is a complex one which needs elucidating in some detail. It is clear that he was convinced from an early stage that a new international system was required and that he saw in this the means of obtaining both personal glory and power and prestige for his country. Later, in common with other statesmen, he came to pin a variety of additional aspirations upon the League, including resisting the Bolshevik threat, underwriting the peace treaties, democratising the world, establishing a new economic order (with a pre-eminent role for the United States) and ending the colonial system. However he had few, if any, well-defined ideas as to the actual form of the new organisation which was to bring about this diplomatic revolution.

Even before the war, Wilson had shown some interest in novel means of securing peace. His first Secretary of State, Bryan, had promoted a series of bilateral treaties whose principal feature was an agreement that, should a dispute arise, the states involved would observe a moratorium of one year to permit investigation and attempts at arbitration before resorting to war.[20] This unlikely notion that a 'cooling-off' period might lower temperatures sufficiently to prevent war was to reappear as Article 12 of the Covenant. A more significant early influence was an abortive attempt by Wilson and his close adviser, Colonel House, to sponsor a Pan-American Treaty in which an important element would be an article committing all parties to 'a common and mutual guarantee of territorial integrity and of political independence under republican forms of government'.[21] A similar wording was to be used in the last of Wilson's famous Fourteen Points on the peace settlement in January 1918.[22] House later claimed that he had all along seen this treaty as a model for a future European settlement.[23] Significantly, in November 1918, when the Director of the Inquiry (Wilson's group of researchers and advisers on the peace settlement) was searching for relevant information, he asked Secretary of State Lansing for a copy of the treaty, offering revealingly to 'use it as a possible form of general international agreement without indicating that it was in contemplation an agreement for this hemisphere'.[24]

The idea of mutual guarantees of independence and territorial integrity appeared in Wilson's first public endorsement of the concept of a League of Nations on 27 May 1916, when he advocated

> a universal association of the nations to maintain the inviolate security of the highway of the seas for the common good and unhindered use of all the nations of the world, and to prevent any war begun either contrary to treaty covenants or without warning and full submission of the causes to the opinion of the world – a virtual guarantee of territorial integrity and political independence.[25]

The reference here to a possible League role in maintaining freedom of the seas was not likely to gain the support of the British government, given its traditional insistence upon naval hegemony. Anglo-American clashes over the purpose of the League were also foreshadowed in an Inquiry memorandum in December 1917, which called for a League 'for the attainment of a joint economic prosperity including equal opportunity upon the highways of the world and equitable access to the raw materials which all nations need'.[26]

Wilson's notion of mutual guarantees had much in common with the collective security principle, as did a later comment that the old-style balance of power needed to be replaced by a 'community of power'.[27] However, Wilson had gone over his May 1916 speech shortly before delivering it and erased any reference to the possible use of physical force against transgressors, thus stopping short of endorsing the fundamental prerequisite of a collective security system.[28] This reflected his reluctance to go beyond high-sounding generalisations to any specific formula for a League of Nations. The reasons for this reluctance, which persisted right up to 1919, are complex. Firstly, he was justifiably afraid that the Senate might refuse to ratify any treaty which appeared to commit American troops to upholding the New Diplomacy.[29] Secondly, he was particularly unwilling to make public any detailed project for a League on the grounds that this would stir up controversy. This was why he frequently resisted pressure to reveal his own ideas for a League both from unofficial League enthusiasts and also from House, who was anxious that public discussion should crystallise around Wilson's plan for a League rather than someone else's.[30] Thirdly, one of the few consistent elements in Wilson's approach to the League from 1916 to 1919 was his insistence that it needed to be an organic 'living thing', that the 'administrative constitution of the League must grow and not be made; that we must begin with solemn covenants covering mutual guarantees of political independence and territorial integrity . . . but that the method of carrying those mutual pledges out should be left to develop of itself, case by case'.[31]

It was also true, however, that while Wilson brushed aside most designs for a League that emanated from private or allied sources – or even from his Secretary of State, Lansing – his own thinking on the League displayed considerable uncertainty and confusion. Most British schemes for a League revolved around the idea of an institutionalised great power Concert, and the first draft constitution of a League offered to Wilson by Colonel House in July 1918 had similarly excluded smaller powers. Wilson rejected this proposal that the League should be a great power club but continued to insist that it should be 'virile' without seeming to appreciate that the presence of small states could be a source of impotence.[32] Precisely what was to be the foundation of this virility was never made clear by Wilson. Moreover any definite ideas he might once have had as to the purpose of the League had become so diluted by 1919 that it is hardly surprising that so many conflicting and unrealistic expectations came to be attached to the League by less eminent observers.

Sometimes Wilson spoke as if the League's peacekeeping objective was to be achieved mainly by open diplomacy and the pressure of public opinion:

> My conception of the League of Nations is just this, that it shall operate as the organised moral force of men throughout the world and that whenever or wherever wrong and aggression are planned or contemplated, this searching light of conscience will be turned upon them and men everywhere will ask, 'What are the purposes that you hold in your heart against the fortunes of the world?' Just a little exposure will settle most questions. If the Central Powers had dared to discuss the purposes of this war for a single fortnight, it never would have happened.[33]

On other occasions his original emphasis on mutual guarantees (which was reiterated in Article 10 of the Covenant) was claimed to be the 'backbone' of the League, without which it 'could hardly be more than an influential debating society'.[34] He could still, however, claim to the American Senate that Article 10 was 'binding in conscience only, not in law', and just before the Peace Conference had said privately that he expected economic sanctions to be the main weapon to be used against aggressors.[35]

Wilson also indulged in the tendency in common with others so widespread during the last six months of 1918 to graft on to the League additional functions which diminished its fundamental security role. One such instance was the responsibility undertaken by the League in its 'mandates' system for the former enemy colonies. The fifth of Wilson's Fourteen Points had called for an adjustment of colonial claims, taking into account the interests of the populations. When House attempted to interpret this point to the United States' allies during his missions to Europe in October 1918, he took it a stage further: 'It would seem as if the principle involved in this proposition is that a colonial power acts not as owner of its colonies but as a trustee for the natives and for the society of nations.'[36] A British Foreign Office memorandum in November suggested that certain colonial areas might be administered by individual powers under a League of Nations mandate.[37] As late as 10 December Wilson, in discussion with his Inquiry team, believed that it was possible for the German colonies to become the common property of the League and be administered by the smaller nations.[38] However, when General Smuts published his detailed plan for a League, Wilson enthusiastically endorsed his basic idea of a mandates system, although Smuts excluded from this the former German colonies in the Pacific and Africa as being 'inhabited by barbarians', whereas Wilson was to argue at Paris that they too should be amongst the League's mandated territories.[39] By the time of the Peace Conference the mandates question, which had started life as a peripheral issue, had become so important to Wilson that he could maintain in his arguments with the other major powers that the League 'would be a laughing stock if it were not invested with this quality of trusteeship'.[40]

Wilson's lack of a clear and comprehensive blueprint for a League, together with his evasiveness on the issue, were such that as late as 6 January 1919 the chief British Cabinet supporter of the League, Lord Robert Cecil, had 'little idea of what the President's conception of a League really involved'.[41] None the less the popular depiction of Wilson as 'father of the League' has some validity. His chief contribution, however, was not so much in being the originator of the Covenant[42] but rather lay in his insistence throughout 1918 that some edifice bearing the title 'League of Nations' should be created, that the League should be the first item on the Paris agenda and that it should be an integral part of the peace treaty.[43]

The drafting of the Covenant

Part of Wilson's problem was that he had come to distrust his own State Department and in particular his Secretary of State, Robert Lansing, whom he considered to be too cautious and legalistic in his approach to the League.[44] Lansing differed from the President firstly in the importance each attached to the League – Lansing insisted that the prime necessity was to push for the democratisation of authoritarian countries[45] – and secondly in his conception

of the League. Whereas Wilson's thinking, vague though it was, entailed a *positive* commitment by all League members to employ sanctions against aggressors, Lansing proposed a strengthening of
existing diplomatic devices, such as arbitration and commissions of
inquiry, but only a *negative* commitment by the powers to refrain
from the use of violence in settling their disputes.[46] The result of the
growing acrimony between the two was that Wilson refused to consider any analyses of the League idea that emanated from the State
Department. Hence, at the start of 1919 all that Wilson had at his
disposal in the way of detailed guidance on the League was a brief
draft covenant drawn up by House in July 1918 and an equally short
revision of this which Wilson himself had produced.[47] House's version was full of resonant phrases about 'honourable' and 'dishon-
ourable' international behaviour and, while Wilson had avoided
this temptation, his draft suffered from his inability to translate his
ideas into precise terminology that could not be torn into shreds by
the legal advisers of other governments. Despite the disdain felt by
most of the British Cabinet towards the League idea, considerably
more thought had been given in official British circles to its concrete implications, and several covenants existed by 1919, of which
Smuts's was the most detailed. The French and Italians had also
produced their own versions of the League by then.

The underlying principles and assumptions about the nature of
the new international order, as they emerge from these documents,
may be summarised as follows.

1 Collective Security

Although this term was not used until much later, its central theme –
deterring potential aggressors by agreeing in advance to oppose
them with a united front of all other states – was present in all of the
deliberations of 1918–19. The collective security idea had been discussed in earlier international conferences, such as those after the
Napoleonic wars, but its immediate origin lay in the belief that the
First World War would have been prevented had Germany been
aware beforehand of how extensive the opposition to it would
become. However, there were vast differences amongst the allies as
to what a collective security system entailed in practice. The French,
once they had become convinced of Wilson's determination to

make the League the cornerstone of the entire settlement, pressed strongly for an international army to be created under a permanent general staff. The Wilson and House drafts placed most of their emphasis on the employment of an economic blockade – the weapon that had been effectively used during the war. Smuts, on the other hand, argued that economic sanctions alone would not be sufficient to deter a powerful state unless, as a last resort, they were backed by military force, but he was unwilling to go as far as the French in this direction. There were also voices raised against the whole concept of collective security. As early as May 1916 Sir Maurice Hankey, Secretary to the War Committee in Britain, argued strongly that the promise of security held out by such projects was 'wholly fictitious' and likely to foster dangerous illusions, especially in Britain.[48]

2 Justiciable Disputes

A common assumption in most drafts was that there was a clear distinction between international conflicts where a legal solution was possible and those where it was not. The former were defined by Smuts in this way:

> Justiciable disputes are those which concern matters of fact or law which are capable of a legal or judicial handling. They involve mostly the interpretation of treaties or some other question of international law; or questions of fact, such as the situation of boundaries, or the amount of damage done by any breach of the law.[49]

It was widely believed that an extension of the existing legal remedies, such as arbitration, could take place under the auspices of the League, and Wilson and Smuts both proposed compulsory arbitration systems to that end. The Phillimore Report, while accepting arbitration in certain circumstances, laid greater stress on the use of conferences of major powers in the event of crisis, and this was to be a consistent element in all later British proposals. The final British draft of 20 January 1919, which was a synthesis of several earlier proposals, including a draft submitted by Lord Robert Cecil, did however, call for a permanent international court to be established.[50]

3 Crisis Management

Understandably enough, most draft covenants were not really designed to prevent all conceivable wars but rather looked back to the origins of the one which had just ended. This was seen by some to have developed from a relatively minor crisis through a series of stages until it was out of control. Hence there were several proposals for some means of interrupting this relentless process of escalation. Suggestions included compulsory moratoria while peaceful means of settling disputes could be tried, as well as public discussions of the matters in dispute, since Wilson believed that the secrecy of traditional diplomacy had been partly to blame for the war.

4 Disarmament

A related set of proposals derived from the view that the arms race before the war had helped to heighten international tension and that the League, therefore, needed to develop some system of arms control. This was to become an abiding concern of international organisations, albeit one fraught with enormous difficulties. Schemes advanced in 1919 ranged from that of the French, who were chiefly interested in ensuring German disarmament, to the British, who were mainly concerned with achieving the abolition of conscription, and the Americans, who wanted a general arms-limitation agreement, including the abolition of the private manufacture of weapons.

5 A Great Power Concert

A persistent theme of several members of the British Cabinet, as well as of the Foreign Office, was that the only realistic means of bringing more stability into international relations was to build upon the practice of great power consultation that had developed during the nineteenth century. One line of thought favoured the continuation in peacetime of a body like the Supreme War Council, which would have meant setting up the equivalent of a great power directorate of international affairs. An ambitious variant of this approach, proposed by the British government in October 1918, called for joint allied control of postwar economic reconstruction. This, however, was vetoed by the Americans, who felt with some justice that such a scheme would entail allied control of food and raw materials, which would inevitably be provided mainly by the United States.[51] Less radical ideas involved an institutionalised Concert of Europe, with either an arrangement for continuous consultation amongst the powers or an agreement amongst them to confer together at times of crisis. The common feature in all such proposals was that they excluded smaller states from any significant role.

6 Functionalism

The approach to international organisation known as 'functionalism' holds that political integration amongst states can best develop from more limited attempts at cooperation in specific functional areas – principally those relating to economic welfare. Although functionalism as a systematic theoretical framework did not emerge until the work of David Mitrany in the 1930s and 1940s,[52] its central argument was advanced by Smuts in his 1918 pamphlet:

> An attempt will be made in this sketch to give an essential extension to the functions of the League; indeed to look upon the League from a very different point of view, to view it not only as a possible means for preventing future wars, but much more as a great organ of the ordinary peaceful life of civilization, as the foundation of the new international system which will be erected on the ruins of this war and as the starting point from which the peace arrangements of the forthcoming conference should be made. Such an orientation of the idea seems to me necessary if the League is to become a permanent part of our international machinery. It is not sufficient for the League merely to be a sort of *deus ex machina*, called in in very grave emergencies when the spectre of war appears; if it is to last, it must be much more. It must become part and parcel of the common international life of states, it must be an ever visible, living, working organ of the polity of civilization.[53]

The idea that the League should not simply concern itself with security matters but should embrace a wide variety of additional functions (including some taken over from existing institutions) did not appear in Wilson's first draft of the Covenant, nor in the Phillimore or House proposals, and it was not fully developed in Smuts's paper. However, it gained momentum in the weeks before the Conference and during the actual Paris debates. One particular suggestion that was taken up by Wilson and others in this period was that the League should be involved in the development of international standards to apply to labour conditions.[54]

7 Organisational Principles

There was widespread agreement by the end of 1918 that the chief organs of the League should be an executive council, a deliberative assembly and an administrative secretariat, but considerable differences still existed as to the constitution and functions of each of these. The British, including their strongest supporter of the League, Lord Robert Cecil, wanted a Council of great powers only, with the other states confined to a very clearly subordinate role. Colonel House also favoured excluding the small states, but President Wilson was not willing to countenance this. Smuts and the Italian delegation independently suggested the novel device of having both permanent great power and non-permanent small power members of the Council, and this won Wilson's approval, appearing in his second attempt at a draft covenant, dated 10 January 1919.[55] However, the draft Covenant that was actually presented to the first session of the Paris Commission on the League on 3 February restricted places on the Council to the great powers, together with any smaller states they cared to invite – making small power membership an occasional privilege rather than a right. It was to take a great deal of pressure from the small nations before the powers accepted the Smuts–Italian formula.

Likewise, the nature and composition of the Assembly were far from settled as the delegates came together in Paris. The eventual role of the Assembly, which provided the model for the United Nations General Assembly, evolved in the years after the Conference, rather than being finally decided at Paris. In 1919 the British saw the Assembly as a talking shop that would meet very infrequently

and would be composed either of parliamentarians or of representatives of the public. This was in line with earlier notions that the
League should provide a forum for what Wilson had termed the
'organised opinion of mankind'. During one of the meetings of the
Commission on the League in February, Cecil inadvertently revealed his country's view of the true status of the Assembly when he
declared that England would probably 'send a leader of the Labour
Party, someone who would be the spokesman of religious interests
and, he hoped, a woman'.[56] For others, such as the Italians, the Assembly was to be taken more seriously and given powers to formulate and develop international law. The Italians also made the
unusual proposal that Assembly decisions could be taken on the
basis of a two-thirds majority vote rather than the unanimity which
was eventually required by the Covenant.

The functions to be allotted to the League Secretariat were much
less controversial, with earlier ideas that it might be given certain
political powers quickly being forgotten. The Secretary-General
(given the grander title 'Chancellor' in most early drafts) was essentially to be an administrator and coordinator of the activities of the
League with those of other international organisations. The Secretariat was to have the role of gathering information, both in a
general sense and, more importantly, whenever states referred disputes to it. One indication of the relative absence of conflict
amongst the powers over the Secretariat came when a meeting of a
special Organisation Committee – set up under House to draw up
details of the administrative structure of the League – was able to
conclude after only eight minutes' discussion.[57]

The League Covenant contains elements which embody all these
principles, but it would be a mistake to see the League simply as an
attempt to translate these ideas into their appropriate institutional
forms. The Covenant that finally emerged in 1919 represents the
outcome of a bargaining process involving many disparate elements
and contending interests. It was, first and foremost, a compromise
between the British and American viewpoints: one which managed
to patch over the only partially concealed suspicions each nurtured
about the other's true intentions. The extent of differences
amongst the allies is illustrated by a report sent to Woodrow Wilson
on 12 December 1918 by E.M. Hurley, his representative in the allied discussions on shipping and food distribution. Referring to the
European leaders, he wrote:

What they are thinking about, as you are probably already aware, is the increased power of our shipping, commerce and finance. In every conversation the commercial question has come to the front . . . . The British are fearful that under a League of Nations the United States, with its present wealth and commercial power, may get the jump on the markets of the world.[58]

Nor did the British delegation speak with one voice: Hughes, the Australian Prime Minister, led a vociferous group which opposed any scheme to place the former German colonies under any form of international control.

Another complicating factor and, with the Bolsheviks, one of the two important but unseen presences at Paris, was the domestic American opposition to the League, led by Senator Lodge. Here too Anglo-American rivalries were apparent, but this time it was the Senate's opponents of the League who suspected Britain of plotting to dominate it. Despite this Lodge was secretly in contact with official British circles, who were left in no doubt of his belief that Wilson would not be able to obtain Senate ratification of the Covenant.[59] Apart from its apprehensions regarding British power, the Senate had several specific objections to the draft Covenant presented to them at the end of February after the League of Nations Commission had decided upon it. These were that domestic affairs were not explicitly excluded from the League's auspices, that the special relationship between the United States and Latin America, as embodied in the Monroe Doctrine, was not officially acknowledged in the Covenant, that the United States might be saddled with mandated territories against its wishes, and that the procedures by which states could withdraw from the League needed to be clarified. Later – after the Paris peacemakers had met most of these objections – opposition crystallised instead around Article 10 of the Covenant, which contained a diluted version of Wilson's long-cherished principle of guarantees of territorial integrity and political independence.

The Bolshevik Revolution had already made an important, if unwitting contribution to the League before 1919. By stealing most of Wilson's New Diplomacy clothes, including his demands for a peace without annexations and for open diplomacy, Lenin had compelled Wilson to concentrate all the harder on the one item the Bolsheviks had left him: the League of Nations. The Fourteen

Points speech was itself made in response to the Bolshevik challenge, and there is more than a hint in British discussions of the League that it would have to be taken more seriously than many thought because it had come to represent a key element in the established powers' riposte to Bolshevism.[60] An even more specific rejoinder to the Russian Revolution was the creation of the International Labour Organisation, which won favour partly as a means of appeasing restive elements in the trade union movement who might otherwise be attracted to Communism.[61]

Three phases of bargaining over the Covenant took place in Paris. The first was in the weeks before the opening meeting of the League of Nations Commission on 3 February and involved primarily the British and American delegations. Next came the first series of meetings of the Commission, during which the basic draft of the Covenant was agreed. The final stage witnessed the reconvening of the Commission on 22 March to consider the series of amendments which Wilson wished to introduce following his return from the United States.

Wilson had insisted from the start that the establishment of the League should be the first item on the Paris agenda, an objective which Lloyd George, for his own reasons, decided to support, thus laying the foundation for Anglo-American collaboration in the actual drafting of the Covenant.[62] The ultimate fruit of this was the 'Hurst–Miller draft' of the Covenant: the version finalised by the British and American advisers on which the subsequent discussions were based. However, before the long drafting session between Britain's Cecil Hurst and the American David H. Miller on 1 February, a series of parliamentary negotiations had taken place involving Wilson, House, Lloyd George and Cecil. The Australian, Canadian and Italian leaders also had some influence on the eventual draft.

Debate during this period revolved around two draft Covenants prepared by Wilson on 10 and 20 January. Cecil found that by adopting a somewhat liberal interpretation of his brief from the Imperial War Cabinet much of what Wilson had in mind could be accepted in a reworded form.[63] However, a number of crucial differences remained between British and American approaches which needed to be resolved. Wilson initially advocated a rather complicated system of compulsory arbitration for international disputes but found no difficulty in retreating from this position. Cecil's alternative suggestion was for a Permanent Court of International

Justice, which he saw not only as an appeal court to which disputes between states could be referred but as a general court performing a wide range of useful functions in relation to all the lesser international organisations.[64] Similarly Wilson was able to accept with seeming equanimity a substantial amendment to his proposed system of guarantees of independence and territorial integrity. In the British alternative wording, which eventually appeared in the Covenant, the League members merely 'undertook' to respect and preserve territorial integrity and independence, rather than 'guaranteeing' them. One of the considerations which influenced the British in this was a desire not to see the territorial status quo frozen by international law.

Other issues proved more troublesome. Opposition to Wilson's proposals on mandates came not so much from Britain as from the Dominions, and several bitter confrontations were to take place before this question was resolved. A more fundamental Anglo-American conflict of interests was involved in Wilson's proposals for the League to be given powers to enforce the freedom of the seas and for discrimination in international trade to be outlawed. The British also found unacceptable Wilson's plan to give minor states significant representation in the League Council. The Hurst–Miller compromise managed to reduce all these points of contention to innocuous formulae, but this led Wilson, realising with dismay the extent to which his original ideas had been watered down, to make an unsuccessful eleventh-hour attempt to have the Hurst–Miller draft discarded in favour of one which more truly reflected his own approach.[65] As if to prove that the Hurst–Miller draft was a genuine compromise, shortly before this Lloyd George had also made an abortive attempt to abandon what he regarded as over-ambitious conceptions of the League and return to the earlier British idea of an institutionalised great power Concert.[66]

The League of the Hurst–Miller draft envisaged power as being concentrated in the hands of an Executive Council of the United States, Britain, France, Italy and Japan, who could invite any other member to attend should its interests be directly affected by the matter in hand. Collective security was provided for by a general undertaking to respect and preserve against aggression the territorial integrity and political independence of members, and by a specific agreement that states involved in a dispute would not resort to armed force until they had submitted their conflict to arbitration or inquiry by the Council. Breaking this latter agreement was to be regarded as an act of war against all other League members, who were to respond immediately by severing economic and financial relations with the offending state. The Council was to examine the logistics of military sanctions. All League members had the 'friendly right' of bringing to the attention of the Council any matter which threatened international peace. A permanent court was to be set up with competence to hear cases deemed to be 'suitable for submission to arbitration, and which cannot be satisfactorily settled by diplomacy'. The League was to have responsibilities in the field of disarmament, although these were left somewhat vaguely defined. The principle that partial disarmament was essential for the maintenance of peace was acknowledged, and the Council was required to formulate plans for the reduction of armaments and to look into the feasibility of abolishing compulsory military service. Where control of the arms trade was necessary 'in the common interest', this was to be supervised by the League.

Articles 17–20 of the Hurst–Miller draft broadened the League's range of responsibilities. Article 17 declared that the well-being of the peoples of the former enemy colonies was a 'sacred trust of civilisation' but made no stipulation that the colonies should become League Mandatories. The stress of this Article was rather on preventing the individual colonial power from enjoying exclusive rights to exploit the economic resources of the colonial territories and from being able to draw upon the colonial peoples to build up its army. Article 18 affirmed the need to establish fair working hours and conditions of labour, while Article 19 guaranteed the freedom of religion. Article 20 contained all that was left of Wilson's original dream of granting the League powers to supervise the freedom of the seas and promote free trade. It read in full: 'The High Contracting Parties will agree upon provisions intended to secure and maintain freedom of transit and just treatment for the commerce of all States members of the League.'[67]

Much of the Hurst–Miller draft found its way into the final Covenant, but a number of significant changes were made during the sessions of the League of Nations Commission from 3 February to 14 February and after Wilson's return from the United States on 14 March. A united front presented by the Brazilian, Serbian, Belgian, Chinese and Portuguese delegates forced Cecil to back down from his opposition to small power representation on the Council, with four places for such states being eventually agreed on. What was now an 'undertaking' to preserve the independence and territorial integrity of all League members was further diluted after renewed pressure from Cecil. In his view this Article still implied that the existing territorial status quo was frozen by law, which would make it more difficult to carry out such later territorial adjustments as might be needed in the interests of international order. More seriously, if the obligation had any concrete substance, he thought an automatic commitment to go to war to uphold it was entailed, which Britain was not prepared to accept.[68] Eventually Cecil agreed to an amendment of Wilson's which stated that in the event of aggression it would be left to the Council to 'advise the plan and the means by which this obligation should be fulfilled'.[69] This effectively rendered the Article innocuous because any action under it would have to be unanimously agreed by the Council, but this was still not enough to prevent the Article from later becoming one of the chief obstacles to the Covenant's ratification by the American Senate. Cecil's other concern, that the territorial settlement might become unduly sacrosanct, was met by a new Article (number 19 in the Covenant) which provided for the periodic revision of international obligations.

The disarmament article was subjected to detailed scrutiny, which led to one significant change.[70] Wilson had allowed his original call for the abolition of conscription to be toned down in the Hurst–Miller draft to meet Italian objections. Now the French declared their total opposition to any reference to this subject and so it was dropped. However, Wilson was able to secure the addition to the original article of an assertion that the private manufacture of armaments was 'open to grave objections'.

What were, in principle, the most important articles of the Covenant, those laying down the League's right to concern itself with any threat to peace, the provisions for peaceful settlement of disputes and the mandatory sanctions to be imposed against violators of these agreements, were all passed with few major alterations.[71] The French tried to raise again their proposal that some kind of International General Staff be created, but without success. The sole concession made to the French position was the establishment of a permanent Commission to advise on military matters. A greatly changed mandates article was also passed without much discussion, largely because its provisions had been worked out in advance during several acrimonious sessions before the League Commission of-

ficially commenced. The new Article set out clearly the principles
that the League as a whole had an ultimate responsibility for the
former enemy colonies, and that not just the 'well-being' (as in the
Hurst–Miller draft) but the 'development' of these colonies was a
'sacred trust of civilisation'. The division of the mandated territories into three types according to their readiness for self-government was the central theme of the new mandates provisions.

The mandates article provided one instance where the Covenant
ran counter to the central orthodoxy of international relations: the
principle of each state's absolute sovereignty in its own domain –
including its colonies. Another attempt to assert the existence of
international standards of behaviour which, by implication, limited
the freedom of governments to do as they pleased domestically was
less successful. Wilson had proposed an article in which the League
members agreed not to interfere with the free exercise of religion,
nor to discriminate against people adhering to any particular religion or belief.[72] This was generally acceptable, but problems arose
when Japan's representative, Baron Makino, tried to graft on to it a
statement opposing discrimination against aliens on account of
their race. This was the only significant Japanese intervention in the
Commission meetings, and Wilson had, in fact, been advised as
early as November 1918 that the Japanese intended to raise the
question of racial equality.[73] The Japanese proposal was anathema
to the Australians and other members of the British empire delegation, who saw it as potentially threatening their policy of refusing
coloured immigration. As Makino had hinted strongly that he regarded acceptance of his proposal as a necessary quid pro quo for
Japanese support for the religious equality article, both in the end
had to be dropped.

Two important sets of amendments were inserted in the Covenant after Woodrow Wilson's return to Paris on 14 March from his
unsuccessful mission to win over the Senate. Wilson had been advised during his visit that four key changes to the draft Covenant
might suffice to win him a Senate majority:

1. A specific affirmation that the Monroe Doctrine, one of the
    traditional pillars of American diplomacy, was not affected by
    the Covenant.
2. An explicit recognition of states' exclusive jurisdiction over
    their own domestic affairs.

3. Clear provisions by which states could withdraw from membership of the League.
4. An acknowledgement that states could refuse to become mandatory powers should they so wish.[74]

Wilson was clearly going to need substantial support in Paris if these amendments were to be passed without the entire Covenant being opened up for revision. The British were willing to help him out but at a price, which included his agreement to a somewhat weaker disarmament formulation, as had been demanded in a strongly worded Admiralty memorandum.[75] Following discussions between Cecil and the Americans on 18 March a new set of amendments was then presented to the reconvened League of Nations Commission, as a common Anglo-American position, although Wilson proposed his Monroe Doctrine amendment separately.[76]

The final stages of the drafting process remained, but these added little of substance to the Covenant as revised by the British and Americans. Perhaps the most significant change stemmed from another British initiative, which increased the emphasis on the League's role in matters other than security by making it the central coordinating and directing body over several other functional organisations. In other respects the last discussions did not augur well for the League. Further limitations were written into the collective security provisions, leading the French to declare that they would be obliged to depend on separate defensive alliances.[77] The Monroe Doctrine amendment was passed only with enormous difficulty and the Japanese failed again to have even the most innocuous reference to racial equality accepted. More generally, such optimism as had been present in earlier meetings had become soured by the 'sauve qui peut' atmosphere now prevalent in Paris and by the increasing likelihood that the United States would not ratify the Covenant.[78]

Conclusion

As a legal document the Covenant had many deficiencies. Some articles were ambiguous or contradicted other articles. The crucial provisions for collective security were full of loopholes. However, the criticisms of this nature that were made at the time (and are still occasionally repeated in the literature on the League) were misguided. States did not operate within the confines of a fully developed legal order, where, like tax evaders, they were merely engaged in an unending search for legitimate ways of attaining their ends. The fact that the Covenant could be interpreted as permitting some kinds of aggression in certain sorts of circumstances was immaterial, although anyone witnessing the battles in Paris over the precise wording of this or that clause might be forgiven for thinking otherwise. The significance of weak or ambiguous formulations in the Covenant was not that these might permit wars which a stricter wording would have prevented, but that they accurately reflected the doubts felt by most states about committing their security to the new system.

Indeed the League had, in a sense, failed in its primary purpose even before it had officially started, when London, Washington and Paris agreed to a tripartite system of alliances to guarantee French security, thus bypassing the League mechanism. When these alliances proved abortive following American failure to ratify the peace treaties, France continued to seek security outside the League framework. Hence in the all-important field of great power relations the League had effectively been ignored from the outset. It remained to be seen whether it might still have a role to play in less important aspects of peace and security as an alternative to traditional diplomacy.

Apart from its role as a provider of collective security, the League may be said to represent two points of departure in the history of international relations. Firstly, it embodied a limited consensus as to the existence of certain international standards of conduct which could be given some status in international law. More generally, it expressed an intention to extend the role of international law itself as, in the words of the Preamble to the Covenant, 'the actual rule of conduct amongst governments'. Secondly, it was an acknowledgement of the increasing range of common functional interests shared by states and the need for more effective centralised supervision of these. The subsequent history of international organisation was to be much concerned with both of these developments.

2 The League of Nations

At one level, the history of the League of Nations is synonymous with the often-told story of the failure of the Western democracies to oppose the aggression of the Fascist regimes and prevent world war. The international order established at Versailles was inherently unstable because the temporary weakness of Germany and Russia meant that the balance of power upon which it was founded was essentially artificial and impermanent and would come under increasing strain as those two states regained their strength. In so far as the League was associated with that order, it too would come under threat. Since the founders of the League always saw it as, above all else, a provider of collective security, there can be no real objection to an assessment of the League in these terms. However, at another level – the one with which we are most concerned here – the League was also an episode in the history of international organisation. Viewed in this light, what is most remarkable is that, far from the disastrous failure of the League leading to a hiatus in the growth of international institutions, it was followed by an unparalleled increase in their number and range of functions. So, while *an* organisation was discredited between 1919 and 1939, international organisation as a significant process in the relations amongst states may be said to have become firmly established during the same period. To understand how and why this was the case, four distinct aspects of the League need to be considered: its collective security operations, its role as cornerstone of the international legal order, its function as overseer and coordinator of a variety of economic, social and technical activities, and the development of its principal institutions.

The League and international security

As many people have pointed out, certain basic flaws were always inherent in the abstract concept of collective security. It required states to be united in their determination to resist aggression, yet if such unity of purpose existed the reason for it would have vanished.[1] A dubious assumption is implicit in the concept – that it will always be perfectly clear that aggression has been committed and which state is the guilty party.[2] Only a collective security pact capable of bringing effective sanctions to bear could hope for success, yet states are unlikely to establish such an obvious threat to their own monopoly of power.[3]

But those who controlled the League were practical statesmen not philosophers, and logical problems such as these are not the last word on the League's security functions, or its failure. The principal European leaders (if not Woodrow Wilson) had always seen the League as, at best, an institutionalisation of older methods of managing international relations, such as the balance of power and the Concert of Europe, rather than as the basis of a wholly new international order. Even these more cautious conceptions of the League failed to materialise when the absence of the United States, following the failure of the American Senate to ratify the peace treaty, prevented an effective balance of power from being built, and the assertiveness of smaller states both in the Assembly and in their demands for representation on the Council obstructed a return to an old-style great power Concert. This meant, as Lord Balfour noted in 1925, that conflicts amongst the major powers arising from 'deep-lying cause of hostility' were beyond the League's effective influence.[4] This problem was exacerbated by the fact that certain other great powers were not members throughout the League's life: Germany was not admitted until September 1926 and left in October 1933, the Soviet Union did not join until September 1934, Japan withdrew in 1933, Italy left in 1937 and several Latin American states were also absent for various periods. Yet a substantial security role remained, and it was the development of this in the 1920s which made the first ten years of the League appear at the time to be so promising.

The first difficulty encountered by the League was how to define its precise powers in peace and security matters. One complicating factor was the continued existence for several years after the war of the allied Ambassadors' Conference, which sometimes seemed to be a rival (and intrinsically more powerful) agency for ordering postwar international relations. This problem first arose when the League was asked to consider Yugoslavia's incursion into Albania in

1920, which some members doubted its competence to do when the issue was already on the agenda of the Ambassadors' Conference. On this occasion Albania declared that the League was the true successor to the European Concert (which had originally settled the Albanian question in 1915) and so it alone had the right to pronounce on Albanian affairs.[5] However, during the Greco-Italian crisis of 1923, Mussolini was able to claim that the League had no right to consider the matter because Greece had brought it before both the League and the Ambassadors' Conference, and the latter had precedence in Italy's opinion.[6]

Some of Europe's more tradition-minded diplomats were at first disinclined to grant the League any more responsibility than absolutely necessary. In 1921, for instance, Lord Curzon reproved the Persian Foreign Minister for writing to reassure the League's Secretary-General that a recent Anglo-Persian agreement was not incompatible with the Covenant. The only effect of such a letter, he maintained, would be to afford the League a pretext to sit in judgement on Persia's sovereign right to interpret its own treaty obligations in any way it chose.[7] Similarly, the allied powers in early 1920 refused to refer the Adriatic question to the League Council, arguing that to do so would imply that there was complete disagreement amongst the allies which diplomacy was unable to overcome and that a reference to the League under Article 11 (which mentioned situations threatening war) would 'start rumours of war unnecessarily'.[8] Taken at face value these observations seemed to negate the whole purpose of the League, which had been set up as a centre for diplomacy and as an alternative to war.

The withdrawal of the United States was followed by a widespread move to water down the crucial collective security provisions of Articles 10 and 16. The Canadian delegation presented a resolution on Article 10 to each of the first four Assemblies, initially in an attempt to have the Article deleted from the Covenant, later with the aim of having a restrictive interpretation placed on its stipulations. All these resolutions failed, but the Fourth Assembly version only received one negative vote and most governments came to accept it as an authoritative interpretation of their real commitments under the Article. A British Foreign Office memorandum in 1926 suggested that, whenever the League Council had to determine the Article 10 obligations of League members, it should have due regard for the 'geographical situations and special conditions' of each state, and that members themselves were free to decide whether they would contribute to any military action under Article 10, with Council recommendations merely being 'taken into consideration'.[9] The provisions for automatic sanctions in Article 16 were similarly weakened by a number of Assembly resolutions interpreted by the Foreign Office to mean that sanctions were not obligatory, although states should 'co-operate loyally' in any collective action under Article 16.[10] Conversely, efforts to strengthen the League's collective security provisions were generally doomed to failure. Cecil was unable to secure the adoption of a Treaty of Mutual Assistance, which would have made collective security operate on a regional rather than a global basis, and have ensured that sanctions under this system would be more effective.[11] In 1924 the 'Geneva Protocol', which would have provided for compulsory arbitration of disputes, also failed, primarily because of British objections.[12] The success of the high-sounding but toothless Kellogg–Briand Pact in 1928 and the more important Locarno Treaty in 1925 did, however, help to create an illusion that the League was being strengthened rather than weakened. The Locarno Treaty involved Britain, France and Germany in a series of mutual guarantees of the Franco-German and Belgo-German frontiers (but not Germany's eastern frontiers), while the Kellogg–Briand Pact was a declaration by the foreign ministers of the USA and France, eventually signed by all but a few states, which renounced war as an instrument of policy. The Locarno Treaty marked a high point of cooperation amongst the European powers but the other document was soon forgotten after the failure of an attempt by Britain and France in 1929 to have the Pact incorporated into the League Covenant.

As the League came to be a more familiar fixture on the international landscape, so the powers began to make greater use of it for a vast range of purposes, although there were still some who, like Lloyd George, privately bewailed the results of this trend: 'It [the League] should have been much more informal, like the Supreme Council. As it was, it had weak links spreading everywhere and no grip anywhere.'[13] In general, however, after this initial wariness had diminished, the powers developed the habit of passing on for League consideration a range of disputes and other international problems which for various reasons they were unable or did not wish to resolve by normal diplomatic means. For instance, in 1920

London brought the dispute between Sweden and Finland over the Åland Islands before the Council because it saw this as the safest way of dealing with an issue of some delicacy (given Soviet interest in the Islands), without causing dissension amongst the Western powers.[14] Here one concern was to use the League to give an aura of legitimacy to the territorial distribution which had resulted from the break-up of the Tsarist empire. The same aim was apparent in an attempt by the allies to place the short-lived breakaway state of Armenia under League protection, although on this occasion the League Council declined the allied request, arguing that the League did not have the resources to undertake tasks of this magnitude.[15]

Even Lloyd George discovered a use for the League in 1921, when he threatened Yugoslavia with League sanctions during a conflict between Yugoslavia and Albania.[16] Lord Balfour was later to claim that the peaceful settlement of this dispute had only been possible because both states could accept the disinterestedness of the League's bodies, including the Commission of Inquiry which was set up to investigate the matter.[17] This was a fairly typical example of the self-congratulatory tone which accompanied some of the League's successes in the 1920s and which helped to create a popular faith in the League's efficacy that was in fact founded on illusion. In this case it had been a great power ultimatum to a smaller state which had forced a settlement and one, moreover, in a situation where both sides had been genuinely anxious to reach a border demarcation.

Other issues were passed to the League by the Supreme Council or the Ambassadors' Conference: sometimes because the powers didn't want to spend time on them; sometimes because the questions involved were intractable and handing them over to the League was a convenient and legitimate way of evading responsibility for them; occasionally because they were an unwanted source of friction amongst the powers themselves; and sometimes because they genuinely called for a lengthy process of impartial investigation. Numerous border disputes in Eastern and Central Europe, Anglo-French differences over Upper Silesia, the Saar Territory and French nationality policies in Tunis, and the problems of stabilising the international economy, all ended up with the League Council for one or more of these reasons. Its normal workload also included countless smaller problems arising out of its peace treaty responsibilities for various minority populations.

The resolution of questions of this kind led Britain's Foreign Secretary, Austen Chamberlain, to declare in 1925 that his respect for the League had increased now that he had seen it at work, not 'on one of those great problems which excite most attention but on those little problems which if we do not settle them might be a great trouble in the world'.[18] This raises the difficult question of how to assess the value of much of the League's work in the 1920s. The League existed in part to prevent minor crises from escalating into major confrontations between the powers, but one can only speculate as to whether any of the crises of the 1920s contained the seeds of a larger conflict which the League could therefore be said to have averted. However, the more ambitious claims made for the League during this period were probably unjustified. Sarajevo had led to war in 1914 because many circumstances had combined to produce an atmosphere of war-preparedness in Europe. In the 1920s almost the opposite conditions prevailed.

A number of conflicts during the 1920s were referred to the League by one of the disputants, of which the most serious were between Greece and Italy in 1923, Greece and Bulgaria in 1925, and Bolivia and Paraguay in 1928. Other incidents involving hostilities included a recurring clash between Poland and Lithuania and a dispute between Britain and Turkey concerning sovereignty over the province of Mosul on the Turkey–Iraq border.

The Greco-Italian incident began in August 1923 when three Italian diplomats were assassinated in Greece, prompting Mussolini's government to send a bellicose ultimatum to Greece with a set of demands which included the payment of a 50 million lire indemnity within five days.[19] When the Greek government did not submit immediately, Italian troops occupied the Greek island of Corfu, whereupon Greece appealed to the League Council. To most objective eyes the injured party in this case was Greece, with Italy clearly having violated the Covenant by its immediate recourse to arms. The case was thus an important test for the League, since Italy still had pretensions to great power status. However, France was at this time involved in a somewhat similar action to Italy's, having occupied the Ruhr in an attempt to enforce payment of Germany's reparations bill, and was in any case in no mood to condemn a fellow great power in order to bolster some abstract principle of collective security. The Council therefore contented itself with passing the matter to a Commission of Inquiry of the Ambassadors' Conference, simultaneously prejudging the result by ordering Greece to deposit 50 million lire in a Swiss bank pending the Commission's findings.[20]

The contrast with the Council's handling of the Greco-Bulgarian affair two years later was instructive. This began in September 1925 when Greek troops crossed into Bulgaria after a shooting incident on the border. Strong diplomatic pressure from Britain and France, acting through the League Council, brought about a rapid ceasefire and a Commission of Inquiry was appointed to investigate the causes of the conflict and the amount of reparations which should be paid. In contrast to the Greco-Italian dispute, when the Council in effect determined in advance both Greece's responsibility and that Italy should receive the full indemnity demanded, the Council in 1925 declared that 'all necessary care and deliberation should be employed in ascertaining the facts and fixing the amount of reparations due'.[21] Moreover, whereas in the Corfu incident a legal commission went some way towards condoning Italy's premature resort to force, in the Greco-Bulgarian conflict Briand, then President of the Council, stated as a general principle that 'in the case of a territory violated without sufficient reason reparations are due, even if at the time of the event the party committing the violation believes that the circumstances justified his act'.[22] However, although the outcome of this affair was hardly the triumph for collective security it was claimed as at the time, it did illustrate the advantages of the existence of the League in a crisis involving two small states where the great powers had no vital interests and so could act in concert. The Bulgarian government was confident enough to be able to instruct its troops not to resist the Greek incursion once it knew that the League Council was taking up the matter. Even Greece, which could justifiably feel aggrieved at the double standards which seemed to apply to similar behaviour by great and small powers, was partially appeased when it received economic aid, arranged through League auspices.[23] Both Greece and Bulgaria benefited from the appointment of a small group of observers to arbitrate over any frontier dispute for two years after the ceasefire – a forerunner of contemporary UN peacekeeping operations.

The Bolivia–Paraguay conflict, which developed into a major war in the 1930s, revealed that the League's sphere of action was mainly limited to Europe and that it could do little in Latin America without the support of Washington. When the first fighting occurred in

1928, the matter was placed before the Council by the League Secretary-General, Sir Eric Drummond, in a rare use of his personal
initiative.[24] However, the Council merely reminded the two sides of
their Covenant obligations and passed the issue on to a pan-American institution, which unsuccessfully attempted to resolve the dispute by arbitration.[25] When the conflict reached the level of full-
scale war in 1933 – a war in which 100 000 were to die – the League
was more extensively, although equally ineffectively, involved. It
sent out a Commission of Inquiry, attempted vainly to bring about
a conciliation, appointed a special Advisory Committee on the matter and tried to enforce a ceasefire by organising (with some success) an arms embargo first against both sides, then against
Paraguay alone after it had rejected Assembly proposals on the
war.[26] Although the United States participated in the arms embargo, it refused to join either of the investigative bodies and it was
clear to the disputants that these lacked credibility without an
American presence.[27]

By the end of the 1920s the League had developed a number of
techniques which it had used with varying degrees of success in several conflicts. There were established routines for investigating
disputes, conciliating the parties and keeping the peace in the aftermath of the fighting. These had, on occasion, even been backed by
the threat of sanctions. Yet, as the major crises of the 1930s un-
folded, the League seemed increasingly irrelevant, to a point where
such a momentous event as the loss of statehood by one of its own
members, Austria in 1938, could take place virtually without comment from the League. But in most cases it was not so much that the
League did nothing – the 1930s witnessed the entire range of
possible League responses to crises – but that what was done was
always too little or too late.

The limitations of the League were perhaps demonstrated most
clearly in the first great crisis of the 1930s, when Japanese troops
overran Manchuria in 1931.[28] Japan had a legitimate military
presence in Manchuria to protect its interests in the South Manchurian Railway, and it was an explosion on the railway, allegedly deto-
nated by Chinese soldiers, which sparked off the Japanese move
into Manchuria. Although it was revealed years later that the whole
incident had been engineered by the Japanese army as a pretext for
the invasion, blame at the time appeared to be more evenly divided.
The League Council at first hoped to be able to deal with the issue

in much the same way as it had handled the Greco-Bulgarian conflict – as an 'accidental' outbreak of fighting which both sides wanted to be peacefully resolved. China appealed to the League under Article 11 of the Covenant, where the emphasis was on conciliation, rather than immediately resorting to the collective security and enforcement provisions of Articles 10, 15 and 16. The Council's first move was to call for a ceasefire and withdrawal of Japanese troops. When the Japanese did not withdraw and further Council meetings (attended for the first time by an invited American delegation) were fruitless, it was decided on 10 December to send a League Commission under Lord Lytton to investigate the dispute. Meanwhile Japan's advance continued, and in January 1932 new fighting broke out in Shanghai. This led China to make a fresh approach to the League, this time invoking Articles 10 and 15 and appealing to the Assembly rather than the Council. The Shanghai affair proved to be merely a temporary episode, but Japan, increasingly dominated by militarist elements, established a separate puppet state in Manchuria, 'Manchukuo', on 9 March. Nearly seven months later the report of the Lytton Commission was published. Although it refused to countenance international recognition of Manchukuo, it called for Manchuria to have autonomous status within China, with a significant Japanese influence over its administration. The report strove to maintain a similar evenhandedness throughout, but its adoption by the Assembly on 24 February 1933 was followed on 27 March by Japan's withdrawal from the League.[29]

The Manchurian crisis brought into sharper focus than any previous conflict the range and complexity of the problems faced by collective security in general and the League in particular. The first area of confusion concerned whether Japan could be identified as a clear-cut aggressor. Throughout the crisis Japan was acknowledged to possess legitimate interests in Manchuria and, especially at the beginning, many were inclined to believe that the Chinese had brought the conflict upon themselves[30] – a belief bolstered by frequent Japanese assurances as to their limited intentions, which the Council had little option but to accept.[31] Secondly, and inevitably in a crisis sparked off by a great power, a variety of larger political considerations outweighed the immediate issue for the other powers. Britain and France were anxious not to take any action that would be opposed by Washington, while in the United States the State Department was influenced by the possibility that League opposition to Japan might have an adverse effect on the domestic balance of power in Japan between civil and military factions.[32] None of the powers was really willing to confront Japan, while, in accordance with a long tradition, one section of the British Foreign Office seemed more concerned initially lest French duplicity might enable Paris to gain some advantage over London in its relationship with Japan.[33] A third problem, and one for which the institutionalised character of collective security was partly responsible, was the considerable delay in implementing the various stages of the League's consideration of the matter. Japan was able to use a range of delaying tactics including legal quibbles throughout the crisis,[34] while the length of time taken for the Lytton Commission to be constituted and arrive in China occasioned bitter complaints from the Chinese.[35] Finally, the crisis clearly revealed the Eurocentric nature of the League. Several influential British diplomats argued, in effect, that the fundamental principles on which the League was based were not applicable to this conflict because the Japanese had not yet 'assimilated the ideas of international relations which have guided British policy since the war',[36] and because, given Japan's special rights in Manchuria, 'the ordinary canons of international intercourse have no application in Manchuria'.[37]

The crisis which effectively broke the League as a force of any significance in the important political questions of the time was the Italian invasion of Ethiopia on 3 October 1935. Although Ethiopia was a sovereign member of the League, Mussolini's government had long seen it as occupying a special, quasi-colonial position in relation to Italy. As early as 1926 Ethiopia had had occasion to protest to the League because of an Anglo-Italian agreement over the exploitation of Ethiopia's economic resources. In 1928 Italy and Ethiopia signed a treaty which included provisions for arbitrating any fresh dispute that might arise between them, but the crisis of 1935 occurred essentially because Mussolini no longer had any interest in a peaceful settlement of disputes with Ethiopia and was determined upon a course of annexation. It began with clashes between Italian and Ethiopian soldiers in the Wal-Wal region of Ethiopia in December 1934. After an initial show of reluctance, Italy was eventually persuaded to seek a peaceful solution under the terms of the 1928 treaty. However, Italian pressure on Ethiopia continued unabated, with a build-up of troops in neighbouring Italian Somaliland and a series of delaying tactics designed to prevent the commencement of the arbitration procedures. On 16 March Ethiopia appealed to the League under Article 15 of the Covenant, which dealt specifically with disputes which had not proved amenable to arbitration or judicial settlement.[38]

For France and, to a lesser extent, Britain, the Ethiopian crisis from start to finish posed a number of genuine dilemmas which strongly influenced their actions after this point. If Italy under its imperious leader were pushed too far this could lead to a great power conflict, with the inevitable risk of a general conflagration, in the name of an organisation whose purpose was to prevent war. Moreover the real danger in Europe, as was becoming ever more apparent in 1935–6, was Hitler's Germany, and Italy was a significant factor in the European balance of power whatever side it might eventually support. On the other hand, should the prestige of the League be seriously damaged by great power inaction over Ethiopia this might have equally unfortunate consequences, including a widespread increase in insecurity. As France's Prime Minister, Pierre Laval, put it in July 1935: 'France's entire European policy is based upon the League of Nations. The League of Nations is the basis of the Locarno Treaty, which is an essential element of French security, and it is within a League framework that the agreements which bind us to our friends in Central Europe are inserted.'[39]

So when Ethiopia appealed to the League in March, the initial Anglo-French response was to renew efforts to have the affair settled by arbitration rather than by the League Council. Mussolini was now prepared to feign a willingness to accept arbitration, especially as he believed that he had received a number of signals from Britain and France suggesting that they might acquiesce in an eventual Italian conquest of Ethiopia.[40] Hence the League Council did not effectively take up the Ethiopian crisis until September, although Britain and France had in the meantime been involved in informal negotiations with Italy.[41] They had also begun to consider the prospects and likely consequences of applying military sanctions against Italy should Article 16 of the Covenant eventually be invoked. Laval and Sir Samuel Hoare, Britain's Foreign Secretary, privately agreed that sanctions should be limited to economic and financial measures to be applied 'cautiously and in stages'.[42] But in public Hoare made a strong speech at the Assembly in the hope that this might deter Italy from the action it was so obviously contemplating. During September a number of League Committees were established to investigate and try to resolve the dispute, while the Commission of Inquiry into the Wal-Wal incident reported its findings on 3 September, which effectively exonerated both parties. Another League Committee (investigating one of Italy's pretexts for the legitimacy of its pressure on Ethiopia) recommended on 18 September that a League Commission should be appointed to promote internal reform in Ethiopia. But the futility of all such gestures of conciliation was demonstrated when Italy launched its invasion on 3 October. Four days later the Council decided that Italy had gone to war in violation of its Covenant obligations, and on 11 October the Assembly appointed a Committee to coordinate the imposition of sanctions.

From this point, the international response to the invasion proceeded at three different levels, which were not always in harmony with each other. At one level, the various League institutions and special Committees concentrated primarily on the sanctions question. At another, Britain and France, while also involved in organising sanctions, continued their behind-the-scenes efforts to obtain an agreed settlement, efforts whose course was critically influenced by important differences between the two powers.[43] At the third level, public opinion, which had been so strongly emphasised by Woodrow Wilson when the League was established, played an important, though by no means always a helpful role, and one in which the different national publics, especially in Britain and France, did not speak with the same voice.

The principal economic sanctions imposed were an embargo on exports of war materials to Italy, a prohibition of all Italian exports and a ban on the granting of any loans to Italy. Although inevitably these measures were not universally observed, they did inflict a significant degree of damage upon the Italian economy. However, it soon became clear that for Italy to be forced to withdraw from Ethiopia more severe measures would have to be considered. Debate at Geneva came to focus on the prospects of imposing two additional sanctions: prohibiting oil exports to Italy and closing the Suez Canal to Italian shipping. The second was never a real possibility: Britain and France, who controlled the Canal, both regarded this as clearly a military rather than an economic sanction and one that would very probably lead to war.[44] But an embargo on oil was another matter and was very nearly enforced.

The League Coordinating Committee on sanctions advocated an embargo on oil on 9 November. Romania, which supplied 40.6 per cent of Italy's oil, and the Soviet Union, which supplied 16 per cent, both agreed to support an embargo so long as it was universally observed.[45] Supplies from another important source, Iran, were effectively controlled by Britain, so prospects for a successful embargo looked good. But although the American Secretary of State, Cordell Hull, had publicly supported the idea of an embargo, Sir Samuel Hoare had very serious doubts as to whether American oil producers would not take advantage of the United States' non-membership of the League to make up any deficiency in Italy's oil imports caused by an embargo.[46] More important, however, was the constant fear in both London and Paris that an oil embargo might provoke Mussolini into a 'mad dog act' – that is a declaration of war.[47] Britain was also concerned that, should this happen, she would not be able to count on the support of France, which was going through a period of political turmoil and where public opinion, partly influenced by newspaper campaigns, appeared hostile both to Britain and to any idea of war with Italy.[48] It was largely these considerations, combined with worries about Britain's lack of military preparedness, that led to the abortive 'Hoare–Laval Pact' in December, by which the two powers would have attempted to settle the crisis on terms favourable to Italy.[49] A contemporary interpretation by a British diplomat present at the meeting between Hoare and Laval suggests that calculations about the longer term security of Europe were a major factor:

> To force France against her will to fight would have meant a definite break of the Anglo-French understanding and therewith risked the end, not only of the League of Nations but, far more serious, of European civilisation. Europe would have been left at the mercy of Germany when the time came for Berlin to move.[50]

However, opinion in Britain, which was strongly pro-Ethiopian, forced Hoare to resign when details of the Pact were revealed, and eventually at the end of February 1936, after a League committee of experts had concluded that a universally supported oil embargo would prove effective against Italy within three and a half months, Britain decided to support oil sanctions. This caused consternation in France, coming as it did at the same time as the developing crisis over Germany's remilitarisation of the Rhineland. But French apprehensions proved to be premature as resistance in Ethiopia quickly collapsed before oil sanctions could be introduced. On 10 May the Ethiopian emperor, Haile Selassie, cabled the League that he had decided to end the war, prompting, amongst many other responses, Guatemala's immediate withdrawal from the League because 'events have demonstrated the impossibility of putting into practice the high ideals aimed at when the League was founded'.[51]

The Ethiopian crisis deserves the relatively detailed coverage it has received here because of its impact on the League and because it represents the only fully genuine collective security action undertaken by either the League or the UN. It also demonstrates some of the inherent problems of the central theme of collective security – that states undertake a general and open-ended commitment to unite against any aggressor – in a situation where action against one state could jeopardise the balance of power against another, far more dangerous aggressor. In the event the chief error of the powers, particularly Britain, lay in their inability to reach a clear-cut decision either for or against firm opposition to Italy. The best illustration of this does not involve sanctions but the other side of the coin: assistance to Ethiopia. In 1930 the League had passed a draft Convention agreeing to give financial support to states suffering aggression but this had never come into force.[52] Ethiopia appealed for financial assistance on 1 November 1935, arguing that 'relying upon the guarantee of collective security embodied in the Covenant, the Ethiopian Government had created neither arsenals nor arms and munitions factories'.[53] Britain's ambassador to Ethiopia strongly urged the government to support the Ethiopian request, but Sir Samuel Hoare replied that as the League as a whole (which was waiting for a lead from Britain) refused to agree to a collective loan to Ethiopia, Britain would not do so unilaterally.[54] Ethiopian military resistance to Italy was, in fact, surprisingly effective for some months,[55] and after the ceasefire Ethiopia's delegate to the League argued strongly that lack of financial support to purchase weapons and munitions had been the decisive factor in the Ethiopian defeat.[56]

A final illustration of the problems faced by the League in its efforts to promote international security is to be found in its pursuit of disarmament: seen by many in 1919 as an essential component of an effective collective security system. An early success in arms control was achieved at the Washington Conference of November 1921, when each of the major powers agreed to limit its naval strength by keeping it within a predetermined ratio vis-à-vis the other powers. However, this agreement was reached outside League auspices and when the League attempted to fulfil its commitment under Article 8 of the Covenant to promote general disarmament measures, it immediately encountered some fundamental problems. Some of these were of an essentially technical nature, such as how to compare different types of armaments for arms limitation purposes, how to distinguish between 'offensive' and 'defensive' weapons and how to supervise commitments to disarm to ensure that they were fully executed. But the fundamental political problem was that agreements to limit arms at the levels current at any given time would please only those who were basically satisfied with the status quo at that time, while they would be unacceptable to those, such as Germany, who wished to revise the existing order and whose current military strength was well below its true potential. All of these issues came to a head at the League's Disarmament Conference which met from February 1932 until the end of 1934 (although its effective end was in October 1933 when Hitler took Germany out of the Conference and the League). The Conference, which was attended by an American delegation, was always overshadowed by the Manchurian crisis and even more by the tightening Nazi stranglehold on Germany but even before Hitler became German Chancellor in January 1933 the Conference had failed to produce any results other than to confirm a 1925 agreement that poison gases should be prohibited in warfare. The Conference had merely served to confirm the fact that substantial disarmament, like collective security in general, required an atmosphere of mutual trust – an exceedingly distant prospect in the Europe of the 1930s.

After the Ethiopian crisis the League lingered on with increasing irrelevance until 1946. Its last act in the collective security field, one that blended petulance and farce, came at the end of 1939 when, with all due solemnity, it expelled the Soviet Union for its attack on Finland. Hitler's aggressions, the Spanish Civil War and even Turkey's annexation of part of Syria in 1936 had all taken place with only marginal League involvement. Many explanations and excuses have been offered for the League's failure: it lacked universality, with the United States never a member and Germany, the Soviet Union, Japan, Italy and several Latin American states absent for various periods; it had to cope with crises of extraordinary magnitude and frequency at a time when the popular mood in the democracies was against war and the worldwide depression made even the cost of economic sanctions seem intolerable; the association of the League with the Versailles Treaty made it automatically unpopular in Germany; the Covenant was a flawed document from the start, with too many ambiguities and loopholes for would-be aggressors; or alternatively it was too ambitious and always impracticable in a world of sovereign states. From another perspective, to talk of the League's failure is meaningless when what really happened in the 1930s was that Anglo-French diplomacy failed in the face of relentless aggression, with the League merely one of the instruments available to the two powers. If so, it was never an instrument in which they seemed to invest much confidence: the combined annual budget of the League, the ILO and the Permanent Court was seldom greater than 6 million dollars – barely the cost of a single cruiser. The 'realistic' argument that the same lack of solidarity amongst states which seemed to make a League of Nations necessary also doomed it to failure may well be correct. It may have been unrealistic to hope for substantial disarmament or any significant diminution of their sovereignty from the powers. But it was perhaps not unduly idealistic to expect that they would at least enable the League to perform its limited functions without the constant need to justify every expense to the world's treasury officials.

The League and international law

In a strict sense the League's role in relation to international law should not be distinguished from any of its other functions. The Covenant was part of international law and the central theme of all aspects of the League's work was that states should be guided by rules of conduct. So whenever the League attempted to carry out its peace treaty obligations to minorities by organising plebiscites or investigating disputes; whenever it tried to decide rules and guidelines to govern international economic relations or such matters as the postwar refugee problem; when it drew up international conventions on environmental and ecological questions, such as the regulation of whaling or controlling the pollution of the seas by oil; when it devised more comprehensive international regimes in areas like communications and transit, preventing the spread of epidemics, or controlling the drug traffic: in all such work it was undertaking tasks which, at the very least, had important implications for international law. But apart from such activities, which in strict legal terms provided 'evidence' of the existence of a rule of international law, rather than actually creating law in themselves,[57] certain aspects of the League's work had a direct and longer term influence upon the role of law in international relations.

A major innovation was the creation of the Permanent Court of International Justice. This had received relatively little consideration prior to the Peace Conference, being one of several ideas which only gained momentum during the negotiations in Paris.[58] The Court, which commenced operations in 1922, consisted of eleven (later fifteen) judges selected by both the Council and Assembly to 'represent the main forms of civilisation and the principal legal systems of the world'.[59] The Court had the capacity to make judgements on disputes brought before it and to give 'advisory opinions' when requested by the League. These opinions were not formally binding upon states but in practice acquired almost as great a legal significance as the actual judgements. The Court heard 66 cases between 1922 and 1939, of which 28 were requests for advisory opinions; 50 of the cases were filed before 1932. States had the option of declaring in advance their acceptance of the Court's jurisdiction of certain classes of dispute, an option taken up with various reservations by 40 governments, with jurisdiction otherwise being voluntary.

Many of the cases stemmed from friction arising out of the peace treaties, especially where Polish-German relations were involved. Some created significant precedents, as when a 1928 advisory opinion on the courts of Danzig appeared to imply that individuals had rights under international law, thus rejecting the traditional doctrine which only accorded such rights to states.[60] However, the Court was not (nor was it really intended to be) a major force for peace and stability. As with any legal system, the effectiveness of international law is in direct proportion to the existence of order and a sense of community in the society which it serves.[61] Rather, the importance of the Court was threefold. It showed that a standing international court did have a part to play in promoting orderly international relations in conditions where there was already a strong underlying desire for order. It was a significant landmark in the gradual acceptance by states that rules had a place in international politics. It also developed a body of jurisprudence which played a part in the adaptation of international law to changing circumstances – which, in a sense, acted as a new source of international law itself.

Although the League was far from being an international legislature, other aspects of its work did have some significance for the creation of international law. Before 1939, 120 international conventions were concluded by the League not to speak of 80 agreed by the ILO.[62] This did not mean that they automatically became binding upon states since they all required (and often failed to obtain) ratification by the sovereign body of each state; but they were none the less important in bringing about subtle changes in the process of law formation in international relations. Traditionally law had 'emerged' from the practice of states. Now, without the old system being displaced, a new element had been introduced (as had been the intention of the Hague Conferences) in which both the general principles and the fine details of international law were debated by states, with attempts being made to arrive at a consensus view. Such a view could not fail to be regarded as important evidence of the existing state of international law, even if it was not, strictly speaking, law itself.

An attempt was made to give the League a more clear-cut role in defining and coordinating the current rules of international law, but this was opposed as 'a very dangerous project' by no less a League supporter than Lord Robert Cecil.[63] However, following an initiative from smaller states, a committee of experts was later set up to begin the codification of international law in such areas as nationality, territorial waters and the rights of aliens.[64] A conference on codification was held at The Hague in 1930, but this was generally admitted to be disappointing and the next Assembly abandoned the attempt at codification.[65]

The League's most intimate involvement with international law came in the various experiments in international administration of the interwar years. Apart from its responsibilities in economic and other functional areas, which are considered shortly, the League administered the Saar Territory, supervised the government of Danzig, and oversaw the mandates system.

The Saar Territory was an economically important area on the Franco-German border which was claimed by both countries. The League governed it for 15 years, at the end of which it organised a plebiscite, as required by the Versailles Treaty, to determine the wishes of the inhabitants. The League's governing Commission of five members had full powers during its administration, with the League Council only empowered to intervene in emergencies. However, the inhabitants had the right (of which they made the fullest possible use) to petition the Council directly. Because of the impending plebiscite everything the Commission did acquired from the start a heavy political content amongst the mostly German-speaking population.[66] The plebiscite, as expected, gave the Territory back to Germany, with a massive Nazi campaign making the result even more inevitable.[67] The League administration, though always unpopular with the Saarlanders, had in fact been both fair and efficient, but ironically the only real beneficiaries of this were the Nazis, who thus gained an orderly and profitable addition to their domain.

The port of Danzig was established as a free city in order to meet Polish demands for access to the sea without actually ceding the city, with its mainly German population, to Poland. It was not directly governed by the League but placed under its protection, with a High Commissioner to act as mediator in disputes. This ensured that Danzig had a complicated and unwieldy governmental structure, with the elected Danzig government, Polish officials with various rights and powers including control over foreign policy, the semi-independent Habour and Waterways Board and the League High Commissioner all occupying separate positions of power. The League Council was itself available as an appeal court of the last resort, although in practice Danzig's problems were the most constant items on its agenda, especially before June 1925, when the procedure was changed to allow the High Commissioner to deal directly with the experts and technical agencies of the League.[68] Matters came to a head with the Nazification of Danzig that commenced in 1933. The position of the High Commissioner, as the sole buffer between the Nazis and their victims, became increasingly difficult. For a time the League Council attempted to support the High Commissioner, Sean Lester, in his efforts to uphold the League's authority and the Danzig constitution. But, as he complained in 1936, 'each meeting of the Council during the past year was followed by an intensification of the policy which has been deplored by the Council'.[69] By 1937, after Lester's departure for the Secretariat, the Council had effectively abandoned Danzig to its fate.

Article 22 of the Covenant had distinguished between three categories of mandate for the former enemy colonies, taking into account 'the stage of development of the people, the geographical situation of the territory, its economic conditions and other similar circumstances'. The detailed implications of this were later worked out in a series of charters adopted by the Council, which in each case gave the mandatory power 'full powers of legislation and administration', with the common requirement that it provide an annual report on its administration to a League Commission of eleven experts on colonial affairs. The different types of mandate were listed as C mandates (South-west Africa and Germany's Pacific territories) which were virtually indistinguishable from colonies, B mandates (other African colonies of Germany) where several restrictions on the mandatory power were laid down, and A mandates (Palestine and Trans-Jordan, Syria and Lebanon, Iraq) which had a wide range of different provisions. The charter for Palestine, for example, included the requirement to put into practice the Balfour Declaration, which had promised a Jewish national home there. The Iraq mandate stipulated that Iraq should be given its independence as soon as possible.[70]

Several problems were evident in the mandates system from the start. It did not bring about a new order for colonies as a whole since it applied only to former enemy colonies. This made the mandated territories appear, with some justice, to be merely spoils of war. The fact that the League Commission was given only marginal and indirect powers of supervision added to the impression that what was really going on was a form of covert annexation by the victorious powers. There was virtually no consultation in advance with the peoples living in the territories, in sharp contrast with the care that was taken to ascertain the views of the new nations and minorities in Europe. But despite these flaws advice from the Mandates Commission was generally taken seriously by the mandatory powers, partly because of the extreme tact employed by the Commission in its dealings with the powers.[71] Seen from the 1990s, when colonialism is all but finished, the mandates system may seem paternalistic and hypocritical. Yet it did serve to focus public attention upon the colonies and help to create the climate of opinion which later made decolonisation inevitable.

The economic and social functions of the League

From one perspective the League was simply the international reflection of the expansion of governmental powers and functions domestically. As governments came increasingly to concern them-selves with wider issues than raising revenue and defending the realm, so they employed ever greater numbers of officials in ever more complex bureaucracies to deal with these matters. And so it was inevitable that they responded to the international dimensions of these problems in the same manner: by establishing interna-tional bureaucracies. This, rather than collective security, was the true growth area in international organisation, with more than 60 per cent of the League's budget going to its economic and humani-tarian work by 1939.[72]

It is part of the tragedy of the League that its complete failure in security matters was matched only by its inability to affect the rise of economic nationalism and the ensuing global economic crisis of the 1930s. Here, however, it had the partial excuse that it was not originally intended to play a substantial economic role. Apart from Article 16, which imposed automatic economic sanctions against aggressors and required states to give each other mutual support to minimise any loss caused by sanctions, the sole reference in the Covenant to economic matters is a few words in Article 23 calling for equitable treatment of the commerce of all League members. The other economic functions grew out of the needs of the time, the most urgent of which in 1920 was reconstruction. The League did enjoy some success in this field, particularly in the case of the financial reconstruction and stabilisation of Austria, a problem handed over to the League after the powers had failed to reach agreement on it elsewhere.[73] The Financial Committee of the League was involved in similar exercises in Hungary, Bulgaria and Greece.

However, the more deep-seated problems of the world economy eluded all attempts at international solution whether within or out-side the League framework. Between 1920 and 1933 several major conferences on global economic affairs were held under League auspices, while a variety of so-called 'technical' committees consist-ing of experts in economic and financial matters were in almost constant session. An American delegation attended many of these meetings. One of the biggest conferences, in 1927, adopted resolu-tions which recognised global economic interdependence and set out certain fundamental principles (for example the removal of im-port and export restrictions) that were thought to be central to im-proving growth and reducing unemployment.[74] But governments paid little attention to these eminently sensible proposals, as even the League's own self-congratulatory ten-year progress report was obliged to recognise.[75] The last of the great economic conferences, held in London in 1933 in circumstances of desperate worldwide crisis, failed after five weeks when the United States, the only state with the necessary economic power to make a stabilisation scheme work, refused to become involved.[76] After this the League's agencies tended to concentrate on narrower research activities.

Economic reality in the 1930s dictated that unless Washington were prepared to assume the kind of responsibility for underwriting the global economic order that it did after 1945, there could be little hope of any real progress. The predominant liberal-capitalist ideology insisted on the need for international competition – despite the prevalence of national economic protection – while the emergence of alternative ideologies provided an additional source of disharmony over economic matters. For instance, at one point a special League committee was set up to examine 'economic aggression', which was seen as arising from the supposedly unfair advantage of countries with state-controlled enterprises.[77] However, to set against its failure to influence national economic-policy formulation, the League probably did constitute a necessary stage in the transition between an international free-for-all and the system which lasted for 30 years after 1945. It compiled an enormous amount of essential information, enabled an exchange of ideas and experiences and revealed some of the technical and structural difficulties that would have to be overcome if a new economic order was to work.

The League was rather more successful in its other 'technical' activities. It established major institutions such as the Health Organisation and the Communications and Transit Organisation, as well as numerous committees on such matters as the drug trade, refugees, the traffic in women and children and intellectual cooperation. The important non-members of the League, including Germany, participated in most of these activities from the start. Although the new technical organisations did not supplant all of the existing international unions, as had originally been intended, they did make a significant contribution to the development of international regimes in their respective fields. For instance, the 1921 Barcelona Conference on Communications and Transit adopted a Convention on freedom of transit across international boundaries which achieved a high level of subsequent ratification, although another Convention on international waterways failed to be ratified.[78] Other conferences reached agreement on a wide range of lesser communications issues, although in some instances they met with complete failure, as in 1931. In health matters the League continued and expanded the work done by earlier sanitary authorities to such effect that it provided the model for the UN's World Health Organisation. It established new procedures for combating epidemics, sent out several large medical units to China, standardised a great number of medicines, stimulated interest in nutrition problems and initiated studies of child welfare, public health training and many other subjects.[79] The League was similarly active in a wide range of other technical areas, although, as ever, the League agencies were constrained by lack of adequate financial support. The comparative success of the League in its functional work led the Bruce Committee, which investigated possible reforms in this area in 1939, to propose that all this part of the League's work should be brought under the supervision of a single agency, to be called the Central Committee for Economic and Social Questions – a proposal taken up when the UN was established.

Special mention should be made of the International Labour Organisation as the only significant part of the League structure to survive intact after 1945. Originally envisaged as a safety valve against the spread of Bolshevism, its constitution gave it potentially far-reaching functions, a fact of which its energetic first Secretary-General, Albert Thomas, took fullest advantage. Its Constitution began with the firm, if debatable, assertion that 'the League of Nations has for its object the establishment of universal peace, and such peace can be established only if it is based upon social justice'. Hence, apart from its basic role in attempting to improve working conditions, the ILO was given some responsibility for pursuing such reforms as the prevention of unemployment and the provision of an adequate living wage. Its influence, such as it was, upon states was enhanced by the fact that most of the non-members of the League, including the United States, did join the ILO. Perhaps more significantly, the trade union movement was a powerful ILO constituency with a strong interest in promoting the ILO's cause. The ILO had no powers to compel states to meet the minimum international standards of labour legislation set by its conferences, a fact which went some way to explaining the general willingness of states to take at least some notice of its conclusions.

The structural framework of the League

One aspect of the League which had, for better or worse, a lasting impact on future international organisations and on the wider conduct of diplomacy was the structure of its principal bodies, the Council, Assembly and Secretariat. In each case the basic pattern set in the League was maintained in the UN as well as in several regional organisations.

The Council's prospects of becoming an institutionalised great power Concert had vanished when the Peace Conference accepted the principle of four Council seats for smaller states on a non-permanent basis. There had been a brief period dating from the 1925 Locarno agreements when it had seemed that an informal Concert system might be emerging out of regular meetings between the British, French and German Foreign Ministers. But to some extent these sidestepped the formal Council sessions rather than utilising them, although the three Foreign Ministers did begin the practice of attending the Council in person during this period.

Once the principle of small power membership of the Council had been first conceded, it inevitably made the acquisition of such a place a matter of prestige and even, for some states, a major foreign policy goal. The Assembly had decided in 1920 that the main criterion in the allocation of non-permanent places should be equitable geographical distribution.[80] But this did not dispel the competitive attitudes of the smaller states concerning Council places, and only accentuated an already evident tendency towards the formation of regional blocs in the Assembly and the other League bodies. This issue came to a head with the crisis in 1926 over Germany's admission to the League (and an automatic Council seat) which led to claims for permanent Council membership from Brazil, Poland and Spain. An attempt was made to appease them by increasing to nine the number of non-permanent seats (which had already been increased in 1922 to six), to include a new category of three 'semi-permanent' seats, whose holders could be re-elected by a two-thirds majority of the Assembly. This did not satisfy Brazil and Spain, who both resigned from the League, although Spain returned within two years.

Another aspect of the Council which worked against any prospect of it functioning as a high-powered international directorate was its obligation to deal with a mass of detailed work arising out of the peace settlement. The finer points of the problems of Danzig, the Saar and a host of minorities all became monotonously familiar to the Council during the 1920s, one reason, perhaps, why the Soviet Union was to insist that the Council's UN successor should confine itself to security matters. Later the Council acquired an unforeseen role as one of the actual arenas of conflicts amongst the powers rather than an agency for effecting compromises amongst them. This tendency was inevitably strengthened by the public sessions of the Council, which were originally hailed as a victory for Woodrow Wilson's 'open diplomacy' philosophy.

In contrast to the determination shown by the smaller states at the Peace Conference to have a significant influence upon the composition and powers of the Council, the Assembly had received very little attention, largely because it had always been seen as the lesser of the two bodies.[81] In most eyes the Assembly was to be essentially a forum for discussion through which Wilson's 'world public opinion' would make itself felt, especially as it was envisaged that the three Assembly delegates permitted for each state would not be government officials. None the less, despite the generally low expectations of the Assembly, it was allocated a number of functions in the Covenant which gave it the potential for developing a significant role in the future. Article 3 gave it the capacity to deal with 'any matter within the sphere of the League or affecting the peace of the world'. Article 11, which in later years tended to be invoked in preference to the more stringent collective security provisions of Articles 10, 15 and 16, gave members the 'friendly right' to bring before the Assembly, as well as the Council, any circumstance threatening international peace. There was also a provision, added as an afterthought to Article 15, for disputes to be transferred from the Council to the Assembly, if so required.

However, these formal provisions were far less important in establishing the Assembly's significance than a series of precedents set in the first Assembly, which opened on 15 November 1920. The most crucial of these was the Assembly's decision to meet every year, as against the assumption at Paris that meetings would be held only every four years. The delegates at the first Assembly were generally leading statesmen, rather than the assorted representatives of various walks of life who were originally supposed to constitute it. This inevitably gave it a much higher political awareness and a collective determination not to accept a subordinate role. The first fruits of this came when the Assembly appropriated for itself the overall financial control of the League, a responsibility that had not been specifically allocated by the Covenant.[82] This immediately gave the Assembly something of the aura of a parliament as well as a means of intervening in almost every aspect of the League's work. In some instances the first Assembly gave itself this right more directly, as when it requested the Council to present future Assemblies with a report on its work in the previous year and when it referred to its committees such matters as the League mandates, which were supposedly the sole responsibility of the Council. Finally the first Assembly immediately captured the public imagination: it had a glamorous air about it and seemed to be the repository of the remaining early idealism which had surrounded the League concept.

During its lifetime the Assembly tended to be the principal initiator of much of the day-to-day business of the League. Its committees not only promoted various projects in the League's technical agencies and drew up many international conventions but also formulated potentially important proposals in the security field, such as the abortive Geneva Protocol. It also requested the Council to pursue various matters, and in general saw itself as the overseer of all aspects of the League's work. On important political questions the requirement for Assembly votes to be unanimous sometimes prevented action, though nothing like as often as had once been feared.[83]

Only three disputes were directly referred to the Assembly, with results which in general did not suggest that such a large organisation could play a useful role where tact and diplomacy might be needed more than verbal belligerence. This was particularly the case of the first dispute, the fighting in Shanghai during the Manchurian crisis, where a highly nationalistic and sensitive government such as Japan's could hardly be expected to take kindly to criticism from smaller states. The Assembly debates were one of the factors leading to Japan's withdrawal from the League, as they were also in prompting Paraguay to withdraw after the Bolivia–Paraguay dispute had been referred to the Assembly. The third instance, the Soviet invasion of Finland, came when the League was already virtually irrelevant, although its action in expelling the Soviet Union was likewise an expression of moral indignation rather than a well-thought-out attempt to resolve the crisis.

Despite its role as initiator and supervisor of general League policy, the Assembly's real significance still lay in its performance of the
function for which it was principally designed: an international
forum for the expression of 'world public opinion'. The Assembly
did not feel itself to be restricted in any way as to the subjects it
could legitimately discuss, and for the first time most major issues
could be debated by the community of states as a whole. Views inevitably differ about the value of this exercise. One contemporary
observer writes that as time went on the Assembly 'tended to lose its
parliamentary character altogether. The "declaration", carefully
prepared, neatly typed and often monotonously read, took the
place of speeches. The proceedings became not only decorous but
dull.'[84] But to another writer, the Assembly was 'very much what the
representative body of an international organisation should be' and
the influence of the small powers generally 'temperate and constructive'.[85]

The third part of the League's structure was its Secretariat. The
Covenant had nothing to say about the recruitment of the Secretariat or how it was to perform its various functions. Many assumed
that officials would be recruited from the existing body of national
diplomats and that these would retain a primary allegiance to their
state rather than to the League. The first Secretary-General, Sir Eric
Drummond, attempted from the start to establish a rather different
principle, borrowed from his experience in the British Civil Service,
which made League officials responsible to the League rather than
to their own countries and called upon governments to accept that
their nationals had to pursue the League's interest during their
period of office. In return officials themselves were supposed always
to act impartially. Another principle laid down at an early stage was
that members of the Secretariat should be drawn from as wide a
geographical area as possible.

Inevitably practice did not always match the theory. Places on the
Secretariat assumed a political significance from the outset, as the
major blocs in the League strove to ensure that their interests were
well represented. For instance, when the Frenchman Joseph Avenol
replaced Drummond as Secretary-General in 1933, Italy, Germany
and the smaller states as a whole each demanded and received the
'compensation' of an additional place on the Secretariat.[86] Moreover,
as Drummond's biographer notes: 'In a sense, Secretariat Positions
and places on temporary or permanent League bodies . . . were a

type of spoils system manipulated both to pay off political obligations as well as to assure the continual loyalty or assistance of a particular power.'[87] A worse problem was that some members of the
Secretariat blatantly pursued the interests of their own countries.
This was especially the case of the fascist states, but even Drummond himself maintained close links with the British Foreign Office, frequently informing London about his Secretariat business
and sometimes about his dealings with other powers.[88] He was also
given access to confidential documents by the Foreign Office – a
useful privilege in view of the League's lack of a diplomatic service
of its own but one that inevitably gave him a somewhat Anglocentric
view of affairs.[89] In general, however, Drummond worked to prevent any suspicion that he was simply allowing the League to be
used as an instrument of British policy. A more common problem
with the Secretariat, especially under Avenol, was that it tended to
see the first interest of the League as survival intact without the withdrawal of any of its members, especially the important ones, which
meant that it normally supported the advocates of appeasement.

In two respects the Secretariat demonstrated the value of having
a permanent body of international officials. It frequently served as
a useful and necessary channel of communication between the
many parts of the League, including the national delegations. And
over the years it became a repository of information and experience
concerning the unique problems of international organisations.
Indeed it may say something for the validity of the concept of the
impartial international Civil Servant, not to speak of the continuity
between the League and the UN, that many League officials later
took up employment with the UN.

Conclusion

That the failure of the League did not doom the whole process of
international organisation is, as has been remarked, at first sight
surprising. There are three main reasons why the powers should
not have thought it futile to try again with the United Nations. The
first is that it was easy to point to various defects in the Covenant
and to believe that these could be remedied in the subsequent
organisation. If in addition the United States became a member,
the overall imbalance of power that had made the war possible

could be decisively corrected. Secondly, it was clearly going to be increasingly difficult for the major powers simply to ignore the voices of the smaller states in matters where the latter felt they had a significant interest. The League had provided one means of catering for this new element of 'international democracy', and it was difficult to envisage how else but in an international organisation meeting continuously all states could accept that their views had an equal chance of being heard.

Finally, the League had been established as a response to several clearly perceived problems and these showed no sign of going away. Indeed the tasks which seemed to require cooperative international solutions had grown in number, as even the briefest comparison of the Covenant with the UN Charter indicates. It was possible to see the League not as having failed but simply as having made a start, if not an especially promising one. This was clearly the case in such areas as the development of international law and the range of issues arising out of economic interdependence, but even in relation to international security matters the League had developed a variety of peacekeeping mechanisms which could, perhaps, be built upon.

3 The American-led, Cold War United Nations, 1945–1960

The creation of the United Nations

Two things were clear in the minds of the wartime allied leaders: they would create a new collective security system and they would not build it on the League structure.[1] This was because the League had been discredited by failure and was unacceptable to the two superpowers: the Soviets because of their humiliation at being, in effect, expelled in 1939; the Americans because they wanted to avoid the old battles that had surrounded the question of League membership.

Churchill and Roosevelt initially played with the idea of a series of regional bodies under an overarching four-power World Council, but were persuaded to abandon it by their foreign ministries. Once universalism had won out, and although '[w]e pretended we had a *tabula rasa*, and were receiving direct inspiration', the new organisation 'bore a most embarrassing resemblance to its predecessor. Again and again, without any direct reference to what had transpired during twenty years at Geneva, we arrived, surprisingly, at results that might seem to have been modelled on the earlier organisation.'[2]

Significant elements of successful pre-existing international machinery, such as the International Labour Organisation, were adopted without fundamental alteration. And the structure of the UN, with its Secretariat, Security Council and General Assembly, mirrored the equivalent organs of the League. Both organisations were firmly based on the principle of voluntary association amongst sovereign equals, and many of the commitments are virtually identical. But the immediate context in which the Charter was drafted was different in three ways.

It differed, firstly, in that the drafting of the Charter was much more professional and considered. Its general outline had been agreed by the end of the Moscow Conference in October 1943. Exceedingly complex negotiations between professional diplomats at Dumbarton Oaks in August–September 1944 worked out many of the details, but the sensitive issue of the Security Council veto was left to the top-level Yalta meeting in February 1945. At Yalta the 'big three' – the USA, USSR and UK – agreed that on all but procedural matters, Security Council decisions required the affirmative votes of the permanent members. (However, in decisions regarding peaceful settlement, parties to a dispute had to refrain from voting.) This settled, the authors of the Yalta agreement united to impose it on the San Francisco conference of April–June 1945.[3]

The second contextual difference was that the UN was deliberately created before the end of the war. This was because the 'big three' wanted to cash in on wartime unity. They feared postwar disunity both at home (the Americans were worried about a resurgence of isolationism) and among the allies. They also wanted to avoid the 1919 mistake of linking the new organisation with the peace treaties.

Thirdly, and according to one of the drafters, '[n]othing . . . was so original in the Charter as the manner of its making'.[4] The San Francisco conference, which was attended by 50 states,[5] took place in an unprecedented glare of publicity under the pressure of popular demand for a vigorous attack on the evils of international life. Never before had 'such vital problems'[6] been subject to such a procedure: all proposals were subjected to the fullest discussion, and required a two-thirds vote to be passed. Some 1200 amendments were tabled and the small states won important concessions. The description of the General Assembly's powers was made more definite and it was given the right to discuss and make recommendations on any matter affecting the peace of the world or the general welfare of nations.[7] The powers of the Economic and Social Council (ECOSOC) were significantly altered and its dignity was enhanced by making it one of the UN's principal organs. The conference added a Declaration Regarding Non-self-governing Territories (chapter 11). It drafted two lengthy chapters (12 and 13) on trusteeship, which had not been discussed at Dumbarton Oaks, and in so doing strengthened the system that had been submitted by the sponsoring powers and France. It also established the Trusteeship Council as a major organ.

Differences from the League

As has been mentioned, there were fundamental similarities between
the UN and the League. But, within these elements of continuity,
there were significant differences of shape and emphasis between the
two organisations. More particularly, there were five important respects in which the UN Charter represented measures which were
regarded as an improvement on the Covenant of the League.

The first such change concerned the powers of the Security Council and the veto.[8] This led to the main contest at San Francisco. After
a tussle in which the Soviet negotiators tried to insist that a dispute
could not even be discussed without the unanimous consent of the
permanent members (only after the matter had been taken to
Stalin did they back down), the medium and smaller powers protested vigorously against the whole concept of the veto. However,
the great powers in effect told them no veto, no UN.[9] In the eyes of
the 'big three', the greatest improvement over the League was that
the UN would be unequivocally based on the principle of great
power concert. The veto was justified partly because the Security
Council was intended to focus its attention on the maintenance of
international peace and security, leaving most other matters to the
General Assembly. The veto was also felt to be warranted because of
great power interests and because the lessons of the past demonstrated the need for agreement amongst the major powers if the
organisation were to act effectively. As the British Commentary on
the Charter put it, their consent was

> imperative . . . since they will have the main responsibility for
> action. It is also clear that no enforcement action by the Organi-
> sation can be taken against a Great Power itself without a major
> war. If such a situation arises the United Nations will have failed
> in its purpose and all members will have to act as seems best in
> the circumstances . . . the successful working of the United Na-
> tions depends on the preservation of the unanimity of the Great
> Powers; not of course on all the details of policy, but on its broad
> principles. If this unanimity is seriously undermined no provision
> of the Charter is likely to be of much avail.[10]

Of course, the veto also meant that great powers could prevent
international measures being taken against their allies, but this was

nothing new. However, in deference to the objections of Canada and other 'middle powers', states providing troops for peace enforcement were allowed to participate when the Security Council took decisions on any question 'concerning the employment of contingents of that Member's armed forces' (Article 44).

A second difference from the Covenant was that whereas the latter had been more British than American, the Charter was fundamentally based on principles advocated by the USA. The Americans were the keenest on establishing the UN and they did more extensive preparatory work than their partners. London was sympathetic to American views because of American power, because Britain wanted to be sure of American participation, and because of the problem of getting Senate approval of the Charter.[11] However, the political realities underlying the veto, and the UN's nature as an organisation in which states would pursue national interests, was hidden from the American public. In the US the UN was sold in such a simplistic and 'wilful' welter of idealistic hyperbole that 'it often seemed as if the U.N. flag was about to be hoisted over the Congress, or the U.S. flag over U.N. headquarters'.[12] This may have drowned possible objections to UN membership, but one historian believes the tension between public and private governmental attitudes was a major cause of the Cold War.[13] It has been said that Roosevelt privately envisaged the UN providing 'the orderly international setting that America's open-market economy demanded for continued success'.[14] He has also been seen as hoping that the UN would provide 'a means of bringing the Soviet Union into the family of nations and of continuing to promote Soviet cooperation at low as well as high levels of government'.[15] Certainly all three members of the Grand Alliance were vividly aware of the importance of continuing their wartime collaboration. But it meant that the UN – if it worked – would be a continuation of that alliance.

A third difference from the Covenant, which emerged in wartime deliberations in Washington and London, was that it gave the new organisation a greatly enlarged role in economic and social matters. There were several reasons for this. One was an awareness that a major international effort would be needed to meet the immediate problems of postwar economic reconstruction. Another reason was a widespread feeling that some international safeguards should be instituted to counter the blatant and extreme violations of human rights of the kind committed by the Nazis. It was also generally believed that war might result from economic conditions. And, of course, the League had been very successful in functional activities. The Soviets did not share the Anglo-American enthusiasm for all this, maintaining that the UN should focus on security concerns and not be 'encumbered' in this way.[16] However, at the 1943 Moscow Conference they agreed to the creation of a *general* organisation and at Dumbarton Oaks in 1944 they agreed that the UN could handle economic and social problems.

The Soviet attitude towards the new organisation was similar to that of France in 1919: they were preoccupied by the German threat which, they believed, could only be countered by a favourable balance of power. But a UN with military teeth might shore up their security. Another Soviet fear, indicative of the gathering Cold War clouds, derived from their dismal experience of the League. This was that pro-Western members might gang up against the Soviets in the General Assembly. When the US suggested that certain non-belligerents (for example, Egypt, Ireland and some Latin Americans) should be UN founder members, Stalin pressed for the admission of all 16 Soviet republics. This was later reduced to two and Byelorussia and the Ukraine duly became founder members. However, the accompanying negotiations caused serious embarrassment to Roosevelt – he secretly persuaded Stalin and Churchill to agree that the USA could likewise have three Assembly seats but backed down after serious criticism following a press leak. The Soviet Union's unsuccessful demands for an absolute right of veto on all matters also reflected its concern lest the UN become an instrument of hostile powers.

The fourth difference from the Covenant, which reflected changing times, was that the Charter has a different philosophical air. Whereas the League's roots lay in the nineteenth-century liberalism of the night-watchman state, the UN reflected the twentieth-century liberalism of the welfare state. Decisions in the General Assembly and Security Council are taken by majority voting.[17] However, General Assembly resolutions are *recommendatory* and do not commit states, whereas Security Council decisions are binding on all UN members. This made the Security Council a much more powerful body than the League Council and it breached the legal doctrine that a state cannot be bound without its express consent.

The League had been idealistic about the possibility of changing international life. The UN emphasised accepting the world as it is. The Covenant was planned to cope with an accidental war, the

Charter to deal with deliberate wars begun by wicked men. Even the location of the organisations reflects the contrast. The League was based in beautiful, peaceful surroundings intended to create an atmosphere conducive to calm discussion. The UN built its headquarters on the former site of slums and slaughterhouses in bustling, cosmopolitan New York.

The fifth difference from the Covenant was the way in which the UN marked several steps forward in terms of the expectations of states, the kind of claims made upon international organisations and the issues on the international agenda. One such advance was the importance attached to economic, social and welfare issues, which were regarded as a matter of common concern and thus made the responsibility of the General Assembly (which is supreme in all matters other than security).

A changed attitude to imperialism was also evident. Mandates were replaced by closely supervised trust territories. Instead of the League's paternalistic references to the 'sacred trust of civilization', 'advanced peoples' and 'peoples not yet able to stand by themselves', the Charter clearly emphasised the responsibility of colonial powers 'to promote . . . progressive development towards self-government or independence' in accordance with 'the freely-expressed wishes of the peoples concerned'.[18] These carefully chosen words meant that independence was an option, not an obligatory goal: there was no inkling of the oncoming rush of decolonisation. Nonetheless, the 'Declaration Regarding Non-self-governing Territories' was a tremendous advance and it helped usher in a new era and a new international agenda.

Frequent references in the Charter to promoting human rights reflected the world's abhorrence of Nazi genocide and with it an expansion of international concern. Traditionally, the treatment of individuals within states was not regarded as a matter of international concern. The Charter upheld this principle in Article 2, paragraph 7, which prohibited UN intervention in matters 'essentially within the domestic jurisdiction of any state'. The only exception to this rule is when the Security Council is engaged in enforcement measures under chapter 7. But a conflict soon arose between Article 2.7 and the provisions concerning human rights. States facing criticism on human rights questions frequently invoked Article 2.7, but gradually the non-intervention principle in this area was to some extent eroded.

The early years: Cold War disputes and the collapse of the Charter system

The Cold War between the US-led West and the Soviet-led East was already perceptible by the time the Charter came into force in October 1945. Because of Cold War tensions, the most important intended change from the League did not materialise: the idea that the Council should be something like a great power directorate foundered on the shoals of superpower mistrust. The clearest manifestation of super-power hostility was the 279 vetoes cast in the Security Council during the Cold War period. These, it has been argued, 'rendered the UN powerless' to deal with many conflicts that arose.[19] Most vetoes in the first, 1945–60 period, were cast by the Soviet Union because of her friendless position in the Security Council – in the 1940s the only other Communists on the Council were Poland and Ukraine; in the 1950s the Council contained no Soviet allies.

There is a sense in which the frequent use of the veto indicated the Security Council was operating as intended when the big powers fell out. Moreover, on the whole these vetoes did not ham-string the UN.[20] However, the numerous Soviet vetoes provided the USA with superb propaganda. Since America could count on a ma-jority of votes in the Council, it developed the tactic of introducing resolutions which were patently unacceptable to the USSR, thus in-ducing vetoes. Sometimes the same resolution was introduced more than once.[21] The number of vetoes was also multiplied be-cause some resolutions were voted on in parts. This was represented in the West as Soviet obstructiveness.

In this climate it was impossible to create the envisaged UN ma-chinery for the maintenance of international peace and security. Since East and West did not trust each other to carry out military action on behalf of the UN, the Military Staff Committee talks about the creation of a UN force broke down in 1948. The Security Council also played only a limited role in the pacific settlement of disputes since the US preferred using other fora such as the OAS.

The first dispute to come before the Security Council showed that the Charter system had already been undermined. In 1941 the allies had occupied Iran but, unlike Britain and America, the Soviets did not withdraw when the war ended. In January 1946 Iran com-plained about the Soviet presence and its sponsorship of separatist movements in the north. Put on the defensive, and suspecting

Anglo-American collusion with Iran, the Soviets rejected Iran's complaint. The USSR then tried to put the West on the defensive by alleging that Britain was interfering in the internal affairs of Greece. (Since Britain was determined to prevent this strategically important country falling within the Soviet sphere of influence, British troops had been sent to Greece in 1944 to prevent a Communist seizure of power.[22]) The crude and blatant nature of the Soviet complaint led to a bitter Security Council debate. Then, in March 1946, when heavy US pressure prompted Iran to raise once more the question of the presence of Soviet troops, the Soviets staged their first walk-out. The Secretary-General, Trygve Lie, made his first attempt to claim more than administrative powers, by presenting the Council with a legal memorandum on the matter which was read out – but ignored. The USSR made difficulties about its troops leaving, demanding autonomy for Iranian Azerbaijan which, as a Soviet-controlled puppet, would enable them to put pressure on neighbouring Turkey (which was strategically important to the West). However, the dispute was resolved peacefully and by early May the troops were gone.

In February 1946 Britain had routed the USSR when the Security Council discussed Greece, but the Greek civil war remained a matter of concern. In December 1946, Athens complained that Albania, Bulgaria and Yugoslavia were aiding Greek communist guerrillas. A fact-finding commission reported in favour of Greece and therefore incurred the Soviet veto. The US then managed, in September 1947, to set an important precedent by transferring the question to the General Assembly. The Assembly established an eleven-nation Special Committee on the Balkans (UNSCOB), nominally to assist the four governments to cooperate in settling their disputes, but in practice acting as 'chronicler of Communist iniquity'.[23] It left when the threat faded at the beginning of the 1950s. As in Iran, the UN served as a valuable diplomatic tool for the West, legitimising its arguments and objections and providing useful anti-communist propaganda.

The Korean War and the question of collective security

In the Korean War, the UN moved from being simply a forum for diplomatic pressure and propaganda to playing a forceful role in a

way not envisaged by the drafters of the Charter. When North
Korea invaded South Korea on 25 June 1950, the US immediately
took the matter to the Security Council. Because the Soviets were
boycotting the Council over the failure to give China's seat to the
Communist regime, the Council was able to adopt an American
resolution calling on members to 'furnish such assistance to the
Republic of Korea as may be necessary to repel the armed attack
and restore international peace and security in the area'. By mid-
September 14 states had sent ground forces for the defence of
South Korea.[24] But the American force commander, General Mac-
Arthur, was carried away by virulent anti-communism and military
success and provoked the entry of China into the war. The UN suf-
fered near-disastrous reverses and, with the Soviets now back in the
Security Council, the United States raised the issue in the General
Assembly. Under the Uniting for Peace Resolution of 1950, the As-
sembly authorised itself to consider any threat to the peace if the
Security Council was blocked by the veto.[25] The following year, at
America's instigation, China was condemned as an aggressor. The
war dragged on until July 1953 when an armistice agreement restored the status quo ante.

   The American propaganda machine portrayed Korea as a collective security operation.[26] There are three arguments in favour of
this interpretation. Firstly, the UN took strong action against aggression. Secondly, a UN-commanded force was established after
the Security Council had condemned North Korea's invasion. And,
thirdly, although the Charter gives the Security Council primary responsibility for maintaining international peace and security, the
General Assembly clearly has a secondary or residual role. It may
not have been collective security as envisaged in the Charter, but it
was pretty well in line with the League's conception that individual
states would contribute as and when they individually recognised
that aggression had been committed.

   The arguments against Korea as an exercise in collective security
essentially revolve around the fact that the USA successfully used
the UN for its own purposes. Firstly, the Security Council was only
able to pass the initial, US-inspired resolutions because the Soviets
were absent. The Charter-makers had assumed that *all* the great
powers had to consent to collective action, which meant that abstention could be deemed to have the same legal force as a vote
against a resolution.

Secondly, the force was a thin veneer to hide US military action. Only 16 out of 60 UN members contributed to it. Most ground troops were American and South Korean (50 and 40 per cent respectively) and the US also provided most of the air and sea forces. The UN command was practically identical with the US Far Eastern Command, sharing the same commanding officer and common headquarters. Moreover, General MacArthur (who enjoyed a remarkable degree of freedom) considered himself a US commander waging war on communism on behalf of the US. Nor were other members fully consulted. Non-US contributors received insufficient information, had inadequate opportunities to express their views, and there was a lack of effective implementation of policies and understandings that had been adopted. When it came to negotiating the armistice, instructions came from Washington and the Security Council played no role. Conversely, and contrary to the theory of collective security, North Korea was not isolated but received considerable assistance (chiefly from China), and the Soviet Union staunchly opposed what the UN was doing.

Thirdly, there was little of the centralised decision-making envisaged by the Charter. It was left up to individual states to decide whether or not they wished to participate militarily in the war or in the economic embargo against China after the General Assembly had condemned it as an aggressor in February 1951.

Fourthly, after crossing the 38th parallel (which divided North and South Korea) in October 1950, the exercise was transformed into a campaign to unite Korea. Only military failure brought the UN back to its original aim of acting 'solely for the purpose of restoring the Republic of Korea to its status prior to the invasion from the north and of reestablishing the peace broken by that aggression'.[27]

Fifthly, the US would have acted anyway as the Korean War was in its interest. This was demonstrated by the US ordering its armed forces to come to the aid of South Korea even before the crucial UN resolution. The US did not act from high-minded reasons. It waged the Korean War because it believed the North Korean attack was Moscow-inspired; because of bitter memories of appeasement in the 1930s; and because the UN offered a splendid opportunity to avoid problems with Congress by acting in conjunction with others under the imprimatur of the world organisation.

The last argument draws attention to frequently voiced assertions that 'proper' collective security is inspired by 'unselfish' considerations of the good of the international community. From a foreign policy perspective, Korea was a typical, national interest/balance of power war which was possible because the UN, like international society, was at that time dominated by the USA. (Even so, acting through the UN to some extent tied Washington's hands and at crucial moments the General Assembly exercised a restraining influence.) But the student of international organisation is confronted with the problem that collective security is an ideal which has never operated as envisaged. Accordingly, as in the preceding discussion, it is a matter of determining not *why* action was taken but *how far* that action meets the criteria of collective security. Most commentators believe the arguments against Korea as a collective security operation outweigh those in favour.

An important legacy of the Korean War, and another consequence of US dominance of the Cold War UN, was the parody of Taiwan continuing to sit in China's Security Council seat for 22 years after the establishment of the (Communist) People's Republic of China (PRC) in 1949. The Korean War intensified already strong American hostility to Beijing and (as has been mentioned) the General Assembly, prompted by the US, condemned the PRC as an aggressor. Selective sanctions were imposed against it. Thereafter, for two decades the United States used its dominance in the General Assembly to prevent the discussion of the question of China's seat. As the General Assembly became third world dominated and the US lost its assured, automatic majority, Washington resorted (in 1961) to having the question of Chinese representation declared an important question. This required a two-thirds majority and kept Taiwan in the UN for another decade. Meanwhile, the PRC showed no obvious keenness to join the UN and did itself no favours by falling out with the USSR, by going to war with India in 1962 and by instigating the brutal and chaotic Cultural Revolution. Only in 1969 did votes for the People's Republic start picking up. Eventually, on 25 October 1971 the US suffered what it regarded as a humiliating defeat: Taiwan was expelled and replaced by the PRC. The US cut off aid to third world states which voted contrary to its wishes and, when he later aspired to become Secretary-General, remembered the Tanzanian delegate's triumphant dance in the aisle.

In the Uniting for Peace Resolution, America had sought to capitalise on its dominance in the General Assembly by trying to turn

that organ into a body that could authorise collective security operations. This soon proved unfeasible and Washington turned back to
alliances, such as NATO, for its security needs. However, the prestige of the General Assembly rose at the expense of the strife-ridden
Security Council. This was because the US continued being more or
less assured of voting majorities in that organ and because weaker
states were keen to increase the authority of the Assembly. And so,
while the Security Council lost work and went into decline, the
General Assembly came to be seen as *the* important organ. Here
friends could be won, people influenced, actions legitimised and
denounced, and substantive issues discussed.[28] At long last
Woodrow Wilson's ideal of a 'world public opinion', which none
could ignore, however much they might dislike it, seemed to have
reached fruition.

The UN and disputes arising out of the ending of colonialism

The Cold War did not prevent the UN playing a useful role in several disputes arising out of the end of colonialism, although the
Cold War contestants tried to make capital out of such disputes
when they came before the UN. Both superpowers were anti-colonial in principle, and in the 1940s the UN facilitated such decolonisation as was already under way; also the colonial powers sought the
organisation's help in respect of conflicts arising out of the decolonisation process. One of the earliest examples of UN mediation,
which also indicated the UN's powerful anti-colonial thrust, was in
1947 when the Dutch colonial authorities clashed with the de facto
Indonesian republican government. In the first of many such
claims by colonial powers, the Netherlands said it was a domestic
matter, falling within Article 2.7 of the Charter. The Security Council successfully evaded this assertion and appointed a three-nation
Good Offices Committee to try to conciliate the two parties. A truce
was arranged but quickly violated by the Dutch. The Council then
upgraded the Committee into a Commission for Indonesia and
gave it greater powers. After strong US pressure, the Netherlands
agreed in March 1949 to grant speedy independence to Indonesia.
    In this instance the existence and character of the UN clearly in-
fluenced the behaviour of the two principal actors – the Nether-

lands and the USA – and also the eventual outcome. The USA did not want to upset or humiliate the Netherlands, but Washington was worried about Communist influence in the region and was unwilling to allow Moscow the propaganda victory of being seen as the greatest friend of liberation movements. The mere fact of UN membership forced the USA to take a stance on what might otherwise have been regarded as a 'far-away dispute'.[29] The Netherlands was affected by the rising tide of criticism, especially from Asian countries who were willing to organise sanctions. The UN played a valuable role in defusing and settling the crisis and, thanks to it, the Dutch government escaped from an uncomfortable situation in a face-saving way.

The UN also played a part in bringing to independence the former Italian colonies in Africa. In 1948, when the major powers had failed to reach agreement upon this matter, they passed it over to the General Assembly which decided Libya should become independent and Somaliland should be a trust territory administered by Italy. Despite opposition from Eritrean Muslims, the General Assembly accepted Emperor Haile Selassie's claim to Eritrea and in 1950 agreed to what would later prove to be an uneasy federation with Ethiopia. (Forty years later, after a long civil war, Eritrea secured its independence.)

Two other disputes arising out of decolonisation produced considerable and long-lasting strife: Palestine and Kashmir. In Palestine, Britain's attempts to maintain law and order were frustrated by American meddling, ruthless Zionist terrorism and the sheer costs of keeping a large portion of the British war-weary army in that territory. The Cabinet could see no solution:

> The essential point of principle for the Jews is the creation of a sovereign Jewish state. And the essential point of principle for the Arabs is to resist to the last the establishment of Jewish sovereignty in any part of Palestine. These, for both sides are matters of principle on which there is no room for compromise. There is therefore no hope of negotiating an agreed settlement.[30]

Britain turned to the UN. In August 1947, after three months' investigation, the majority of the members of a Special UN Committee came up with the well-worn suggestion that Palestine be partitioned into an Arab state, a Jewish state and a UN-administered

Jerusalem. (The minority recommended a federal state with Jerusalem as its capital.) The Jews welcomed the partition plan since the balance of advantage was in their favour. The Arabs, however, were implacably opposed to the creation of a Jewish state. Britain had earlier warned that it would not enforce a solution unacceptable to both sides. Believing the plan to be an inequitable recipe for disaster, and in the faint hope that announcing its imminent withdrawal might 'induce a sense of realism and offer the prospect of a settlement',[31] Britain declared it was abandoning the mandate. Thereafter Britain took no part in UN discussions on Palestine and sullenly let events run their course prior to its departure on 15 May 1948.

Thanks to strong-arm US tactics, the General Assembly approved the partition plan, and a UN Commission for Palestine was set up to implement it. Underwriting the settlement required enormous resources which only America had. But while President Truman insisted that any American commitments should take place only within a UN framework, a UN force in Palestine might well result in Soviet troops being legitimately introduced into the Middle East. In addition, there was the conflict between the demands of America's major ally, Britain, and the powerful Jewish lobby. Opinion at the highest levels was divided. The Policy Planning Staff under George Kennan (one of the most influential US policy makers between 1946 and 1949), thought the partition plan should be ditched. Firstly, this was because of the damage it was doing to relations with Britain and the Arab world; and, secondly, because the US might find itself drawn into a potentially enormous commitment to Israel. However, pro-Zionist opinion found greater favour with the President, who was in any event predisposed towards a Jewish state.

As it turned out, the UN Commission never left New York. The Soviets tried to sponsor a UN force to implement partition and the US responded by proposing a temporary trusteeship in Palestine, leaving open the way for partition at a later date. Nothing came of either scheme. Instead, events ran their uninterrupted course. The Jewish community in Palestine declared that Israel would come into existence at midnight on 14 May 1948. A few minutes later President Truman granted immediate recognition without consulting or informing anyone. All the members of the Security Council were worried that the bloodletting that followed the creation of Israel might escalate dangerously. So the Security Council used tough words, demanding a four-week truce which was obtained with the assistance of unarmed UN officers. When fighting broke out again a month later, the Security Council ordered an indefinite truce and brought in more officers to supervise it. But the situation remained precarious. Peace treaties were impossible. The presence of international officers – later known as the UN Truce Supervision Organisation (UNTSO) – became a permanent fixture.[32] And several UN officials were killed during the 1948 fighting, including the UN mediator, Count Bernadotte of Sweden.

The problem of Kashmir was a legacy of Britain's hasty partition of India. Following independence in August 1947, the situation became increasingly inflammable. A large force of Pathans crossed the border from Pakistan, leading the Hindu ruler of Muslim Kashmir to accede to India, which then provided military help. Finding its army confronting Pathan tribesmen, India protested to the Security Council that Pakistan was interfering in Kashmir. Pakistan protested that its hands were clean and that India was violating self-determination and oppressing Kashmiri Muslims. The Security Council despatched a Commission which obtained the parties' agreement to a ceasefire (coming into operation on 1 January 1949) and used a small group of military officers to watch over the ceasefire and prevent minor incidents getting out of hand.

Since neither India nor Pakistan renounced their claim to the whole of Kashmir, the officers remained after the delineation of the ceasefire and became known as the UN Military Observer Group in India and Pakistan (UNMOGIP). A few dozen UNMOGIP soldiers were still there as late as 1995, monitoring the 500-mile partition line (which India claims is an international frontier) and assisting the parties to live at peace. Although there is frequent tension, and India and Pakistan have several times come to blows, neither party is constantly thirsting for war. India grudgingly accepts the presence of UNMOGIP (despite insisting since 1972 that it has no function) while Pakistan sees UNMOGIP as a symbol of its continuing grievance.

An alternative approach to security: peacekeeping[33]

It was not until the late 1950s that it was recognised that the UN was engaging in a distinctive activity which, while not envisaged in the

Charter, was immensely helpful in threatening situations. At the time, the Secretary-General, Dag Hammarskjöld, often referred to peacekeeping as 'preventive diplomacy'. This reflected his belief that peacekeeping was a diplomatic method whose purpose was chiefly to prevent the Cold War seeping into conflicts. However, although peacekeeping did do this, it has a wider role. Peacekeeping 'refers to the international help which is sometimes sent to an immediate problem area' when conflicting parties 'wish, at least for the time being, to live in peace'.[34] In retrospect, it can be seen that this was what the UN did in Indonesia, Palestine and Kashmir. However, the concept of peacekeeping is much misunderstood as many people confuse it with collective security. But the idea behind peacekeeping is closer to counselling than enforcement action. This may be understood by looking at the four characteristics of peacekeeping.

Firstly, it must be noted that notwithstanding its pacific character, military personnel are to some extent utilised in a peacekeeping operation, and often compose at least its core. This is because military people are usually available for immediate despatch to trouble spots. They are acceptable to the local military with whom they will have to deal, and military expertise is usually needed. Tight discipline must be maintained in a sensitive spot on foreign soil and the authoritative approach of the military can be very useful. Such peacekeepers come from countries with no immediate interests in the dispute. Thus, during the Cold War the troops who constituted the backbone of peacekeeping came from the Nordic countries, Canada, India and Ireland.

The second, vital, characteristic of peacekeeping is its values (or principles): peacekeeping consists of behaviour which is non-threatening and impartial. Peacekeepers are not in the business of using or threatening force. They are thus lightly armed, using weapons only in self-defence and to assert freedom of movement. Only if they behave with manifest impartiality and in a non-threatening way will they be trusted by all disputants. Thus peacekeepers do not take sides, whatever their private feelings or those of their states. If they do not behave in this way, they will at least be seen as a party to the dispute, with the consequence that they may be attacked or asked to leave.

Thirdly, peacekeeping fulfils three functions. *Defusion* helps to reduce an immediate crisis by enabling disputants to withdraw in a face-saving way, by helping to avoid a crisis escalating to war, or by deterring third parties from intervening. Once in place the force may help to settle future crises. UNTSO and UNMOGIP served this function. *Calming* activity helps to keep a potentially dangerous situation quiet, just as a bandage protects an open wound. Peace-keepers may also stop things getting worse by dispelling each side's anxiety about the other's intentions, and helping to prevent incidents. Sometimes, the wound is so deep that, as with UNMOGIP, peacekeepers are in for a long stay. Peacekeeping to *settle or resolve* disputes occurs when an impartial third party is required to ensure that each party honours its side of an agreement. For example, to maintain order during a plebiscite, or to oversee a plan for national reconciliation, or to administer a disputed territory prior to handing it to one of the disputants without the other losing face.

The final characteristic of peacekeeping refers to the context in which it operates. It is in all key respects one of cooperation. There must be an authorising body such as the Security Council or General Assembly which decides to establish the operation, determine its duration and, if need be, extends its mandate. Then states must supply resources and funds for the operation. And states hosting peacekeeping operations must give their consent and be willing either to settle their dispute or desist from hostilities for time being. If consent is withdrawn, the force must be removed. Otherwise sovereignty would be infringed; contributing states would probably withdraw their troops; and the non-cooperation or hostility of the host state would quickly make peacekeeping untenable. Unless all the immediate parties to a dispute are willing to cooperate, peace-keeping cannot work. If only one side cooperates peacekeeping may be seen as not partial, and much of its *raison d'être* will be lost.

The first UN Emergency Force (UNEF I) in the Sinai – often regarded as the beginning of peacekeeping – illustrates these characteristics. It began as a defusing operation when Britain and France invaded Egypt in 1956. Since British and French vetoes blocked Security Council action, the General Assembly used the Uniting for Peace procedure to discuss the Suez crisis. The majority supported a Canadian suggestion that the British and French troops should be replaced by a UN force. But in order that all concerned could put their own interpretation on what had happened, the exact way of replacing the British and French was left vague. No one was deceived that Britain and France were being forced out of Egypt, but they kept some dignity. After they and the Israelis had gone, UNEF's 6000 troops from ten countries sat on the Egyptian side of the Egypt–Israel border, Israel having rejected their presence. The force remained a calming presence until 1967 (diminishing in scope as the years went by), helping to prevent incidents and reducing anxiety.

The UN operation in the Congo from 1960 to 1964 illustrates the way in which the Cold War continued to dominate the UN in the security field. It also marked the culmination of the USA's manipulation of the Cold War UN, and illustrates the pitfalls of straying from the tenets of peacekeeping.

Having been thrust precipitately into statehood on 30 June 1960, the former Belgian Congo (now Zaire) immediately disintegrated into bloodshed and chaos following a mutiny by the Congolese army. Without the permission of the Congolese government, Belgium began intervening to restore law and order. The Congolese government appealed to the UN for protection from Belgian aggression.

UNEF I had given a powerful impetus to the idea that despite the breakdown of collective security, the UN could play a significant role in the maintenance of international peace. The despatch of an observer group to the Lebanon in 1958 had further whetted this appetite. Thus, the Security Council hardly batted an eyelid at despatching a 20 000-strong peacekeeping force to the Congo although, by the peacekeeping standards of the day, it was huge and tremendously expensive.

By September the UN Operation in the Congo (ONUC) had easily supervised the withdrawal of Belgian forces. But ONUC's more important purpose was to defuse a potential new area of Cold War conflict by interposing a neutral, UN force which would isolate the country from superpower ambitions. Other than France (who sympathised with Belgium) the chief external powers all initially supported ONUC. For the superpowers, it was their first involvement in Black Africa and both invested considerable energy and prestige. The US, whose commitment was greater than that of any other state apart from Belgium, paid 45.5 per cent of the costs as well as giving a large amount of bilateral assistance and logistical support. Washington had long been a supporter of peacekeeping in principle, and using the UN seemed an ideal way to avoid the Congo becoming 'a kind of whirlpool of great power politics and conflicting world ideologies'.[35] For its part, the Soviet Union was keen to make political capital by having Belgium branded an aggressor, gaining a friendly Congolese government and parading its anti-colonialist credentials. Unfortunately, the Congolese Prime Minister, Patrice Lumumba, had a mercurial personality and leaned clumsily towards Moscow, encouraging Western fears of Soviet intervention. The Secretary-General, Dag Hammarskjöld, sympathised with Western worries and when the central government collapsed in September 1960, ONUC responded in a way that weakened Lumumba's position. Later that month (with, it is said, the help of the US Central Intelligence Agency) Lumumba was deposed in an army coup and the ensuing Mobutu government closed the Soviet embassies. Moscow's anger at this boiled over into fury when Lumumba was captured and handed over to his enemies to be murdered, and some states withdrew their peacekeeping troops.

Instead of defusing the crisis the UN had deepened it by sacrificing its impartiality. The West was not unhappy at the way things had gone, but the Soviet Union was livid. Hammarskjöld was bitterly attacked by the USSR, which refused to have any dealings with him and demanded the Secretary-General be replaced by a three-man *troika* consisting of representatives of the West, the East and the non-aligned.

In February 1961 the Security Council authorised ONUC to use force as a last resort to prevent civil war, leading the Congolese government to suspect the UN of attempting to take the country over. However, in effect ONUC's role in cooling down the Cold War crisis was over by the end of 1960. In August 1961 (possibly assisted by American money and persuasion) Washington's favoured candidate, Adoula, became Prime Minister.

A complication of the Congo crisis was the secession of the copper-rich province of Katanga which was very important to the Congolese economy. The Katangese had no overriding sense of loyalty to the Congolese state and were encouraged by Belgium in their greed to keep the profits of the copper mines. But this violated the principle of territorial integrity and, had it succeeded, would have offered a dangerous precedent for would-be secessionists elsewhere. It was also seen as a neo-colonialist move by the Soviets and the non-aligned.

Because UN members were more interested in achieving political goals than adhering to peacekeeping principles, the Secretariat decided in mid-1961 that ONUC should arrest and expel foreign mercenaries from Katanga. In August, September and December ONUC used force. However, it was not until decisive military action at the end of 1962 that Katangan secession was ended. By taking sides in a major domestic conflict the UN had violated key peace-keeping tenets.

The Congo episode was therefore controversial in a variety of ways. Partly this reflected the fact that until then the political nature of peacekeeping had not been fully understood. When ONUC was despatched, there was no anticipation that force would be used or that a hundred-odd UN fatalities would be suffered. But the use made of ONUC, including its anti-Katanga moves, was an ominous sign of the wedge-like potential of peacekeeping forces. Once a force gets involved in internal turmoil, there is no knowing where it might end. It was a lesson the international community heeded for many years. The Congo operation was the culmination of America's manipulation of the UN: the US tipped the scales in favour of moderates over extremists, and in favour of a unified state; and also provided the logistical, diplomatic and financial support which made the operation possible.

The Soviet Union was the chief loser, and its belief that Lumumba had been deposed by a UN force directed by a pro-Western secretariat coloured future Soviet attitudes to peacekeeping. Lumumba's deposition was also seen as a cautionary tale. Africans in particular were apprehensive about the perils of hosting peacekeepers: in the late 1960s the Nigerian President did not want UN involvement during his country's civil war because he feared a UN force might remove him. All subsequent UN peacekeeping forces had mandates which were limited in time so that the 'big five' could veto their extension. Also, many states and the Secretariat itself were hesitant about future UN excursions into a law and order role.

The Congo operation led to severe financial troubles. Until then peacekeeping costs had come out of the regular budget. But, despite a ruling from the International Court, 32 states, including France and the Soviet Union, did not pay their assessed contributions. By 1964 arrears stood at $100 million and there was a major crisis since, under Article 19 of the Charter, a defaulter is at a certain stage deprived of its vote in the General Assembly. Had this been applied, the Soviet Union would probably have left the UN. This was averted by avoiding formal votes for a year. Then the US conceded that the General Assembly would not apply Article 19 on this occasion. According to one observer, America's retreat on the constitutional issue was 'the end of an era: the end of American hegemony within the UN'.[36]

The rise and fall of two Secretaries-General

To discharge his office effectively, a Secretary-General must be trusted by the UN's members, especially the most powerful. When national interests clash, he must walk a political tightrope between the claims of opposing sides. In the paranoid atmosphere of the Cold War UN, the balancing act was particularly delicate. The first two Secretaries-General spectacularly failed by sacrificing their impartiality – and hence their perceived trustworthiness – when major Cold War conflicts engulfed the organisation.

The first Secretary-General was Trygve Lie of Norway. He was a dynamic man, full of initiative and very ambitious for his office and for the UN. He adopted an active role from the outset, declaring in September 1946 that under Article 99 it was his duty to inform the Council of threats to the peace and, if the Council did not act, he must. By July 1948 he was exercising, unchallenged, the right to present his own amendments to resolutions before the Council. However, he offended the USA (in 1946 over Iran), incurred British criticism (over the Berlin crisis in 1948) and Soviet enmity (over Korea). During his last few years in office, he was completely ignored by the Soviets in their official contacts with the UN and in its attendant social life.

When Lie's term expired in 1951, he did not seek reappointment, but the Western powers felt that, as a matter of principle, it was important to support Lie. President Truman told Lie that America would veto anyone else. After the Soviets had unsuccessfully nominated a Pole and vetoed the reappointment of Lie, the Security Council had to tell the General Assembly that it was unable to agree on a recommendation. After two days' debate, the Assembly reelected Lie. However, the Soviet boycott meant that Lie could not effectively discharge his office and he left the UN in April 1953.

Lie was not the best man for the job. He was too brash, hasty, didactic, tactless and, in his quest for the UN-inspired millennium, unrealistic. He left the organisation in a poor shape. The Security

Council chose as his successor Dag Hammarskjöld of Sweden whom they expected to be an untroublesome, quiet, administrative-type Secretary-General. Hammarskjöld immediately reorganised the secretariat, was cautious, and gained a reputation for being financially 'sound'. But he had no more intention than Lie of taking a back seat. He also had tremendous gifts. He combined ingenuity, subtlety, tact, discretion and great intelligence with deft political skills.

Under Hammarskjöld, and apparently because of him, the UN seemed to flourish. Increasingly, the UN tended to 'leave it to Dag', who seemingly could perform marvels. In 1954 he arranged the release of US airmen who had been imprisoned in China during the Korean war. When the Soviets invaded Hungary in 1956, he was asked to 'take any initiative which he deemed helpful'. During the 1956 Suez crisis he played a very active and effective role and was granted remarkable executive powers in respect of the peacekeeping force that the UN despatched to Egypt. In 1958 the Soviets did not object when he expanded the UN presence in Jordan and Lebanon despite their veto. In 1959 he took the initiative in visiting Laos after allegations that foreign troops had infringed the Laotian border. And in 1960 he was again granted considerable powers in controlling the UN's Congo operation.

Hammarskjöld was able to achieve so much not just because of his genius, but because he took office at an ideal time: Stalin had died, Eisenhower had assumed office and there was a ceasefire in Korea. In the moderate tension that came with a slight thawing of the Cold War, there was an opportunity for him to play a significant role. And in their relief that the UN was making progress in a few areas despite the paralysis of the Security Council, the 'big five' were willing to allow Hammarskjöld to act relatively independently.

However, Hammarskjöld broke his political back by being too independent. In seeing himself as 'a servant of the principles of the Charter',[37] he ignored the vital importance of keeping the permanent members happy.[38] By running the Congo operation as a pro-Western enterprise and giving a nod and a wink to Lumumba's removal,[39] he incurred the wrath of the Soviets. They boycotted him and began touting their *troika* proposal. And it was not only Moscow whom he offended. France was so incensed by Hammarskjöld's attitude towards French policy in Algeria and his role during the Bizerte crisis of 1961[40] that President de Gaulle did not send condolences when Hammarskjöld died. Had Hammarskjöld not been killed in a plane crash in September 1961, the aura that still surrounds his name would probably have dissolved.

The 'non-political' UN

The UN must be distinguished from the wide range of institutions which are known as UN Specialised Agencies, and which have been established to serve various functional ends. Collectively, the UN and the Agencies are often referred to as the UN 'family' or the UN 'system'. But each Agency is an entirely separate international organisation.[41] Some, like the Food and Agricultural Organisation (FAO), were established before the UN. Others were set up as part of the post-Second World War planning. Two of these, the International Monetary Fund (IMF) and World Bank (IBRD), effectively lead a life independent of mainstream UN activities.

Within the UN proper, however, there are also many functional commissions, ad hoc groups, 'programmes' and 'funds'. And two of what the UN refers to as its Principal Organs also have what may be seen as a 'non-political' focus: the Economic and Social Council (ECOSOC) and the International Court of Justice (ICJ). But this does not mean that attempts will not be made, as in the case of ECOSOC, to use such bodies for political ends; nor that even the most non-political body of all – the ICJ – is removed from the impact of major political phenomena such as the Cold War.

ECOSOC was modelled on the 1939 Bruce Report which, it has been said, encapsulated 'the finest achievements and highest ideals of the League'.[42] It was intended to be the chief coordinator of the UN's economic and social activities and was given special responsibility to promote respect for, and observance of, human rights and fundamental freedoms.

Unfortunately, ECOSOC grew into a sprawling and complex organisation. This was due to its broad terms of reference and multiplicity of functions, combined with the early decision to pursue 'every social and economic objective in sight, with an extravagant faith in the virtue of words and resolutions and in the value of proliferating committees and commissions'.[43] Subsidiary bodies include commissions, committees and working groups on statistics, population, social development, human rights, preventing discrimination and protection of minorities, the status of women, narcotic drugs, science and technology, development, crime prevention, transnational corporations and human settlements. Thanks to effective log-rolling, a West European Economic Commission was followed by Asian and Latin American Commissions, nominally supervised by ECOSOC. Also formally under ECOSOC auspices, but in practice autonomous, are such bodies as the United Nations Children's Fund (UNICEF), the Office of the High Commissioner for Refugees (UNHCR), the Industrial Development Organisation (UNIDO), and the UN Development Programme (UNDP).

In the Cold War UN, the work done in some of these fields was relatively uncontroversial. But negotiating and proffering advice on important social and economic questions provided a wide opening for superpower tensions. Profound ideological divergences over economic doctrine deepened the rifts between states whose representatives had scant respect for the Charter – or reality – in airing antagonisms and prejudices as they sought to score debating points. 'Few harsher punishments could be devised for a modern Prometheus', says Nicholas, 'than to read through the verbatim records [of ECOSOC and many of its subordinate bodies] . . . it would certainly cure him of any pride in the collective wisdom of mankind'.[44] Discussions of social questions, such as freedom of information or religious persecution, put the Soviet Union on the defensive. For example, a 1953 report into forced labour was used by the US to condemn Soviet penal legislation. The Soviets responded by condemning the report as 'a collection of forgeries and fabrications' and criticising its failure to condemn 'the extensive practice of forced labour which existed in the United States'.[45] On the other hand, the Soviets courted Afro-Asian favour by holding the US up to ridicule on such questions as racial discrimination. Non-governmental organisations (NGOs) offered further complications: in 1954 the pro-Soviet Women's International Democratic Federation had its consultative status with ECOSOC withdrawn after a disagreeable debate and the United States caused controversy by being reluctant to grant visas to representatives of such organisations.

The conflict between East and West robbed ECOSOC of the basis which would have made possible effective cooperation. In economic matters, the US had a profound impact since many development programmes were effectively dependent upon US financial support. However, as the UN became third world dominated there was disenchantment with ECOSOC's acceptance of the Western view of a minimalist role for functional agencies. As will be seen in the next chapter, other fora became more important.

Because the Permanent Court of International Justice (PCIJ) was regarded as one of the League's greatest achievements and successes, in 1945 it simply changed its name to the International Court of Justice (ICJ) and its continuity was symbolised by the last president of the PCIJ becoming the first president of the ICJ. However, the Cold War climate was unpropitious for the Court. From the beginning, and up to a point in contrast with the League, law played second fiddle to politics. This was shown in the first dispute taken to the General Assembly, India's 1946 complaint about South Africa's treatment of people of Indian origin. There were good grounds for thinking India's complaint could not even be discussed because it was a domestic matter falling within Article 2.7 of the Charter. Western states wanted to seek the Court's opinion. But India succeeded in keeping it in the political arena of the General Assembly – and won the day.

During the Cold War, the ICJ languished. In its 24 years, the PCIJ delivered 32 judgements and 24 advisory opinions, all of which were accepted. By contrast, after 45 years, the ICJ had given only 33 judgements and 19 advisory opinions. The first dispute to go to the Court, the 1947 *Corfu Channel Case* was inauspicious. Two British warships had been damaged by mines laid by Albania. The Court ruled that Albania must compensate Britain but it refused to do so. Since then judgements and advisory opinions have been rejected by all the permanent members other than Britain, as well as by Bulgaria, Hungary, South Africa, Italy and West Germany.[46] In addition, far fewer states accepted the compulsory jurisdiction of the Court under the system known as the Optional Clause. And those who did accept the Clause tended to make such sweeping reservations that in the late 1980s there were said to be 'only eleven countries which really adhered to the compulsory jurisdiction of the Court'.[47]

This gave rise to a common perception that the ICJ was irrelevant and needed reforming. But in itself there was nothing wrong with the Court. In an international society marked by pessimism, divisiveness, high levels of tension and ideological rivalry (which extended to the content of international law), the Court could not play a significant role. The fact that the fortunes of the Court revived at the end of the Cold War, emphasises that its effectiveness is related to the international context in which it operates.

Conclusion

The UN was intended to be an improvement on the League. But its fate during the Cold War is a reminder that it is not the machinery or constitution of an organisation that is crucial, but the attitude of its members and the international climate. All UN members sought to use the organisation to further their national interests, but the US was most successful because of its dominance in international society. The superpower quarrel prevented the creation of the intended security machinery, and permeated all aspects of the UN system. But this did not prevent the UN playing a useful role in some disputes, and the development of peacekeeping sometimes helped states live at peace.

Moreover, the UN had quickly established itself as a vital adjunct to diplomacy. As a club of sovereign states the UN, unlike the League of Nations, was very much a going concern after 15 years. In fact, one of the most notable things about the UN during this period is that despite the most acute international tension, those states in the minority made no move whatsoever to leave the UN. Evidently, the idea that the world should be equipped with an organisation which included all states was one whose time had come. The next two decades, when the UN was dominated, in numerical terms, by the states of the third world, only served to emphasise this far-reaching change in international life.

4 The Third World UN, 1960–1980

The decline in US dominance of the UN began in 1955 when America lost its 'automatic' two-thirds majority in the General Assembly. For in that year, after much superpower wrangling, 16 new members were admitted. (Until then Security Council vetoes or a lack of the required number of positive votes barred admission to any states expected to side with either superpower in the Cold War.[1]) Within a few years decolonisation had transformed the UN into a third world dominated organisation. (Out of 114 members in 1964, 57 were Afro-Asians.) In consequence, it was said in the mid-1960s that the UN would have been 'hardly recognisable' to those who were at San Francisco.[2]

Committees, commissions and working groups proliferated on issues that directly concerned the third world.[3] The UN's agenda widened. Soon there were almost yearly conferences on development or development-related issues – for example, the 1974 Rome food conference which produced an ambitious, long-term plan and led to the establishment of the World Food Council. The thrust of the third world UN was in the direction of economic activities. By the early 1980s up to six times more was spent in this field than on international peace and security.[4]

The Soviets courted the third world. Expecting their friendship, Nikita Khrushchev (the Soviet leader from 1958 to 1964) encouraged the enhancement of the Assembly[5] and began the stampede of heads of state to its sessions. But extreme Soviet proposals won no support. Khrushchev felt 'crushed'[6] by the Assembly's support for the US position on the Congo. And he not only 'made a mess of himself'[7] in the famous shoe-banging incident during a colonial debate (in the course of which the Irish President of the Assembly broke his gavel) but distressed the Afro-Asians by his rudeness and seeming lack of faith in the parliamentary system.

Third world states voted with the Soviets only when their views coincided, and in the early sixties the US won twice as much support as the Soviets on Cold War issues.[8] However, as the growth of non-alignment indicates, most new members did not see the Cold War as 'their' concern. They had their own agenda. They wanted to change the largely Eurocentric vision prevailing in the UN and to make it more 'democratic'.[9] ECOSOC and the Security Council became more representative: the former grew from 18 to 27 in 1965 and to 54 in 1973. The Council expanded from 11 to 15 in 1965. But this did nothing to remove the international evils that new states perceived. They had all the righteousness of the weak and only one trump card, their ability to speak out – loudly if necessary[10] – and to pass General Assembly resolutions by overwhelming majorities. An increasingly strident Assembly became a third world campaigning body in which voting victories substituted for fundamental changes.

Anti-colonialism

One prominent third world concern was colonialism. Accordingly, anti-colonialism was a recurring theme of the UN during this period. There was no dispute about the right of the General Assembly, acting through the Trusteeship Council, to exert influence in trust territories, whose administering powers were bound by individual trusteeship agreements. The Trusteeship Council collected annual reports from administering states, received petitions and despatched three-yearly missions to each territory. Its membership was equally divided between administering and non-administering powers. This rendered it insufficiently aggressive or critical for the anti-colonials. Whenever possible, therefore, they used the General Assembly and by-passed the Trusteeship Council.[11] The Assembly heard oral petitioners who had been refused a hearing by the Council, sent its own visiting missions to trust territories, made recommendations (not always in accord with those of the Council) direct to administering authorities, and tried to get the Trusteeship Council to take certain sorts of action. And so the Trusteeship Council declined in business and prestige.

Separately from its provisions about Trusteeship, the Charter had a section (Chapter 11) called the Declaration Regarding Non-self-governing Territories (that is, regarding straightforward colonies). Initially, the colonial powers disputed the General Assembly's right to discuss any information transmitted to the UN under this chapter. However, the anti-colonials succeeded in 1946 in creating a temporary, Special Committee on Information from Non-self-governing Territories. The Committee's mandate and functions were then repeatedly extended and in the 1950s it became the main focus of anti-colonialism. During these years, the General Assembly decided that resolutions on non-self-governing territories did not require the two-thirds majority that had been taken for granted until 1953. The colonial powers' emphasis on the importance of 'progressive development'[12] was criticised as too slow. And the Assembly utterly rejected Belgium's argument that overland empires (such as, so it was claimed, the Soviet Union) were similar to overseas empires.

In 1960 the admission of 17 former colonies gave a big boost to anti-colonialism, and the Soviet Union seized the opportunity to curry friends and make trouble: it proposed a declaration demanding freedom for all colonies within a year. The 43 Afro-Asians took up the idea, modified it, and in December 1960 a draft resolution, called the Declaration on Granting Independence to Colonial Countries and Peoples, was overwhelmingly passed as Resolution 1514(XV). It demanded immediate independence and proclaimed:

> The subjection of peoples to alien subjugation, domination and exploitation constitutes a denial of fundamental human rights, is contrary to the Charter of the UN, and is an impediment to . . . world peace and co-operation.[13]

In 1961, the effort to revoke the legitimacy of colonialism was pushed to an extreme when India 'liberated' Goa from Portuguese rule and the three Afro-Asians on the Security Council supported India, ignoring Article 2.4 which bans the use or threat of force. Then, in 1965, Resolution 2105(XX) comprehensively condemned colonial rule as a threat to international peace and security and a crime against humanity.

Meanwhile, the Committee on Information from Non-self-governing Territories[14] had been wound up in 1963 since the irked colonial powers would have nothing to do with it.[15] By then, the anti-colonials were pursuing their imperialist quarry in other fora: the Assembly's Fourth Committee and the predominantly Afro-Asian 'Committee of Twenty-Four',[16] which was established in 1961.

The latter Committee went on a spree. It collected information and received petitioners – providing they had the 'right' bias. (In 1967 it refused to circulate petitions in which Gibraltarians protested about Spain or residents of Aden complained about interference by the United Arab Republic [as Egypt was then called].) It despatched visiting missions where the colonial power would accept them and, when visits were denied, held meetings in the field, near to the territories. It also compiled its own list of colonial areas to which independence should be granted. (Of the 64 territories listed in a 1963 document 40 were British – mostly small, scattered islands.[17] In 1968 Britain was called on to 'terminate the colonial situation in Gibraltar' within a year – despite over 90 per cent of its population having affirmed their wish to remain British.)

The Committee became increasingly extreme, partly because the fiercest anti-colonials – the 38 subSaharan African states – were frustrated over the 'hard core' colonial areas remaining in Africa. By the end of the sixties, however, there were few trust territories,[18] and such colonies as remained were mostly very small. But the campaign continued. It resulted in irritated Western powers leaving the Committee of Twenty-Four. When Portugal recognised the independence of its former African colonies in 1974, the anti-colonial spotlight focused almost exclusively on Southern Africa. Here the target was not just colonialism (in the shape of the white minority regime in Rhodesia and South Africa's continuing control of South West Africa – Namibia), but the racist policies of Rhodesia and South Africa.

Racial discrimination

Racial discrimination had become an international issue in 1946 when the General Assembly criticised South Africa's treatment of people of Indian origin. Gradually the criticism broadened and when South Africa introduced complete racial segregation in 1952, the General Assembly launched its onslaught. Under the heading 'the question of race conflict in South Africa resulting from the policies of apartheid', Article 2.7 of the Charter was circumvented. In 1961 apartheid was condemned as a flagrant violation of the Charter.[19] In 1962 the General Assembly passed its first resolution calling for sanctions (only the Security Council can impose them), and institutionalised the anti-racist campaign by creating the Special Committee against Apartheid (as it was known from 1970). From 1966 onwards it was assisted by an anti-apartheid centre in the UN Secretariat.

The eleven members of the Special Committee against Apartheid were all from the third world or eastern bloc and they harried South Africa as vigorously as the Committee of Twenty-Four hounded imperialists. (The UN Council for Namibia acted similarly in respect of South Africa's occupation of Namibia.[20]) In 1963 the Security Council called on states to embargo arms sales to South Africa and the General Assembly passed the strongly worded Declaration on the Elimination of All Forms of Racial Discrimination (Resolution 1904[XVIII]). By 1973 12 per cent of all Assembly resolutions attacked South Africa. In 1974 South Africa suffered the humiliation of having its delegates' credentials rejected (which meant they could not appear in the General Assembly or its committees). In 1976 the Assembly began advocating 'armed struggle'. By the early eighties South Africa was being verbally attacked in over half the plenary sessions and criticised in a fifth of the resolutions.[21] South Africa's trading partners were condemned for encouraging racist policies and the Security Council was unsuccessfully called on to apply comprehensive mandatory sanctions.[22]

Rhodesia

Rhodesia came before the General Assembly in 1961 and was one of the first territories tackled by the Committee of Twenty-Four. The latter castigated British colonialism, international monopolies and white settlers for being in league with one another. But it was Rhodesia's 1965 unilateral declaration of independence (UDI) that put it on the front burner. At Britain's behest, the Security Council immediately condemned the 'illegal, racist minority regime',[23] urged states to withhold recognition, called on Britain to end the rebellion and asked other states to break economic relations and apply an oil embargo. This fell short of what the Africans ardently desired and demanded: British military force to defeat the rebels. But Britain made it clear she would veto military sanctions, and the Security Council would go no further than was acceptable to London. Miffed African states staged a walkout when Britain's Prime

Minister addressed the Assembly in 1965. And Commonwealth meetings were so stormy that at one stage the Prime Minister angrily exclaimed that 'Britain is being treated as if we are a bloody colony'.[24]

However, the Commonwealth persuaded Britain to adopt a tougher line. In December 1966, just over a year after UDI, the Security Council applied mandatory sanctions for the first time ever. Nine exports vital to the Rhodesian economy were embargoed on the grounds that the illegal regime constituted 'a threat to international peace and security' (this assertion being necessary for chapter 7 of the Charter to be invoked). Almost a hundred states reported compliance with the resolution and Zambia, which was dependent on Rhodesia for 95 per cent of its transport, was given urgent Commonwealth aid and a British-sponsored airlift of oil. In 1968, at Britain's request, the Security Council approved a total trade ban on Rhodesia. The British navy patrolled the sea surrounding Beira, the port nearest to Rhodesia, but there was much sanctions busting, primarily by South Africa which supplied Rhodesia with oil, and by Portugal (which ruled neighbouring Mozambique). And in 1971 an American Congressional amendment lifted the ban on the import from Rhodesia of 'strategic and critical' materials (chiefly chrome and nickel).

When Rhodesia declared itself a republic in 1970, it again came before the Security Council. The Afro-Asians insisted on voting on a resolution they knew Britain would veto. Having seen the Security Council's sanctions committee paralysed for months because of 'a silly little squabble about its membership', Washington responded to 'openly insincere manoeuverings'[25] by casting its very first veto. But in the mid-1970s the political balance in Southern Africa changed with Angolan and Mozambiquan independence, and nationalist guerrillas gained an increasing military advantage. South Africa in effect told Rhodesia's leader, Ian Smith, to settle and Smith reached an internal agreement in 1978. The world refused to recognise it. By then Rhodesia was taking up practically all the British Foreign Secretary's time and on his first day in the office Lord Carrington announced in 1979: 'We're going to settle it'.[26] Commonwealth pressure, accompanied by an emphatic demonstration of the political and economic costs of going it alone, weighed more heavily in Britain's thinking than the UN. There were other considerations, too – the views of her European partners and the US and (in the eyes of some) the danger of Russian expansion.[27] Building on his predecessor's negotiations, Lord Carrington chaired the Lancaster House talks which led to Rhodesia becoming Zimbabwe in May 1980. In this there was no role for the UN: it was a Commonwealth force which monitored the pre- independence elections.

The 'non-political' UN

In the third world UN, the Western, liberal distinction between what was technical and what was political became blurred. Issue compartmentalisation broke down and everything became 'related to everything else'.[28] This is best illustrated by the events leading to the demand for what was called a 'New International Economic Order' (NIEO).

President Kennedy's proclamation of the 1960s as a UN Development Decade has been described as being 'to economic development what the Declaration on Colonialism was to self-determination'.[29] Thereafter the 'north–south gap' was a major UN issue which gained impetus from the influx of third world members and the arrival in 1961 of a Burmese Secretary-General, U Thant, who regarded the problem as 'the most serious source of tension in the world'.[30] In 1960 the UN created the International Development Association (IDA) to provide loans on favourable terms to third world countries. And in 1962 ECOSOC endorsed Thant's proposals for action in such areas as development planning, mobilising human resources, international trade, development financing, technical cooperation and other aids to development. It also gave full support to the Freedom from Hunger Campaign, the new World Food Programme, and a conference on the application of science and technology to the problems of less developed areas. But although there were some gains, the gap between rich and poor widened and, in terms of assistance and growth, 'the decade was a dismal failure'.[31]

By then the third world's expectations had markedly increased and, being disappointed with ECOSOC's conservative line, it had created bodies in which to challenge the whole American-inspired, liberal trading system. 1964 saw the creation of the United Nations Conference on Trade and Development (UNCTAD) and the emergence of the 'Group of 77'.[32] By maintaining a united front under

the leadership of UNCTAD's first Secretary-General, Raoul Pre-
bisch, the developing states called attention to their trade problems
and the way in which these were aggravated by the developed states
(while successfully keeping attention away from reforms they could
introduce themselves). In this way, they managed to change the
terms of the debate and put the West on the defensive.

Seeing UNCTAD as 'a demand for everything by those who have
nothing',[33] the West ignored such UNCTAD demands as more 'un-
tied' aid, lower tariffs and stable prices for primary commodities.
This prompted much name-calling and recrimination, especially
against the USA, which acted as scapegoat for the West. But two
developments in the early 1970s led the West to take a more constructive attitude towards the problem of development and admit
the inequity of the existing international economy. Firstly, there
was the collapse of the Bretton Woods system, widespread harvest
failures and a major international economic crisis. Secondly, the
quadrupling of oil prices in the wake of the 1973 Middle East War
had a tremendous psychological impact, raising doubts about the
West's supply of raw materials from the South on which it seemed
increasingly dependent. Developing states felt greatly encouraged
and the more radical, led by Algeria, saw the oil crisis as the first
shot in the world economic revolution.

In April 1974, at the sixth special session of the General Assembly,
Southern assertiveness blossomed into full-blown demands for a
New International Economic Order (NIEO). Agreement on practical measures was wellnigh impossible, but two resolutions were
adopted. The first, the Declaration on the Establishment of a New
International Economic Order, combined 'features of a recitation
of past evils, a salutation of present changes in the international
economic power structure, and a manifestation of desired reforms
in the system'.[34] The second resolution adopted a 'Programme of
Action' for the NIEO. This had no substantive weight, being an
enumeration – in emotive and value-laden words – of the aspirations of the developing states and the normative duties of the developed. Later that year, the regular Assembly session adopted a
'Charter of Economic Rights and Duties of States'. This contained
stiff medicine for the rich – in the words of some Western wags, it
was 'all developing state rights and developed state duties'.[35]

However desirable the NIEO might have been, it demanded more
self-abnegation than the rich possessed. The key states required to

offer themselves as sacrificial lambs were those who voted against the Programme of Action. Clearly there was little progress to be made in this confrontational direction. The South therefore changed tack and began moderating its tone as early as the 1975 special session on the NIEO. And UNCTAD IV in 1976 was marked by readiness on both sides to understand the other's problems and recognise the need for cooperation. As the 1970s wore on the prospects of an NIEO vanished. The North came to feel less vulnerable. The oil countries were not willing to use their leverage on behalf of other developing countries. The poor could not create other cartels similar to OPEC. The South's solidarity crumbled in the face of non-complementary short-term interests and the success of the West in drawing in the *nouveaux riches*. The final crunch came in 1980 when there was an attempt to empower the General Assembly to bring all UN institutions into line with development doctrine and fundamentally to reform the IMF. The 1980 special session came to a dismal end 'and effectively derailed "global negotiations" ' on an NIEO.[36]

But the quest for an NIEO did bring modest gains for the South. Structural explanations of underdevelopment achieved credibility and behaviour was affected by standard-setting for development assistance. The IMF introduced compensatory financing facilities and IMF credit was increased. There was a modest increase in participation in the decision-making process of the World Bank. The 1975 Lomé Convention between the EEC and 46 third world states set a new standard in relations between industrialised and developing states. The GATT Tokyo round of 1975–9 allowed some, qualified, trade preference. An International Fund for Agricultural Development was established in 1977. And third world dependence on primary commodities was reduced from over 80 per cent in 1978 to 48 per cent in 1986. But the NIEO had little impact on its intended targets: the Bretton Woods institutions and GATT.

Meanwhile, although there were troubles elsewhere in the UN system (as will be discussed below in respect of the International Labour Organisation), much valuable work was done. For example, the World Weather Watch, launched by the World Meteorological Organisation in 1967, was highly useful and successful and offered no scope for making political hay. Thanks to the World Health Organisation, malaria seemed virtually wiped out and smallpox was eradicated. And due to the Food and Agriculture Organisation, the 'green revolution' dramatically improved food supplies through the introduction of high-yielding cereals. Arguably, the UN system's contribution to the elimination of poverty was a drop in the ocean. But at least something *was* happening. People benefited through having sewers and clear running water in villages. Children were saved from hunger and early death. Education, hospitals and roads were provided in developing states. And, as Thant pointed out, 'a bridge was being built between the North and the South, there was acceptance of a community of interest and recognition of interdependence'.[37]

The impact of the General Assembly's activity

The General Assembly has two levels of activity. One is the private level. Virtually all member states have sent permanent missions to the UN, so that within the geographically confined space of an area around the UN's headquarters there are high-ranking diplomatic posts from almost all the world's states. This is particularly important for third world states which, being relatively poor, cannot afford many embassies. With one in New York, however, they have the opportunity to make private face-to-face contact with the representatives of any other member (as well the few non-members such as the Holy See and Switzerland). As at most conferences, these off-stage discussions can have as much – and, on particular issues, often more – importance than what goes on in public.

But the second level of the General Assembly's activity – its public face – is important, too. Here states can speak for the record, and mount their open diplomatic campaigns. Some of these campaigns have had little effect, or have even been counter-productive. Those who were on the receiving end of barracking in UN committees grew weary of discussions that were devoid of reality and in which they were continually having to resist attempts to expand the UN's authority. Thus the colonial powers withdrew from the Committee on Information from Non-self-governing Territories. Britain ceased participating in Committee of Twenty-Four discussions on Rhodesia. And a 1964 attempt to broaden the membership of the Committee on Apartheid was unsuccessful, as opponents of sanctions refused to join.

States did not alter their fundamental policies just because of General Assembly demands. For example, in addition to criticising the superpowers for discussing arms control outside the UN framework, the General Assembly designated the 1970s and 1980s as 'disarmament decades' and convened three special sessions on disarmament (1978, 1982, 1988). But the main achievements were negotiated elsewhere. Britain did not speed up decolonisation because of the UN,[38] though the anti-colonialist campaign did provide an added justification for its colonial disrobing. The UN did not fundamentally alter Britain's policy on Rhodesia or end racial discrimination in Southern Africa. States whose cooperation was necessary for stiffer sanctions against Rhodesia or South Africa did not change tack or give in to haranguing.[39] And as long as the West felt economically impregnable, discussions over the plight of the developing world often seemed like a dialogue of the deaf.

Furthermore, one impact of sanctions can be to rally populations behind the target governments, and to make those governments more intransigent and antipathetic to anything connected with the UN. This happened in Rhodesia and South Africa. Thus Rhodesia's Ian Smith was led to say: 'There is more justice where Satan reigns than where the United Nations wallows in its sanctimonious hypocrisy.'[40]

However, third world campaigns were by no means always fruitless. A variety of points should be noted. In the first place, as well as demonstrating the depth of moral commitment to a cause, fiery speeches are one way of releasing a real build-up of political steam. It is therefore possible that they may reduce the temptation actually to indulge in hot-headed action. Secondly, the campaigns provided a means whereby the dislike of certain situations could be effectively dramatised[41] and so be given increased prominence. Thus, by such devices as delegates walking out when South African representatives addressed the Assembly, racial discrimination in South Africa was kept in the public eye.

Thirdly, by repeatedly passing resolutions by large majorities, the third world campaigners not only achieved symbolic victories but also had some influence on that amorphous entity known as world public opinion. General Assembly resolutions may be no more representative of world public opinion than, say, *The Times* or the *Sun* is of British public opinion. But they do signal developments in the world's *diplomatic* climate and that in turn helps to set the international agenda. Resolution 1514 and subsequent resolutions, for example, amounted to a de facto amendment of the Charter and the outlawing of colonialism, at least in political terms, and perhaps also in legal terms. This is what is meant when it is said that General Assembly resolutions represent something more than the sum of their parts. It also explains why such importance is regularly attached by member states to getting a majority in favour of their case, or to preventing their opponents from securing a majority. In this way the General Assembly has become an important element in international diplomacy.

A fourth consideration is that public discussion in the General Assembly may sometimes precipitate policy changes by individual states. A state which knows it is going to be attacked may occasionally trim its policy sails in the hope of being able to present a better defensive case. France, for example, rushed a bill on Algeria through its parliament in 1957 in anticipation of the General Assembly debate on that subject. The knowledge that one has to stand up and be counted on an issue in which one's state is not directly concerned may move that state away from its initial inclination in favour of the target state towards the majority view, or at least towards abstaining on the vote. It may be judged just not worth the diplomatic cost to court unpopularity through a gratuitous display of one's personal sympathies. This clearly seemed to happen over South Africa as the Assembly's anti-apartheid tempo heightened. For certain Western states came to opt for abstention on draft resolutions which called for sanctions, rather than allow themselves to be seen as providing comfort to an international pariah. On Rhodesia, too, one state – France – switched its line in 1968 at least partly in response to the intensity of international feeling on the question. Moreover, in the case of some states – those of Asia – hostility to South Africa seems genuinely to have increased as a result of regularly having to vote on the matter in the General Assembly. Through being forced to take a public position, their substantive position underwent change.

Fifthly, it must also be borne in mind that states are always alert to the possibility, on issues which do not greatly interest them, of 'selling' their votes, or bartering them to achieve a desired result on another matter. Thus in the 1950s, with Algeria very much in mind, France supported Britain over Cyprus. And, sixthly, the General Assembly has been increasingly looked to to provide legitimacy for states' policies. The obverse of this aspect of the Assembly's activities is the diplomatic ploy of hiding behind a resolution of the

General Assembly – claiming an inability to act because the Assembly has ruled it out or, where the Assembly is thought to have responded weakly, simply trying to shift the blame for not having acted oneself to the world body.

What all this amounts to is the undoubted fact that the General Assembly has become a diplomatic forum of some significance. It is *not* a legislature. Nor do its votes necessarily have a high moral character. But it is a diplomatic register which states have found it increasingly unwise to ignore, and which they have, when in the majority, tried to use to further their own policies. It is, therefore, the third world states who have benefited most from the General Assembly's public activities. But, naturally, states on the receiving end of the majority's censure were far from happy about this development. Above all, this was true of the world's most powerful state, the US.

American disillusionment and increased use of the Security Council

American enthusiasm for the UN waned as the General Assembly became third world dominated. In 1945 the 'cosmic overselling of the UN'[42] as an 'American organisation' had headed off any possible opposition in Senate. But it contributed significantly to America's stunned reaction when things no longer went its way. Although in the 1960s the great majority of resolutions were still supportive of America's position, disillusion began setting in when, in 1964, third world states would not back the USA over its intervention in the Congo. (America had done this to protect Western citizens.) The US had the same reaction after being criticised by the Committee of Twenty-Four over the handling of its possessions in the Pacific and Caribbean.[43]

Symptomatic of America's declining leadership of, and support for, the UN was President Ford's 1974 warning against the 'tyranny of the majority', and the 1975 appointment of Patrick Moynihan as the United States' ambassador to the UN. A blunt, confrontational man, Moynihan believed the UN was growing 'in a certain kind of ideological authority . . . deployed on behalf of totalitarian principle and practice wholly at variance with its original purpose'. It was time 'the American spokesman came to be feared in international forums for the truths he might tell'.[44] The General Assembly's tilt against Israel – reflected in the 1975 resolution declaring Zionism a form of racism – made things worse since it was interpreted as a thinly veiled attack on the United States. Demands for an NIEO caused indignant outrage.

There was a new American indifference to UN appeals. Aid was cut, Rhodesian sanctions were violated to maintain chrome imports, and America's contribution to the budget was reduced from 31 to 25 per cent. President Carter, who took office in 1977, sought to restore the UN's place in American foreign policy and, by appointing a black civil rights veteran, Andrew Young, as US ambassador to the UN, won 'a two year honeymoon with the Organisation of African Unity and the [African] Front Line states'.[45] But the UN had become the organisation of the underdogs and Carter could not outweigh powerful internal opposition to what was regarded as an unholy Soviet–third world alliance in the International Labour Organisation (ILO).

The 1970s had begun with Congress withholding US budget payments to the ILO because a Soviet was appointed to a senior position. In 1974, and without proper prior investigation, the ILO conference passed a resolution condemning Israel's labour practices in the occupied territories. The same meeting failed to adopt an Expert Committee's report containing several specific condemnations of the Soviet Union.[46] The final straw was when the 1975 ILO conference granted observer status to the Palestine Liberation Organisation. That November Washington gave notice of withdrawal because the ILO had 'become increasingly and excessively involved in political issues which are quite beyond the competence and mandate of the organisation'; had shown 'appallingly selective concern' in respect of human rights'; increasingly demonstrated 'utter disregard' of 'due process' in condemning states without following the correct procedures; and its unique tripartite structure – granting representation to employers, workers and states – had been eroded because some employers and workers were under the thumbs of their governments.[47]

While America worked out its two years' notice the ILO continued causing offence. First the conference blocked a US nomination as vice-president. Then it rejected an American proposal to ensure the observation of due process before states were attacked. And, thirdly, it displayed 'double standards' in not adopting a report critical of Argentina, Chile, Ethiopia and Uganda, while dam-ning Israel by refusing to accept data on labour conditions in the West Bank. Despite pressure from close allies and the State Depart-ment, Carter reluctantly withdrew because the ILO had not taken 'corrective measures . . . to restore that organisation's commitment to its original purposes'.[48]

The ILO survived the loss of America's 25 per cent of the budget by additional voluntary contributions and financial economies. But it wanted Washington back and senior officials noticed 'dramatic' and 'fantastic' changes.[49] Noticeably less rhetoric flew around the con-ference hall. The agenda became markedly 'non-political'. There were no anti-Israeli resolutions. And the ILO tackled the problem of human rights in Eastern Europe by condemning Czechoslovakia and investi-gating trade union policies in Czechoslovakia and Poland. Moreover, the adoption of a secret ballot for some votes enabled individuals to vote according to conscience rather than the dictates of their govern-ments. Satisfied, the USA rejoined the ILO in February 1980.

The enlargement of the Security Council in 1965 from 11 to 15 members shifted the balance away from the P5 (permanent mem-bers). The latter could now be outvoted by non-permanent mem-bers who constituted a majority which could block a resolution with seven abstentions. (This is sometimes called the 'hidden veto'.) Non-permanent members, who now tended to see themselves as representatives of their regional group, began inviting, and giving a hearing to, non-members of the Security Council, thereby contri-buting to a certain amount of 'irrelevancies and invective'.[50] The USA found itself increasingly isolated and, in consequence, re-sorted to the veto.

Nonetheless, the Security Council remained a relative haven to which both superpowers retreated from an awkward and unbid-

Table 4.1   Vetoes in the Security Council to August 1995[51]

	USA	USSR	UK	FRANCE	CHINA
1946–55	0	75	0	2	1
1956–65	0	26	3	2	0
1966–75	12	7	8	2	2
1976–85	34	6	11	9	0
1986–95	24	2	8	3	0
TOTAL	70	116	30	18	3

dable General Assembly. This contributed to an increase in the Council's authority, as did four other developments. Firstly, the P5 recognised the need to agree amongst themselves and engage in genuine diplomacy on a broad, intercaucus basis. Secondly, the Nixon administration, elected in 1968, was inclined to acknowledge Soviet strategic parity and talk the language of the balance of power. Thirdly, this trend was strengthened when the People's Republic took over China's UN seat in 1971[52] and there was a marked improvement in American-Chinese relations. And, fourthly, the 1967 and 1973 Middle East Wars reminded the permanent members, especially the USA, that they shared a *common* interest in avoiding war and that the UN could be useful in this. Apart from the 1971 India–Pakistan war – when Chinese, Soviet and American interests diverged sharply – the Security Council now became a forum for action as opposed to expressions of opinion.

As a result, limited collegiality emerged and the P5 began having private meetings and consultations. There had always been private meetings on sensitive subjects such as electing the Secretary-General. But in the late 1960s regular discussions began to be held on substantive issues. By the early 1970s the Council was also holding 'informal consultations of the whole': off-the-record meetings (governed neither by the Charter nor rules of procedure) at which representatives could speak freely without committing their states. A commodious and well-provided consultation room was built adjacent to the Council chamber, thereby making consultations a symbolically separate replica of formal Council meetings.

The UN and the maintenance of international peace and security

The third world UN had very little impact on the maintenance of peace and security. For, notwithstanding the fact that many disputes arose in the third world, they almost all had a Cold War dimension and so limited the UN's ability to act. And on direct Cold War issues the UN continued to be of little relevance. However, although the UN was shunted to the margins when the superpowers clashed, it could be still valuable. During the Cuban Missile Crisis in October 1962, the USA used the Security Council to embarrass the USSR with photographic evidence of the Soviet missile sites.

Off-stage corridor diplomacy and the Secretary-General's mediation assisted in resolving the crisis. Yielding to U Thant rather than
President Kennedy's ultimatum enabled Khrushchev to save face.
But the US looked to the OAS to legitimise its naval 'quarantine' of
Cuba, and Castro's blank refusal to allow the UN to dismantle the
missile sites was a reminder of the need to take into account the
pride and views of smaller states.

The USSR vetoed a resolution condemning its invasion of
Czechoslovakia in August 1968, and had the newly installed Husak
government remove the item from the UN's agenda. Since the Soviets had no intention of backing down, there was nothing practical
the UN could do. But because of the UN, the Soviets were put in a
very uncomfortable position. The Soviet Ambassador was 'weary,
uneasy and embarrassed'[53] and gave the impression 'that he was
reading out texts which even he could not believe'.[54] Although the
Soviet veto of a condemnatory resolution was a foregone conclusion, desperate filibustering revealed the want of a convincing justification. The fact that ten out of fifteen Council members voted for
the resolution clearly recorded the weight of opinion – as did many
speeches in the subsequent General Assembly.[55]

Over Vietnam, the organisation was quite helpless. This was not
just because Washington would only allow the UN to act as a sound-
ing-board for its claims to be an aggrieved party and tireless seeker
after peace. Hanoi also rejected the UN's competence in what it
considered to be an internal conflict, and Hanoi's friends followed
its lead. The Secretary-General tried to mediate but all efforts were
rebuffed. Almost all states regarded the 1967–70 Nigerian civil war
as a strictly internal matter – the line adopted by the Organisation
of African Unity. Since no state ever took it to the UN, the organisation had no role.

The birth of Bangladesh in the 1971 India–Pakistan war vividly
indicated the UN's impotence when permanent members' interests
were at stake. By June 1971 millions of refugees were flooding into
India from East Pakistan and cholera had broken out in Calcutta.
But the Soviet Union was protector of India, the People's Republic
of China was Pakistan's patron, and the USA was reluctant to take a
strong stand that might damage *détente* with Moscow and *rapprochement* with Beijing. Because of this, they 'did not even discuss the
problem privately'.[56] Thant's 'pleas and warnings to the Security
Council, both privately and publicly, fell on deaf ears'.[57] Only when

war commenced on 3 December did the Security Council meet, but it was blocked by vetoes and passed the matter over to the General Assembly under the Uniting for Peace procedure. The Assembly called for a ceasefire and withdrawal of forces, two weeks before the Security Council did likewise (though without taking a vote). But by then Indian troops had achieved their objectives and Pakistani capitulation was almost complete.

However, while the UN could do nothing when the superpowers fell out, its peacekeeping activities continued making a valuable secondary contribution to peace – with the support not just of the major powers but also of the third world states. The UN Force in Cyprus (UNFICYP) – which, unusually, contained troops from a permanent member, Britain – was despatched in 1964 to try to prevent fighting between Greek and Turkish Cypriots, to maintain order, and to assist in restoring normal conditions. During the next ten years UNFICYP did much humanitarian work but, in the face of considerable intercommunal tension, could do no more than interpose itself on the de facto front lines between the communities, patrol sensitive areas and generally try to keep things calm.

A bungled coup attempt in 1974 led to a Turkish invasion and, later, to the creation of the Turkish Republic of Northern Cyprus. UNFICYP could do nothing about this for it was neither intended nor equipped to resist an army on the march. But it helped defuse the crisis, marginally stemmed the barbarity of the fighting, helped firm-up ceasefire lines and established Nicosia airport as a UN protected area. Since then the force has acted as a buffer on the divided island. It has been argued that by reducing anxiety levels, UNFICYP has removed the necessary spur the disputants need to reach a settlement. And some states withdrew from UNFICYP because of its cost and their frustration with the situation.[58] But UNFICYP remains because of worries about the fearful escalatory propensities of possible hostilities and for the time being all concerned are keen to avoid such a risk.

Peacekeeping again proved useful in 1965 when India and Pakistan came to blows. With the help of the Secretary-General they were able to end fighting over and (in due course) agree on ownership of a desolate, uninhabited salt marsh, the Rann of Kutch. But they ignored Security Council calls for a ceasefire in Kashmir and, in a rare show of unanimity that reflected the perceived seriousness of the threat, the Council despatched Thant to the subcontinent. The intransigence of both sides forced Thant to proclaim his 'helplessness' to the Security Council, which symbolically underlined its support for him by going, as a body, to the airport to welcome him back. After several days' deadlock, both sides found acceptable a Security Council resolution demanding a ceasefire and withdrawal of troops to the positions held before fighting. Thant set up a new, short-term observer group – the United Nations India–Pakistan Observation Mission (UNIPOM) – which assisted UNMOGIP in the vital task of calming things down and supervising the ceasefire.[59] It was not the Security Council that was decisive in obtaining the ceasefire and withdrawal. It was the Soviet Prime Minister, Alexei Kosygin, who negotiated the Tashkent declaration, signed by the two parties in December 1965.

In Egypt, UNEF I had an unexpectedly long life. While the Soviets grumbled, the United States, other Western powers and a number of smaller states welcomed the idea that UNEF I should play a calming role in this dangerous region. For its part, Egypt found it advantageous to have an international buffer between her and her stronger neighbour. As long as Israel and Egypt were willing to live at peace, UNEF I helped them to maintain it. But in the spring of 1967, Arab-Israeli tensions rose dangerously high. This was at a time of Security Council paralysis; the first 1967 Council meeting was held in late May but it adjourned after propaganda and mud-slinging. When war broke out on 5 June, neither Israel nor Egypt called a Security Council meeting. However, it quickly became clear that Israel would massively triumph over Egypt, Syria and Jordan. Leonid Brezhnev, the Soviet leader, wanted to save his allies from worse humiliation and, as he told President Johnson on the hotline, Moscow desired no part in a Middle East war. So the Soviets backed down from insisting that Israel be condemned as an aggressor and the Security Council called for a ceasefire. After six days, Israel had achieved its objectives and the Security Council supported Thant's proposal to send observers to restore a UN presence. Officers from UNTSO were therefore despatched to the Golan Heights between Israel and Syria, and later to the Suez Canal between Israel and Egypt. But although in November 1967 the Security Council unanimously agreed a framework for the comprehensive settlement of the Middle East conflict (Resolution 242), no settlement could be reached. Arabs and Israelis continued living in a state of war, with frequent acts of violence on both sides. UNTSO suffered casualties and the Secretary-General seriously contemplated its withdrawal. But it was a useful buffer as long as the parties did not want fighting to escalate.

The second most dangerous post-1945 crisis occurred when war broke out in the same region, in 1973. After over a week of inertness, the immediate danger of confrontation jolted the superpowers into 'an impressive and rare display of statesmanship and great power unanimity'.[60] Through the Security Council they called for a ceasefire. Fighting broke out again and ominous Soviet troop movements prompted the USA to move its forces and put them on nuclear alert. The mere agreement to send a second UN Emergency Force (UNEF II) to Sinai defused the superpower crisis,[61] but UNEF II's really vital role was in bolstering the fragile ceasefire and defusing tensions on the ground. It then monitored the withdrawal of troops and established a buffer zone in the Sinai. Since both Egypt and Israel wanted to maintain stability, they both cooperated with UNEF II which helped to ensure calm until the Camp David Agreement of 1978 and the Egyptian-Israeli Peace Treaty of the following year. Mindful of its Arab clientele's condemnation of these developments, the Soviet Union then announced it would veto an extension of UNEF II's mandate. The force was therefore quietly withdrawn. Inspectors from a US-manned Sinai Support Mission acted as observers until 1982 when a non-UN Multinational Force and Observers took over after Israel finally quitted Egyptian territory.

Meanwhile, at the end of May 1974, gruelling shuttle-diplomacy by the US Secretary of State, Henry Kissinger, produced an Israeli-Syrian agreement to disengage their forces under the supervision of the UN Disengagement Observer Force (UNDOF) which would then patrol a buffer zone between them. The superpowers jointly sponsored UNDOF's creation as they wanted to limit the possibilities of confrontation via their Syrian and Israeli clients. In less than a month, UNDOF had defused a very hostile situation and, by its continuing presence, helped to prevent accidental conflict on a very dangerous border. (It should be noted that another peace-keeping force – the UN Interim Force in Lebanon [UNIFIL] – was despatched in 1978. It engaged in valuable humanitarian work but was helpless to prevent Israeli incursions and was stuck behind Israeli lines for three years after the Israeli invasion of Lebanon in 1982.)

Secretaries-General

The choice of U Thant of Burma to fill out the remainder of Hammarskjöld's term of office directly reflected the added prominence of new Afro-Asian states. Thant took over when the UN was going through dire days. It was in financial straits, peacekeeping activities were under challenge and Moscow was pushing for a three-man *troika*. Thant's courageous and skilful handling of the 1962 Cuban Missile Crisis defused the *troika* campaign. On his own initiative he provided Khrushchev and Castro with acceptable ways of backing down and engaged in toilsome post-crisis negotiations while the Council remained inactive. In November 1962 no one challenged Thant's election to a full, five-year term of office and he was able to insist on, and obtain, the same authority as previous Secretaries-General. He reluctantly accepted a second term (to begin in 1967) when the P5 'promised him every consideration and virtually pleaded with him from a kneeling position'.[62]

Yet when Thant left office there was a widespread sigh of relief. One reason was the myth that, compared to Hammarskjöld, Thant was inactive, ineffective and lacked character and leadership qualities. In terms of personality the two men were very different. They were from very different parts of the world and, whereas Hammarskjöld operated in a bustle, Thant did so quietly. But perhaps Hammarskjöld had *too much* personality. For he nearly wrecked the Secretary-Generalship while Thant strengthened the office and demonstrated its capacities.

Thant was not lacking in backbone. He made no secret of his views and would not be moved against his will. ('[C]onvincing Mr Thant', said a Soviet diplomat, 'is like fighting your way forward in a room full of mashed potatoes.'[63]) For speaking out over Vietnam he was 'less than popular in the State Department and the White House'.[64] He told the Soviet public on Moscow Radio that they were misinformed about the Congo and not only denounced the Soviet invasion of Czechoslovakia but urged the despairing Czech ambassador to speak out in the Security Council. But, as in 1967 when 'helpless' Western powers 'needed someone else to blame' for the outbreak of the Six-Day War, Thant was attacked for timorousness.[65]

Thant presided over the UN when it was in the political doldrums. The development of sophisticated methods of crisis management between the superpowers robbed him of the space to manoeuvre that had existed for his predecessor. It also made the world less anxious about small wars escalating into superpower confrontations. Nonetheless, Thant probably acted more independently than any other Secretary-General. He went beyond Hammarskjöld in authorising first the use of force and then decisive military action to end Katanga's secession from the Congo (Zaire). Despite French and Soviet wariness and criticism, he extended the Secretary-General's responsibilities in the maintenance of peace. He took the initiative in the 1962 agreement transferring West New Guinea from the Netherlands to Indonesia and the associated despatch of a UN mission (the UN Temporary Executive Authority – UNTEA) to the territory enabling them to avoid handing it over directly to Indonesia.[66] US diplomatic pressure and Dutch recognition that time was not on their side were important in resolving this dangerous crisis, but Thant's role was also valuable. In 1963 he helped work out a disengagement agreement in the Yemeni civil war and obtained the Security Council's blessing to UN observers being posted between Yemen and Saudi Arabia. In 1963 he also persuaded the relevant parties to allow a team of UN observers to determine whether the peoples of North Borneo and Sarawak wanted union with Malaysia rather than Indonesia or the Philippines.[67] The Security Council approved Thant's proposal to despatch UNIPOM in 1965, and in 1970 he mediated on the future of Bahrain, thereby enabling Iran to relinquish its claim and Britain to withdraw from the Gulf. Thant got away with things because he was more circumspect than Hammarskjöld and avoided unnecessary confrontation. When Thant failed, it was because of the parties' attitudes – for example, in 1971 when his warnings of fratricidal strife in East Pakistan were ignored.

Withdrawing UNEF I in 1967 earned Thant much criticism. But failure to accede to President Nasser's demand would have violated the key peacekeeping principle of consent, and few states would have been willing to accept peacekeepers in future. Furthermore, the UN had no right to do what it liked with volunteers who had temporarily donned blue berets; and in any case two contributors had made it clear that, given Egypt's request, they would withdraw their troops. Once more Thant served as an international 'Aunt Sally – the large and conspicuous figure at which things can be thrown both with impunity and with almost complete certainty of hitting the target'.[68]

Thant was not, however, an administrator and the Security Council sought a successor who could put the secretariat in order and tackle the UN's financial problems. After much difficulty, and at the eleventh hour, the Security Council chose Kurt Waldheim of Austria. Ironically, given later revelations about Waldheim's wartime service in the Nazi armed forces, his main recommendation was his 'uncontroversial record'.[69] In the eyes of one of his closest advisers, Waldheim was 'an energetic, ambitious mediocrity' who had 'determination and, on occasion, courage' but 'lacked the qualities of vision, integrity, inspiration, and leadership that the United Nations so desperately needs'.[70] But he 'gave satisfaction'[71] and fared better than his predecessors.

This was, firstly, because Waldheim was spared the types of controversies that faced Lie and Hammarskjöld and he encountered fewer potential banana skins. The continued improvement of the international climate and the unwillingness of parties to use the UN in important conflicts limited his scope. And the People's Republic of China's entry into the UN in 1971 added a powerful supporter of Franco-Soviet determination to keep the Secretary-General on a short lead.

The second reason why Waldheim was less criticised was that states had come to realise that a diplomat's pragmatic, quiet, unshowy approach was best for the job. Waldheim was safe. He did not hector. He was nervous about offending members and conflicted with governments only three times: by speaking out over US bombing of North Vietnamese dykes in 1972; by putting terrorism on the 1972 Assembly agenda – against the wishes of several important states; and in 1976 by publicly calling for a ceasefire in Lebanon and its maintenance as a unified state.

A third reason why Waldheim fared better was because his predecessors had firmly established the office of Secretary-General. They had won the right to address the Security Council, to take charge of peacekeeping operations (under the authority of the Council), to engage in fact-finding and good offices on their own initiative and to initiate peacemaking. Although the Council kept a tight rein on Waldheim, he adjusted UNTSO's observation arrangements following the 1973 Middle East War. When UNEF II took over most of UNTSO's tasks on the Egyptian-Israeli border he put peacekeeping on a sounder financial footing by proposing that UNEF II's costs be treated as part of the expenses of the UN.[72] When Turkey invaded Cyprus in 1974, he asked the President of the Security Council to call a meeting so that he could report on information received from his representative and the UN Force Commander. And with the division of Cyprus, Waldheim turned UNFICYP from a law and order force into a barrier force.

Britain sharply rebuked Waldheim in 1972 when he tried to involve his office in the Ulster conflict and he also failed to negotiate Vietnamese withdrawal from Kampuchea. But he organised a highly successful conference aimed at helping Kampuchean refugees. A 1979 meeting, on Vietnamese refugees and displaced persons, doubled the number of resettlement places, produced $190 million in new funds for resettlement centres, and persuaded the head of the Vietnamese delegation to stop forced departures (then running at 65 000 a month).[73] By working quietly and discreetly, Waldheim claimed to have often 'save[d] a human life, even free[d] whole groups of people from persecution'.[74] The most dramatic instance was when he flew with eight French hostages to Paris in 1977 after arranging their release from the Western Sahara.

Secretaries-General rarely use Article 99 to call the Security Council into session. This is because if states were willing to do anything, they would call a meeting anyway. This was illustrated when Waldheim used Article 99 for only the second time in its history (the first was when Hammarskjöld used it in respect of the Congo) over the US diplomatic hostages in Iran. Iran refused to attend and nothing was achieved. Waldheim then decided to go to Iran at the beginning of 1980 but his position was compromised by an American statement that, if he failed, sanctions would be demanded. After the ensuing nightmare in which Waldheim felt lucky to have escaped with his life,[75] he received public support from the US administration. (But at the same time those who needed someone to blame used the Secretary-General as their whipping boy.) Waldheim also failed to persuade the Security Council to act when the Iran–Iraq war broke out in 1980. This was because everyone hoped the Ayatollah Khomeini would be overturned.[76] In any case, the UN could not curb the bitter war in which egos and the mutual hatred of leaders were decisive.

Conclusion

International society was transformed by the emergence of the third world, but the underlying realities of the game between sovereign states remained unchanged. The main impact of the third world was in shifting the UN's priorities and significantly altering the international agenda by anathematising colonialism, racial discrimination and the North–South gap. The majoritarian impulse and outspokenness of the South made life increasingly uncomfortable for the West (in itself an indication of the significance of the UN). It also contributed to the P5's retreat to the Security Council and that organ's gradual rehabilitation. But the Cold War continued preventing the Council playing a leading role in many international disputes and, 'by a kind of contagion' the UN 'shared in the slump of idealism that Vietnam induced'.[77] By 1980 the slump was turning into crisis.

5 The UN in Crisis and its Rejuvenation, 1980–1994

The 'political' UN in crisis

As the seventies turned into the eighties, the international climate changed unfavourably for the UN. It was unable to play a role in many conflicts because of the unwillingness of the disputants. The revolutionary Iranian Government that seized power in February 1979 ignored appeals from the Security Council and an ICJ ruling demanding the release of American diplomatic hostages. There was fighting between China and Vietnam (whose patron was the USSR). In December 1979 the Cold War flared up when the USSR invaded Afghanistan. And when the Iran–Iraq war began in September 1980, the Security Council idly watched two 'troublesome' states slaughtering each other. The November 1980 election of Ronald Reagan as US President compounded 'a mood of widespread disenchantment' in which the UN was:

> attacked on the grounds that it produces more rhetoric than action, that it is ineffective and often ignored, and that the one-nation, one vote system allows the Third World to dominate decision making – divorcing vote power from the ability to act . . . it has seemed to cope less and less effectively with international conflicts of various kinds, and its capabilities in other areas of international cooperation have also seemed to dwindle . . . [Some critics even asserted] that the United Nations is no longer a useful organisation.[1]

The USA found the UN useful, especially in letting the Secretary-General try to find a solution to seemingly intractable problems such as Afghanistan or Cyprus. And America's disastrous experience in 1982–4 with the Multinational Peacekeeping Force in Beirut was a sharp lesson of the values of peacekeeping. (Both Jeane Kirkpatrick – Reagan's ambassador to the UN – and Reagan acknowledged the UN's past peacemaking and peacekeeping successes.[2]) The Security Council was also the obvious – and safest – place in which to denounce the shooting down of a Korean Airlines jumbo jet that had strayed hundreds of miles off course over a strategic Soviet submarine base.

But America's patience with the snapping and snarling underdogs in the General Assembly had run out. In 1982 it was on the losing side in 133 out of 157 resolutions. In 19 of them, the US was alone; in 18 only Israel voted with it.[3] This contributed hugely to the Reagan administration's tendency to regard the UN at best as 'a troublesome sideshow'.[4] At worst, the US attitude came perilously close to the right-wing Heritage Foundation's belief that 'a world without the United Nations would be a better world'.[5] America's ideologically-minded UN ambassador, Jeane Kirkpatrick, and her associates:

> seemed to see themselves as embattled defenders of the faith, venturing out from their fortress in the U.S. Mission mostly to do battle with the infidel, to chastise offenders, and to worry about the loyalty of putative allies. They did not associate with the Third World or other representatives . . . [and engage in] making friends and building an international constituency. They seemed to be more preoccupied with punishing reprehensible behaviour or trying to score points off the Soviet Union.[6]

US critics believed that in, say, the Middle East or South Africa, the UN exacerbated conflicts and, on balance, did more harm than good. Former envoys wished the UN would 'be towed off into the sunset' and maintained that the Security Council had 'become the captive of a Soviet/Third World working majority and of that bloc's political agenda: anti-Israel, anti-West, anti-US'.[7]

They were not altogether justified in their complaints – which pictured the US as the victim (in voting terms) of all but its close friends. In fact, the General Assembly did not operate on clear-cut bloc lines. Even America's European allies did not support its intervention in Grenada in 1983, for which it was condemned by the General Assembly. But on the other hand, and notwithstanding the general cohesiveness of the Soviet bloc, Poland sided with the US more than Mexico did. In respect of African states, Zimbabwe (although a large recipient of US aid) voted with the US less often than Libya.[8] Moreover, the General Assembly condemned the Soviet presence in Afghanistan, called for the immediate withdrawal of Vietnamese troops from Kampuchea in 1979, and rejected Cuban efforts to designate Puerto Rico a US colonial territory.

It was, however, the Reagan administration's perceptions that counted. Under Reagan, the US tended to operate outside the UN the better to dominate negotiations, avoid embarrassing criticism and exclude the Soviet Union from international settlements. The supposed profligacy of the secretariat, and the UN system generally, provided the means of wreaking vengeance. By the 1980s the UN's longstanding financial difficulties had become acute. This was partly because the UN's burgeoning budget had defied all attempts at reduction. Partly it was due to soaring unpaid dues[9] and the late payment of assessments. Hustled by the Heritage Foundation, Congress passed the Kassebaum Amendment in 1985, requiring America's UN contribution to be reduced from 25 to 20 per cent of the budget unless weighted voting was adopted on budgetary matters. Combined with Congressional cuts in federal spending, this meant that in 1986 the US paid only about 12 per cent of the budget. No one else could – or would – meet the shortfall. (Most states paid between 0.01 and 0.02 per cent of the budget.) With the USA accounting for over 80 per cent of the UN's indebtedness, the UN neared bankruptcy.

The Secretary-General pledged all the UN's reserves to meet deficits. Conferences were cancelled, staff expenditure was slashed and the 1986 General Assembly was reduced from 13 to 10 weeks. At the beginning of 1987 there was less than a week's cash in hand and the year's end saw the Secretary-General forecasting imminent insolvency. US financial delinquency became a considerable embarrassment. America's European allies made clear their disapproval, as did Japan who wanted a permanent Council seat in a viable UN. Other defaulters shamed Washington by announcing they would remit what they owed: China intended to repay nearly $4.4 million, the Soviet Union offered $18 million to UNIFIL, and France (which owed $4.35 million) said it would start paying its full assessed contribution.[10]

However, pulling the financial plug produced results. Kirkpatrick found debates and resolutions becoming more constructive.[11] At the 1986 special Assembly session on Africa, self-criticism was more apparent than attacks on 'imperialism'. A special 'Eighteen-member Group' of the Assembly bowed to America by, in effect, proposing cuts in the secretariat, recommending weighted voting on the UN budget and curbing General Assembly extravagance. (New activities had to be financed out of a small contingency fund or by the redeployment of existing resources. Otherwise they could not be undertaken until contributions were reassessed.) The proposals were accepted in 1986 with quiet Soviet support. (The USSR shared America's desire to keep the reins firmly in great power hands.) Applauding the decision, the American delegate promised to recommend to the President and Congress that the US meet its full assessed contribution and pay off outstanding debts, and the State Department duly invited Congress to modify the Kassebaum Amendment. But Congressional hostility did not abate and only in 1990 did the US begin paying dues in full and gradually started reimbursing its arrears. However, Republican Congressional victories in 1994 led to a renewed assault on the cost of the UN – including peacekeeping – to the American taxpayer, with serious implications for the future financing of the UN.

The 'non-political' UN in crisis

US dissatisfaction with what it regarded as mismanagement, inefficiency, extravagance and, above all, the spread of politics like an 'infection'[12] from the General Assembly to the Specialised Agencies, led it to throw the UN Educational, Scientific and Cultural Organisation (UNESCO) into crisis. America's commitment to internationalism had always tended to be defined in terms of the US way of life and it seemed UNESCO was opposing 'the very principles'[13] upon which the US had built the Specialised Agencies. Since UNESCO was considered marginal to US interests, it bore the brunt of Washington's wrath and was used to fire a warning-shot to the UN system as a whole. UNESCO 'is the intellectual arm of the United Nations system', seeking to 'build peace in the minds of men and to do this through education, science, culture and communication'.[14] Most of its activities are uncontroversial. These include preserving endangered cultural monuments (most famously, the Nubian temples threatened by the Aswan Dam), scientific collaboration (for example research into the environment and preventing desertification), teacher training and literacy programmes (for example, providing education for 100 000 Cambodian refugees). These take up getting on for 80 per cent of the budget. But by virtue of UNESCO's mandate,[15] its other activities make it the 'most political' agency. 'It's unpleasant. It's inevitable, and you have to keep it below the toxic level', said a former senior official.[16]

Politicisation crept in during the 1970s when Britain and America tended to neglect UNESCO[17] while third world states used it to pursue 'explicitly political' matters 'in the guise of debates on UNESCO-type issues'.[18] Serious trouble began with anti-Israeli moves in 1974. It continued in 1975 when Western delegates walked out after the Arabs asked UNESCO to endorse a General Assembly resolution defining Zionism as a form of racism. It came to a head over the proposed New World Information and Communications Order (NWICO) which was ostensibly aimed at countering Western, 'imperialist' control of news reporting.

There were three dimensions to the NWICO campaign. Firstly, NWICO reflected the developing states' resentment that Western news agencies, which provide most international reporting, produced a one-way flow of communication which gave 'a false and distorted' image of developing states.[19] The West responded to this by helping third world countries to improve their communications and information systems.[20] Secondly, NWICO had a significant Cold War dimension. The USSR was its prime mover and much of the debate to 'decolonise' information was clothed in Marxist rhetoric. Thirdly, NWICO would have stringently limited the free flow of information by government 'licensing' of journalists, and making governments answerable to one another for unfriendly press reports. This would, of course, would have been to the benefit of the Soviet Union and other undemocratic regimes. A raw American nerve was touched. What UNESCO described as 'an essential objective for the world community, on a level with the new international economic order',[21] the US saw as a call to 'war' in which it was 'not the future of press freedom which is at stake, but the future of UNESCO'.[22]

Dissatisfaction with NWICO moved on to resentment that the eight states who paid 60 per cent of UNESCO's budget were 'insulted and . . . vilified with anti-colonialist propaganda'[23] in Specialised Agencies that had:

lost touch with economic reality . . . [and were] living in a dream world, immune from the economic problems of the donor countries, from inflation or privation or harsh budget cutting . . . There [wa]s too much travel, too many conferences, too much misuse of resources and too little cutting off of dead wood.[24]

In July 1983, the Reagan administration ordered a 'thorough review' of US participation in UNESCO because of concern over 'a number of controversial issues', 'including press freedom' and the belief that bilateral programmes might give better value than UNESCO.[25] That year's annual conference avoided ideological confrontation. Several contentious resolutions were neutralised. Britain obtained consensus support for a flexible description of NWICO as an 'evolving and continuous process'. And the budget was trimmed (though not enough for the USA and ten other states who abstained on the vote).

Meanwhile, American voices in favour of UNESCO were drowned by a tide of anti-UNESCO propaganda. Congress prohibited the support of any organisation that threatened freedom of the press. The powerful Heritage Foundation insisted 'UNESCO's activities are pretty constantly inimical to American interests and values'.[26] And even the normally supportive *New York Times* said UNESCO had become 'a babel of words notable for their muddiness and dishonesty' and that its every meeting had become 'an anti-Western rally'.[27] In December 1983 the USA gave notice of withdrawal because of UNESCO's 'politicisation' of virtually every subject, its 'hostility' towards free institutions, its 'unrestrained budgetary expansion' and its wasteful management methods.[28]

Britain shared America's view that UNESCO was 'corrupt and useless'[29] and the British press joined in the anti-UNESCO free-for-all. 'Unesco wastes money and does a lot of silly things,' said *The Times*. 'It puts out a good deal of high-minded drivel . . . gets involved in political disputes . . . indulge[s] in the luxury of abusing the developed nations that provide most of its funds. It wastes time and money on pernicious ideas.'[30] In April 1982 the UK demanded several specific reforms including a budgetary standstill, greater priority being given to practical activities in the field (especially education, science and culture),[31] better control by the governing bodies, improved management and personnel arrangements, and proper attention to evaluation.

Vilification of UNESCO came to focus on the Senegalese Director General, Amadou M'Bow. Since he responded to Anglo-American criticism by waging a 'private war' against them,[32] he was a very convenient scapegoat. His long absences from Paris, combined with a reluctance to delegate, were said to make management erratic. '[A]utocratic, vindictive and conflict-seeking'[33] bureaucratic procedures tended to 'stifle initiative, delay decisions and risked setting up paperwork barriers with the real world'.[34] He had 'created an immense mess'.[35] This was not altogether fair. UNESCO had problems before he took office and his dictatorial predecessor had done 'little to suppress the clouds of jobbery and political nonsense which flowed steadily through the portals of the Paris headquarters'.[36]

No doubt M'Bow's head would have been part of the price of Britain and America staying in UNESCO. But neither state really seems to have intended that. Although the Executive Board and M'Bow set up a committee and working groups to consider reform, Washington demanded fundamental constitutional change (to give 'minority' – or Western – opinion an effective veto power) in a space of time that 'was clearly beyond the ability of any 161-member organisation operating a biennial budget and six-year planning term to achieve'.[37] America left in December 1984. A year later, despite considerable success in securing changes and arguments that Britain benefited from membership, the UK withdrew from UNESCO. (Singapore also withdrew in December 1985 because of unhappiness over her assessed contribution.)

With the departure of Britain and America, UNESCO's budget was cut by almost a third. After a struggle, M'Bow was dethroned in 1987 and succeeded by Professor Federico Mayor from Spain. Mayor described UNESCO as being 'like a dinosaur. Its enormous body contrasts with the stunted development of its brain. The solution is either to reduce the size of the body or to enlarge its brain – or preferably to do both at once.'[38] This was easier said than done. Mayor was constitutionally bound by his predecessor's programme and had to tread softly on the eggshells of states to whom he owed his election – the Soviet Union and Africa. However, NWICO was dropped and by 1991 a quarter of the budget was being devoted to eradicating illiteracy. Dr Mayor admitted having 'failed in one-fourteenth of [his] objectives'[39] in that UNESCO's expenditure and personnel continued to be concentrated at its headquarters in Paris.[40]

But staff costs were the lowest in the UN system and UNESCO had become 'an extremely well-run organisation'[41] which was, 'in many respects . . . in the vanguard amongst UN agencies'.[42] A Foreign Office minister admitted that were the UK still in UNESCO, it would not withdraw.[43] But Whitehall departments were not enthusiastic about rejoining and the government placed higher value on the bilateral assistance to which they had switched the funds saved by withdrawing from UNESCO.[44] The question of membership is constantly under review, but as of late 1995 Britain, America and Singapore have not rejoined.

The experience of the ILO in the 1980s contrasts sharply with UNESCO. At the beginning of the decade it narrowly approved an anti-Israeli resolution at the same time as failing to adopt a report citing East European violations of relevant international law. But then the wheel turned full circle. Poland withdrew in 1984, complaining that critical reports constituted interference in its internal affairs. Other Soviet bloc countries supported Poland, alleging that 'the ILO is being turned into an arena for political manoeuvres to serve the interests of certain circles'.[45] And in 1985 the Soviets considered withholding contributions to 'inappropriate' ILO projects and protested about a pro-Western bias.[46] But Soviet foreign policy was about to be transformed by Mikhail Gorbachev and the dispute vanished from sight.

A Specialised Agency which continued to attract unfavourable publicity, however, was the World Health Organisation (WHO). Once it had had high prestige and was considered the 'best-managed' specialised agency; now it had fallen by the wayside of poor management and financial practices. In 1993 inspectors described the overall picture of its technical programs as one of 'organizational fragmentation verging on disintegration'. The consequences included: 'hobbled strategic direction of the organization as a whole, high operational costs and functional inefficiencies due above all to the virtual impossibility to synchronize and coordinate cross-programme processes throughout the Organization'.[47]

Again the man at the top got most of the blame. The US, West Europeans and Nordic states claimed that Dr Hiroshi Nakajima of Japan 'lacked management and communications skills, had mismanaged a political crisis, had caused the departure of the charismatic Director of the WHO AIDS Programme, and that his [1993] re-election had been "bought" '.[48] The controversy over Dr Nakajima's reappointment crystallised and publicised a longer standing underlying malaise about the WHO's role, structure and effectiveness. The outcome remains to be seen.

Unlike the Security Council, the 'non-political' organs of the UN proper (as distinct from its Specialised Agencies) were in general not revivified by the end of the Cold War. A harsher spotlight was thrown on their deficiencies. As the Secretary-General pointed out, piecemeal measures, establishing bureaucracies 'as substitutes for problem-solving and . . . in some cases, to camouflage problems rather than expose them to serious attention' had led to chaos. 'Duplication is widespread; coordination is often nominal; bureaucratic battles aimed at monopolising a particular subject are rife, and organisational objectives are sometimes in conflict.'[49] Some organs were sustained solely because of bureaucratic and member-state vested interests and no longer did useful work even if they had once done so. The Secretary-General recommended introducing a flexible, high-level intercessional mechanism to enable ECOSOC to respond in a continuous and timely way to new developments. But he had no power to bang heads together.

However, one non-political organ of the UN benefited from the new climate: the International Court of Justice (ICJ). With the end of the Cold War, the decline of the Optional Clause began to go into reverse and the ICJ was back in business with a vengeance. In 1992 the Court had ten cases before it, of which two had earlier led to war and six had been brought under the Optional Clause.[50] Moreover, one case, which was the equivalent of four or five normal cases, settled a dispute between El Salvador and Honduras which dated back to 1839 and which had given rise to the four-day soccer war in 1969.[51] The fact that Libya appeared before the Court for the sixth time, and that Iran also sought the Court's protection, testified how widely the Court was valued.

The rejuvenation of the United Nations

In 1985 a senior UN official 'sometimes felt that only an invasion from outer space would be a sufficiently non-controversial disaster to bring the Council back to the great power unanimity that the Charter required in order to make the United Nations effective.'[52] However, the rejuvenation of the Council was already under way.

One indication was that by the mid-1980s, decisions were being taken in unofficial, 'informal consultations of the whole' and formal meetings became a forum for making speeches for the record and rubber-stamping consensus achieved in private, particularly by the permanent members (the P5). Another indication was voting patterns. Between 1980 and 1985, permanent members voted together in 75 out of 119 resolutions. Between 1986 and 1990 they voted together on 93 out of 103 resolutions.

The main reason for the rejuvenation of the Security Council was that the Soviet Union had lost the Cold War. Under the leadership of Mikhail Gorbachev, the USSR improved relations with the USA and China and turned to the UN for protection. The taking of tea and buns in the British Ambassador's apartment encouraged a collegiate attitude amongst the P5,[53] and the Secretary-General, Pérez de Cuéllar, developed a 'remarkable coordination'[54] with the Security Council, helping to persuade it to alter its working practice and to adopt common policies.

The first significant sign of an emerging 'concert' was the July 1987 Security Council resolution ending the Iran–Iraq war. Resolution 598 'took 5 months of negotiation outside the Council but only about 15 minutes to approve'.[55] Although it was mandatory under chapter 7, Iran did not accept it for a year (unlike Iraq which accepted immediately). But when Iran finally accepted defeat, the superpowers displayed their new-found harmony by jointly providing transport for the UN Iran–Iraq Military Observer Group (UNIMOG) which acted as a calming influence, firming up the ceasefire and supervising force withdrawals.

Then, in September 1987 Gorbachev suddenly gave the UN pride of place in his 'new thinking' about Soviet foreign policy. The Security Council should, he said, assume the pivotal role assigned in the Charter, the Military Staff Committee should be revived and, in effect, there should be a UN army. There should also be wider use of peacekeeping, a more independent role for the Secretary-General, greater resort to the ICJ, more authority for the IAEA, a new agency to monitor compliance with arms control agreements and the military situation in areas of conflict, a tribunal to investigate acts of terrorism, and a large role for the UN in respect of environmental, economic and human rights matters.

Sceptical Westerners suspected another Soviet propaganda ploy. However, Gorbachev demonstrated good faith by making a UN expert deputy foreign minister; by clarifying Soviet military expenditures to facilitate disarmament talks; by announcing the USSR had paid off all arrears on the regular budget and was willing to pay what it owed for peacekeeping; and by being willing to let Soviet citizens enter into long-term contracts with the UN. Further, he announced major unilateral force reductions when he addressed the 1988 General Assembly.[56]

In 1988 when Gorbachev decided to rid himself of the 'Afghan incubus'[57] – a major cause of the 'second Cold War' – he turned to UN peacekeeping to save as much face as was possible. Under an agreement guaranteed jointly by the US and USSR, the UN Good Offices Mission in Afghanistan and Pakistan (UNGOMAP) supervised Soviet withdrawal. The Soviets had clearly been defeated but they were respected for acting honourably, holding regular meetings with UN officials and even giving the UN maps of withdrawal routes. By February 1989 the last Soviet soldier had left. UNGOMAP was less successful in its other task of checking the execution of the peace agreements between Afghanistan and Pakistan, but the situation was wholly unsuitable for peacekeeping. The peacekeepers watching over continuing intervention were thus withdrawn in 1990.

The end of the Cold War also made possible the removal of one of the longest thorns in the UN's flesh: South Africa's presence in Namibia in defiance of the General Assembly, the Security Council and the ICJ. Determined efforts in the 1970s had produced an agreement in principle for a UN peacekeeping force to supervise pre-independence elections. However, South Africa stubbornly stayed put until the changed international climate and military defeats forced its hand. By linking Namibian independence with the withdrawal of Soviet-sponsored Cuban troops in Angola, a December 1988 agreement to send peacekeepers to both territories removed another source of Cold War tension. The UN Transitional Assistance Group (UNTAG) in Namibia was a huge operation, costing roughly half the UN's regular budget. It monitored the 1989 elections, oversaw the virtual demilitarisation of Namibia, kept law and order during the election process, engaged in humanitarian work and endeavoured to insulate Namibia from external influences. Thanks to UNTAG, 97 per cent of registered voters participated in free and fair elections which brought to an end a 20-year armed struggle and introduced another member to the UN. In Angola, the first UN Angola Verification Mission (UNAVEM I) confirmed that Cuban troops had been withdrawn by the end of May 1991.

Collective security revived?

The rising prestige of the UN was reflected when the 1988 Nobel Peace Prize went to UN peacekeeping forces. Progress in other conflicts – the Western Sahara, Cambodia and Central America – further enhanced its stature and reflected the harmony amongst the P5. With only three vetoes cast between 1990 and June 1995,[58] the Security Council was finally operating as intended. The crowning glory came in 1991 when the Gulf crisis revived hopes of collective security amidst much talk of a 'new international order'.

Having huge debts from his war with Iran, troubled relations with Kuwait, and his eye on the main chance, Saddam Hussein invaded and annexed Kuwait in August 1990. To his surprise, the Security Council swiftly condemned Iraq's invasion and imposed mandatory economic sanctions under chapter 7.[59] But although sanctions were almost universally applied, they dented neither Hussein's will nor his powerful military machine. Accordingly, the Security Council demanded he withdraw by 15 January or face the might of the United States and its 29 coalition allies. Operation Desert Storm began on 17 January, ended on 2 March and Iraq capitulated the following day. On 3 April the Security Council determined the terms of a peace settlement. Other resolutions condemned the repression of the Iraqi population, established the UN Iraq–Kuwait observation mission (UNIKOM) on the border and ensured that Iraq adhered to the terms of the settlement.

Contrary to assertions that the episode was collective security in action, critics of Desert Storm contended that the UN merely legitimised US action. Their arguments ran as follows. The US (and hence the UN) acted because of America's strategic and oil interests in the Middle East and because America twisted arms to get what she wanted. According to chapter 7 of the Charter, the Security Council and Military Staff Committee should have been in charge. However, the Security Council delegated the monitoring of shipping in the Gulf to the coalition (in Resolution 665), and authorised the coalition to use 'all necessary means to uphold and implement' previous UN resolutions (in Resolution 678). Instead of all members being involved, there was space for neutrality and non-belligerency. Led by an American general, the coalition states flew their own flags, not that of the UN. And although the Security Council received written reports and was orally briefed, it did not meet formally during the military campaign, the ending of which was determined by US officials.

The Gulf War was clearly in the national interest of the USA and, from a foreign policy perspective, it was a typical national interest/balance of power operation. However, that does not necessarily mean that it cannot be an instance of collective security. It is not a question of 'either/or', but one of 'both/and'. The operation meets the criteria of collective security in as much as, firstly, there was clearcut aggression. Iraq had attempted to annex another UN member and despatched its army across an international border in pursuit of this expansionist design. Secondly, Iraq was virtually unanimously condemned. Thirdly, there was powerful resolve in all important quarters to right this wrong, whatever the cost. The US did not act alone. The Security Council was deeply involved, passing twelve resolutions before Operation Desert Storm was launched. The operation was supported militarily by 29 allies, financially by Japan and Germany, and morally by the vast majority of states. Even Libya, Yemen and Jordan participated in economic sanctions. Resolution 678 could hardly have been more authoritative since almost all Council members were represented by foreign ministers and it was implicitly or explicitly accepted by all the P5.[60] Fourthly, permanent UN forces would not have been capable of dealing with a threat from what was the fourth largest armed force in the world. The 'hired gun approach'[61] was 'unavoidable'.[62] And, fifthly, at the end of the war, and for the first time, all P5 contributed troops to the peacekeeping force sent to monitor the Iraq–Kuwait border.

Collective action was possible in the Gulf because of the chance combination of a number of factors: the importance of oil, Kuwait's strategic position, Iraq's unpopularity, the end of the Cold War, the revolutionised attitude of the Soviet Union and the USA's ability to act. Such fortuitous circumstances are unlikely to recur and the UN will probably never get any nearer to collective security.

The 'crisis of expectations'[63]

Between 1990 and 1995, 27 additional states joined the UN,[64] bringing the total membership to 185. Many new members emerged from the breakup of the Soviet empire and were going through considerable political volatility and turmoil. There was also an unprecedented number of humanitarian disasters and emergencies – most of them man-made in developing countries where civil strife was out of control and security severely lacking. In 1993 there were roughly 70 areas of conflict or potential conflict[65] and the Security Council was working at full steam. It held 171 meetings and passed 93 resolutions of which 85 were unanimous and 27 were taken under the hitherto seldom employed chapter 7.[66]

The 'tumult of demands'[67] led to an exponential growth in the number of UN peacekeeping operations. Up to 1987 there had been just thirteen. Between 1988 and 1994, 21 new operations were mounted. Most were internal operations[68] and most of them were in areas where the superpower writ had run. Peacekeeping provided the means of ending Cold War intervention in Angola and Afghanistan and was integral to winding up a bitter dispute in Nicaragua in which the US had been the leading external antagonist.

The blossoming of democratisation and the successful monitoring of free elections in Nicaragua in 1989, led to many similar requests for election supervision.[69] But participants who were not willing to play the democratic game deprived some operations of success. Morocco stalled the UN Mission for the Referendum in Western Sahara (MINSURO) for fear of an unacceptable outcome, and the losing side in UN-supervised elections in Angola resumed military hostilities. Fighting continued in Liberia despite peace accords.

In Somalia and Rwanda peacekeeping ran aground on the shoals of internal strife. Intervention to protect Kurds in the Gulf War shifted the UN further away from the traditional principle of non-intervention as enshrined in Article 2.7 of the Charter. There is uncertainty and dispute over the exact extent of the UN's right to concern itself with the internal behaviour of states, but clearly the Security Council now regarded the gross abuse of human rights as a ground for action.[70] When the UN operation in Somalia (UNOSOM I) failed to safeguard the delivery of humanitarian assistance in a complex and ever-changing civil war in 1992, the US sent a large contingent which the Security Council authorised to use force to protect and distribute emergency aid. In May 1993 UNOSOM II took over. It was a huge, very expensive operation (costing on average $3 million a day) which did valuable humanitarian work. But departing from the key peacekeeping tenets of impartial and non-threatening behaviour led to strife. Scarcely a month after arriving, 25 Pakistani soldiers died in a clash with followers of the Somali clan leader, General Aideed. There followed a futile, sometimes farcical, UN-authorised hunt for Aideed which had to be called off in October. By then Aideed's popularity ratings had soared in Somalia and the US Congress had demanded US withdrawal from UNOSOM II following the death of 56 more peacekeepers, 25 of them American. The departure of the Americans – and West European contingents early in 1994 – led to a scaling down not just of the size of UNOSOM, but also in its purpose, as in effect it returned to the traditional peacekeeping mode. By late October 1994, with the parties in Somalia showing little sign of becoming truly reconciled with each other, it was felt that the Somalis had 'had their chance' and the force was withdrawn in January 1995.[71]

In 1994 the world was horrified when the death (in an aircrash) of the Presidents of Rwanda and Burundi led to genocide and the largest and fastest flood of refugees the UN had seen. In the process, ten Belgian peacekeepers were killed. This prompted Belgium to withdraw its battalion. Also, the headquarters of the UN Assistance Mission for Rwanda (UNAMIR) was attacked. The Security Council's decision to cut UNAMIR from 2500 to a token 270 was hugely criticised even though no states volunteered the thousands of troops that would have been required to stop people intent on bloodshed. The Security Council reluctantly agreed to rebuild UNAMIR. While the Secretary-General fulminated over the difficulty of finding troops, the French (who had been patron of the Hutu government) decided to go in and establish a 'safe-zone' for Hutus in the south-west. The Tutsi-dominated Rwandan Patriotic Front (RPF), which was rapidly approaching the capital, Kigali, bitterly opposed France's action. However, there was no confrontation between the RPF and French forces. But the formation of an RPF government and the departure of the French when new UNAMIR troops arrived in August, prompted a huge exodus of refugees and Hutu soldiers to Burundi and Zaire. As of June 1995, the situation remains volatile and the future of the ravaged country is uncertain.

The lesson that sometimes only military might will force errant parties back to the straight and narrow was given when the United Nations Mission in Haiti (UNMIH) failed to persuade the military regime to return power to the democratically elected government. The Security Council took a new step in treating an internal political crisis as a threat to international peace and security by imposing a mandatory oil and arms embargo. But the regime did not budge and the Security Council authorised the USA to use military force. The US, however, hesitated to risk American lives when vital interests were not at stake. As tension mounted, former President Carter succeeded in negotiating a deal whereby the military government stood down and American forces (later replaced by UN troops) maintained order until the elected government took over.

Elections were also part of a wide-ranging process of national reconciliation in Cambodia. After bitter civil conflict followed by a decade of occupation by Soviet-backed Vietnam (China was backing the other main group), the occupying forces were withdrawn at the end of the Cold War. Tortuous negotiations ensued, eventually resulting in the four Cambodian factions agreeing that the UN should mount a multifaceted peacekeeping operation – a Transitional Authority in Cambodia (UNTAC) – which in effect would run the country for a year. The culminating point of this enterprise was meant to be a government whose legitimacy was accepted on all internal sides. Things did not go smoothly. UNTAC had some sizeable internal problems of its own; one of the main Cambodian factions withdrew its cooperation; and the others complied less than fully with what had been agreed. But the elections went ahead, the turnout was surprisingly high, and a government emerged in which power was shared by several of the factions. This enabled the UN to withdraw its 22 000-strong mission (three-quarters of whom were soldiers, and one-sixth police) at the end of 1993. As Australia's Foreign Minister (who had been closely involved in the negotiation of the agreement) put it, the operation was a 'flawed . . . success'.[72] Cambodia's problems are far from having been ended. But once again the UN demonstrated its use, and its versatility, as a peacekeeper.

The Cambodian mission was conducted along traditional peacekeeping lines, in that there was no attempt to coerce the parties into honouring their promises to cooperate with the UN and with each other. It is not so clear that this is the case in respect of the UN Protection Force (UNPROFOR) in ex-Yugoslavia, which (in early 1995) involved around 43 000 military personnel. It was established in 1992, and not long afterwards chapter 7 began to be regularly invoked in the relevant, and numerous, Security Council resolutions, together with some tough words. However, they applied only to UNPROFOR's activity in Bosnia-Herzegovina, and in 1995 the three separate aspects of UNPROFOR were recognised by its formal division into three operations.

The UN Preventive Deployment Force (UNPREDEP) is along the borders of the Former Yugoslav Republic of Macedonia with the Federal Republic of Yugoslavia (in other words, Serbia and Montenegro). It is small and run on traditional lines. But in as much as it has been mounted to try to stop a problem arising, it has been hailed by the UN as an innovative instance of – to use the words of the Secretary-General in his *Agenda for Peace* – 'preventive deployment'. The problem in question stems from the facts that about one-third of Macedonia's population are ethnic Albanians; that the neighbouring Serbian area of Kosovo is overwhelmingly Albanian; but that Serbia is anxious to put a Serbian imprint on Kosovo because it is very dear to the Serbs on historical grounds. Clearly, there is a possible problem here, which could easily result in the involvement of the neighbouring states.

The UN confidence Restoration Operation (UNCRO) was in Croatia where large Serbian enclaves resisted Croatian rule. A large UN Force therefore was sent to patrol the borders of the enclaves with the rest of Croatia, and watch over the behaviour within them of the Serbs in the hope of discouraging further ethnic cleansing. Chapter 7 was cited with regard to these activities, on the ground that the operation is in keeping with the principles of peacekeeping. However, the Croatian Government resented UN 'interference' and successfully demanded that it be reduced and redeployed.

It is in Bosnia-Herzegovina (which has a Muslim government but large Croatian and Serbian minorities) that the UN appears to have gone beyond peacekeeping.[73] For the Council has given UNPROFOR the right to protect the delivery of humanitarian supplies; banned all military flights in the state's air space; asserted the right to ensure compliance with the ban; established some 'safe areas'; authorised certain measures to protect their civilian inhabitants; and demanded a nationwide ceasefire. In support of some of these objectives the air power of no less a grouping than NATO has been sought and made available. This is far removed from the language of traditional peacekeeping.

On the ground, tough measures have sometimes been taken in response to considerable provocation and promise-breaking. NATO's planes have occasionally been called in and after some peacekeepers were taken hostage, a 10 000-strong Rapid Reaction Force was sent in in mid-1995 to deter future acts of this kind. This constitutes internal enforcement. But on the whole the UN has been very cautious. The Secretary-General has announced that the force is not there to defend territory, or to get involved as a belligerent;[74] with regard to the protection of civilians and humanitarian convoys (the latter hardly connected with peace), negotiation rather than muscularity has been UNPROFOR's order of the day; and generally the force strives to work with the disputants rather than against any one of them. As a high-ranking UN official has said, 'one does not go to war in white-painted vehicles'[75] – this being the colour used by the UN when it is on the road in a peacekeeping capacity. While, therefore, the operation sometimes goes beyond the methods of peacekeeping, on balance it looks more like that mode of behaviour than enforcement.

The most peacekeepers can do when disputants have no immediate intention of living at peace is to negotiate between warring sides or provide humanitarian relief. At worst, they become drawn into the conflict. 'Tougher peacekeeping' is a contradiction in terms. An operation is either non-forceful, impartial peacekeeping or it is enforcement action under chapter 7. It is asking rather a lot of states to be willing to risk lives, at possibly huge expense, in a conflict that does not touch on vital interests. Hence the US withdrawal from UNOSOM II and Belgian withdrawal from UNAMIR. Although in 1995 peacekeeping seemed everywhere to be in crisis, without it things would probably have been far worse and the scale of human suffering much greater. Even when things looked hopeless, the UN did not withdraw completely but, as in Angola, left a presence to act as the organisation's eyes and ears and undertake humanitarian activities until it is possible to assist constructively in a peaceful outcome.

The swelling of the number of peacekeepers – from 10 000 at the beginning of 1992 to 78 000 in October 1994 – brought two more kinds of crisis. Firstly, it was increasingly difficult to find enough militarily efficient troops who were acceptable to the parties. Stalwarts like Canada were reducing their forces and were reluctant to risk casualties in violent situations. The range of contributors grew to over 70, but some troops were distinctly second-rate, and even criminally inclined, in a few cases. Secondly, the UN's financial difficulties were compounded by the apparently endless demand for peacekeeping. In the first half of 1992, peacekeeping costs rose fourfold – from some $700 million to about $2.8 billion.[76] By 1994 they had risen to over $3.6 billion.

The UN is not outrageously expensive. Its headquarters in New York cost roughly the same as the British Foreign and Commonwealth Office and the UN employs fewer civil servants than the city of Winnipeg.[77] In 1992 the combined regular and peacekeeping budgets were lower than the cost of running the New York police and fire departments for one year. But the list of debtors has grown. In March 1994, the USA still accounted for more than half the $490 million owed in arrears. Then came the Russian Federation and Ukraine which could not afford to pay sums based on out-of-date Soviet economic statistics. Late payment is endemic; in August 1993 fewer than ten states were fully paid up. The UN totters. The Secretary-General issues dire warnings and threatens drastic cuts in services. Nothing much is done.

Another potential crisis relates to the reform of the UN's central organ, the Security Council. The new 'concert of powers' and its secret conclaves was resented by egalitarian-minded underdogs. Third world states also objected to its 'Euro-centric'[78] character and the wider interpretation it had given to threats to international peace and security. German and Japanese bids to join the P5 also drew attention to the Security Council's fossilisation of the 1945 balance of power. Although no one queried their claims (though some disputed whether they were yet 'ready' for the responsibility) the jostling of other contestants for this elevated status complicated matters considerably. The General Assembly's request in 1992 that the Secretary-General invite comments on a possible review of Security Council membership opened a Pandora's box and a debate that had remarkable similarity to that at San Francisco in 1945.

The possible expansion of the Security Council to, say, 20 or 25 members, is relatively uncontroversial. There seems also to be no significant criticism of the Council's power of taking binding decisions, or of the veto. But the criteria for having a permanent seat, the ratio between permanent and non-permanent members, and whether the veto should be limited to chapters 6 and 7 are controversial. It remains to be seen whether the UN can avoid a major crisis similar to that when the League Council was enlarged in 1926.

The role of the Secretary-General

In 1981, after six weeks and 16 secret ballots, Kurt Waldheim and his nearest competitor, Salim Salim of Tanzania, withdrew their candidatures for the Secretary-Generalship. Despite an immediate rush of candidates, the Security Council despaired of agreeing on a Secretary-General, let alone a good one. Fortunately for the UN, Javier Pérez de Cuéllar of Peru suddenly emerged as the man acceptable to everyone. A former diplomat with considerable UN experience, he was cast in the Waldheim mould. But his qualities were superior to those of his predecessor. By steering a middle course between the models of Hammarskjöld and Thant, Pérez de Cuéllar won the high opinion of all, even those who did not think well of the UN. He was unafraid of sticking out his neck but, although critical of the big powers in general, did not court the risk of giving serious offence to them individually. In 1986 there was no question about giving him a second term of office.

Like his predecessors, Pérez de Cuéllar inherited problems in the secretariat. Below the top level, 'mediocrity and politically expedient [sic.] appointments predominated'. 'Too many top-level officials, political appointments, rotten boroughs and pointless programs had rendered the Secretariat fat and flabby.'[79] In 1986, when yielding to Washington's demand for weighted voting on the budget, the General Assembly endorsed the 'Committee of Eighteen's' view that the UN was 'too complex, fragmented and top-heavy'.[80] By 1987 senior staff had been cut by almost a third and over the next few years there was, overall, a 13 per cent cut. Morale suffered, especially given the increased workload. But Pérez de Cuéllar failed to reduce the budget or improve the secretariat's administrative functioning.

On the political front, Pérez de Cuellar inherited an office that had considerable influence, which he protected by maintaining his impartiality. Being privy to confidential information, he could privately advise, encourage and warn. Public expressions of his views – for example in his annual reports – were seriously considered by leaders. As a mediator he could play a crucial role when parties were willing to use his skills. Article 99 gives the Secretary-General scope to take initiatives and he had considerable responsibility as head of peacekeeping operations. His position was also enhanced by the revival of the Cold War and the power struggle between the USA and General Assembly.

No eyebrows were raised at Pérez de Cuéllar's independent initiatives over the brewing dispute between Venezuela and Guyana, the 1982 Falklands War, or in sending fact-finding missions and establishing political offices in Kabul, Islamabad, Teheran and Baghdad. By warding off a potentially damaging Arab proposal to challenge the credentials of the Israeli delegation, he 'successfully expanded his office's tradition of independent activism, by demonstrating his capacity to mediate disputes between the various states in the UN itself'.[81] And his appointment as formal arbitrator in the *Rainbow Warrior* affair[82] testified to his and the UN's high standing.

However, Pérez de Cuéllar was criticised for failing to stir the Security Council into action in anticipation of the 1982 Israeli invasion of Lebanon. But had there been any point in a meeting, a member of the Council would almost certainly have called one. The only time Pérez de Cuéllar invoked Article 99 (over Lebanon in 1989) the outcome was unsatisfactory. Indirect use of this article is more effective – for example, producing a confidential memorandum, dropping heavy hints in the right quarters, asking the Council President to call a meeting so that he can make a report, or, during a meeting, drawing the Council's attention to new information and reminding it of his responsibilities and the gravity of the situation. This reflects the fact the Secretary-General has influence rather than power. His actions are also not obvious to those who do not see behind the scenes. Pérez de Cuéllar was 'a man of rare talents' who achieved much 'because he went about his business by stealth'.[83]

Pérez de Cuéllar's high qualities were not fully appreciated. Critics complained that his 'face, voice and style seemed incapable of expressing anything beyond clause 36 of subsection D of UN Resolution 1001',[84] and there were calls for his successor to be 'of a higher caliber'.[85] But any Secretary-General will represent a compromise between the P5. Their collective requirements were satisfied in 1991 by the almost 70-year-old former Egyptian foreign minister, Boutros Boutros-Ghali. He is from Africa whose 'turn' it was to provide the Secretary-General. He speaks French (essential to avoid a French veto). He is a Christian married to a Jew. He was admired in the Egyptian Foreign Ministry for his intellect and courage. And he was widely respected as one of the architects of the 1979 Camp David agreements.

The rising crescendo of demands for reform of the secretariat had put management skills high on the shopping list for the new Secretary-General, but Boutros-Ghali was not noted for them. However, according to Pérez de Cuéllar, the constraints that prevented him from reorganising and updating the secretariat were vanishing.[86]

Boutros-Ghali immediately set about cutting recruitment and trimming the number of senior advisers (while keeping the P5 happy by keeping their nationals), rejigging offices and departments, and making efforts to root out corruption and waste. Unfortunately, in part because of his forceful personality and his abrasive, autocratic style, the morale of the secretariat sank a little lower.

Since the UN is so busy, Boutros-Ghali has a central role on the world stage and is increasingly entrusted with developing and implementing machinery for resolving conflicts. He despatched more fact-finding missions in 1992–3 than in any previous such period.[87] He set up 'interim offices' (combining information, humanitarian and political functions) in a number of former Soviet republics. He took new initiatives to limit conflicts and try to anticipate possible refugee flows and displaced persons. And the Security Council's first summit-level meeting in January 1992 asked him to produce a forward-looking report – *An Agenda for Peace* – which, cautiously interpreted, was welcomed by the 1992 General Assembly. But Boutros-Ghali also came into conflict with the Security Council.

This was partly due to his frustration at the heavy demands placed on the secretariat without receiving the resources he considered necessary. Partly it was because he resembles Hammarskjöld in his keenness to extend his authority, and Lie in sometimes lacking a realistic appreciation of what the UN can do. He offended diplomats – whom he called *fonctionnaires* (bureaucrats) – by reminding them he was not a diplomat but a man of principle.[88] He 'neglected' the P5. He was said to make a point of missing Security Council meetings or keeping it waiting and not fully consulting it. He challenged the Council's priorities and played a major role in pushing for UNOSOM by complaining that the Council focused too much attention on Bosnia while neglecting the catastrophe in Somalia. And when there were discussions about strengthening UNAMIR's numbers in response to the carnage in Rwanda, Boutros-Ghali initially wanted the peacekeepers to be equipped to stop the fighting.[89] *An Agenda for Peace* showed the same lack of realism in proposing 'peace enforcement units'. Moreover, the *Agenda for Peace* not only failed adequately to distinguish peacekeeping from peacemaking but, in suggesting consent might not be needed for future peacekeeping operations, Boutros-Ghali did not recognise that consent is crucial for success in all contexts short of outright enforcement.[90] Developing countries were also unhappy that Boutros-Ghali spent so much time on security issues at the expense of the third world's enormous social and economic problems.[91] The interim assessment is that Boutros-Ghali may not be the best man for the job.

Conclusion

The UN has at almost every turn confounded its founders, developing a momentum and a life of its own in response to political developments. As Claude pointed out, it:

> is no Rip Van Winkle, now awakening and going into action after a long period of dormancy. It has not been stalled and stymied by the Cold War, with its members standing by in frustration, eager for the first opportunity to make it the kind of organisation contemplated in the Charter. Instead, the Organisation has, throughout its . . . history, changed; its members have made it into something other than, something different in function from the 1945 model.[92]

What it is depends upon the members and the nature of relations between them. Good relations are reflected in the greater ease of cooperation through the UN system; poor relations may be ameliorated with the help of the UN; bad relations may exclude the UN from playing any role beyond serving as a means of scoring points. It is not a perfect organisation. It has many weaknesses. It also has considerable strengths, the greatest being the absence of debate about its continued existence or challenges to its fundamental nature as an organisation of sovereign states. It is clear that states value and need it. Through it they can pursue their interests, conduct diplomacy, debate and cooperate – to the extent that they feel able – in achieving the purposes set out in Article 1 of the Charter. As such, it is likely to survive for a long time.

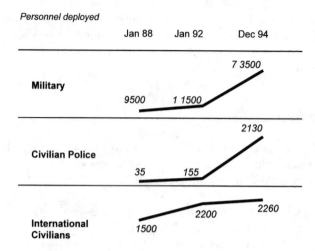

Figure 5.1 UN Security Operations

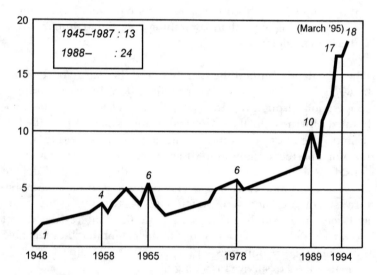

Figure 5.2 UN Peacekeeping Operations

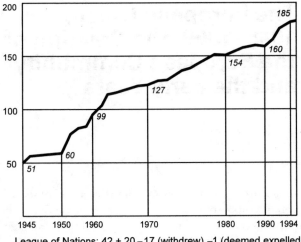

League of Nations: 42 + 20 – 17 (withdrew) –1 (deemed expelled)

Figure 5.3 UN Membership

Table 5.1 UN Financing (1995)

25%– 1	(United States)
10%– 25%– 1	(Japan)
5%– 10%– 4	(France, Germany, Russia, UK)
1%– 5%– 8	
0.35%–0.99%–14	
0.02%–0.34%–64	
0.01%–92	

6 The European Union, 1945–1969: the Creation of the European Community and the Early Years

Introduction

The idea of European integration and the creation of some kind of federation or empire or 'community' of Europe is not new but goes back down the centuries. On the one hand, there have been those who sought to unify Europe through military might – from Charlemagne to Napoleon – whilst on the other, there have been political thinkers who have advocated unity through peaceful cooperation. For example, as early as the seventeenth century the Duc de Sully proposed a federation of states to improve European defence against the Turks whilst a European parliament was proposed in 1693 by William Penn, the English Quaker.[1] Political leaders have perhaps been less visible in promoting European integration but have, at times, been able to see the economic advantages of cooperation in Europe, although this has actually yielded few practical results until very recently. In fact, economic cooperation through abolishing intra-European trade barriers has historically been short-lived or region-specific rather than European, like the nineteenth-century Zollverein.[2]

Nevertheless, in spite of these historical precedents, it was not until the twentieth century that cooperative European integration began to take place on a significant scale. It first began to be taken more seriously in the interwar period when many pro-integration groups flourished. The best known of these was the Pan-European Union, founded by an Austrian count, Coudenhove-Kalergi, which advocated a European federation. However, in spite of much activity and some interest amongst significant politicians of the time such as Beneš, Briand and Herriot and some of the younger generation (who were to be active in giving concrete shape to some of the ideas after 1945),[3] little of consequence was achieved. The customs union established between Belgium and Luxembourg in 1922 attracted minimal interest elsewhere and attempts to extend cooperation to the Scandinavian countries at Oslo (1930) and Ouchy (1932) were not successful.

The most significant official contribution was the Briand Memorandum in 1930[4] which proposed European union of a kind but was vague and ill-defined; it was not well received outside France and was effectively forgotten well before Briand's death in 1932. However, both Briand and Herriot did highlight one theme that was to recur periodically when European integration eventually took off. They set their 'European union' firmly within the framework of the League of Nations. The dilemma of choosing between regional and global organisations and, specifically, the accommodation of the United States, remains very potent today. Returning to the interwar years, the Briand Memorandum can be seen as a high point in the trend, such as it was, towards European integration in the interwar period. The dark years of the 1930s had no place for the idea of European unity. Indeed, it was to take a second world war before European integration and a 'community' of European nation states could begin to become a reality.

The immediate post-war years: 1945–1950

In the mid-1940s it was becoming clear that the movement towards some form of European integration was gathering momentum. Even before the war ended, many were turning their thoughts to the need for postwar cooperation. In 1944 the exiled leaders of Belgium, the Netherlands and Luxembourg announced a customs union which became effective in 1947–8.[5] Also in 1944, there was a joint declaration by various resistance movements proposing a European federal union.[6] Around the end of the war the cause of European unity was espoused by many prominent politicians in continental Europe. Then, in 1946, Winston Churchill called for 'a kind of United States of Europe'. Although it was clear that he only envisaged a loose form of cooperation with Britain as a 'friend . . . and sponsor' rather than a participant, this speech, coming from one of the wartime 'big three', did much to popularise the European idea.[7]

European integration was now an idea whose time had (finally) come. The legacy of the war created a unique situation which made cooperation in (Western) Europe inevitable, although its form and extent were by no means obvious at that time. (This uniqueness of the European experience is important because it explains why efforts to promote regional integration elsewhere in the world have achieved such limited success.) The pressure to cooperate operated through several channels:

- There was an overwhelming desire for peace and prosperity. Specifically, there was a determination that the mistakes made after the First World War would not be repeated after the Second World War and creating a regional European organisation was seen as the best way forward. The depth of feeling underlying this non-economic rationale for European integration still exists (albeit in a weaker form) and has frequently been underestimated by those in Britain who tend to approach the EU from a mainly economic and pecuniary perspective.
- Allied to this was the need to move forward by a route that was not vindictive towards Germany and also allowed reconstruction to proceed there, whilst, at the same time, ensuring the containment of Germany and preventing future outbreaks of German aggression. Many came to realise that the problem of Germany could only be finally resolved within the context of a united Europe. This was appreciated even by the Resistance leaders in 1944: 'Only a Federal Union will allow the German people to participate in the life of Europe without being a danger for the rest.'[8] In fact, they actually foreshadowed the Schuman Plan by calling for the chemical and heavy industries of Germany to be integrated into European industrial organisations so that they could no longer be used for German nationalist aims.
- On the economic front the Second World War had brought Europe to the brink of ruin and there was an obvious need for mutual cooperation to promote reconstruction, recovery and growth. Indeed, this was actively encouraged by the Americans when Marshall Aid was distributed.[9]
- The position of (Western) Europe – caught between the two superpowers (geographically, politically and economically) – gave rise to much concern. Although the decline of the former great powers of Western Europe was not to be conclusively

demonstrated until the Suez debacle of 1956, the weakness of Western Europe and its limited influence even over its own destiny was clear enough in 1945. There was an obvious threat of Soviet domination either through conquest or through Moscow's influence over the Communist parties in France and Italy which seemed close to power. On the other hand, the threat from the Americans was more economic than political: increasing reliance on American technology, the power of the dollar and the rise of the American multinationals were all sources of growing European apprehension. It was increasingly becoming clear that a disjointed and divided Europe was an aberration that had to be consigned to history if Europe was to recover its former status.

- However, the United States also played a more positive role in fostering European unity. While Washington still hoped that the wartime alliance with the Soviet Union would continue in peacetime, regionalist ideas in Western Europe were discouraged, but this policy was slowly reversed as it grew increasingly evident that American hopes were ill-founded. By 1949 it was axiomatic that a Western European community should be created both as a counter to Soviet power and as the best means of resolving the German problem. Moreover, it was urged by some that the 'US role in this matter should not . . . [simply] . . . be one of passive encouragement'.[10] Indeed, discreet American pressure on Western European nations to develop closer ties with each other was evident from January 1947, when a speech by John Foster Dulles advocated a federal Europe.[11]

- The final and most immediate impetus for European integration came from various economic factors. Several European federalists, including Jean Monnet, accepted the functionalist doctrine of David Mitrany that political unity amongst states depended upon the links at lower, mostly economic levels.[12] However, the most directly relevant economic consideration was more pragmatic and arose from a developing crisis during 1948-9 over the allied dismantling of German heavy industry, including its steel-making capacity. Essentially, by 1949, in the face of growing apprehension about the Soviet Union, the Americans had reversed their policy and were no longer advocating the dismantling of German industry. They were seeking to impose this change on the reluctant French who were concerned, not only on security grounds, but also because reversing the decline in German production would lead to overproduction of steel in Western Europe and the prospect of difficulties for their less competitive producers which could severely damage France's prospects for economic recovery.[13] The European Coal and Steel Community (ECSC) was an imaginative way of dealing with these problems.

The ECSC had been preceded by a number of other initiatives designed to strengthen European unity, which mostly fell short of their mark. A major reason for this failure was British reluctance to countenance more than loose consultative arrangements which in no sense involved a transfer of sovereignty to a central authority. In March 1948, the Brussels Treaty linked Britain, France and the Benelux countries in a defensive pact. A month later, the Organisation for European Economic Cooperation (OEEC)[14] was established by 16 European states as part of their attempt to meet the Marshall Aid requirements of greater European economic cooperation. Potentially the most important venture was the Council of Europe, set up in May 1949 with the general objectives of promoting unity in various fields and of protecting human rights. After functioning as little more than an ineffectual debating society for several years, the Council gradually began to acquire a significant role in regard to human rights, although early ideas that members would 'merge certain of their sovereign rights' vanished in the face of stubborn resistance from Britain.[15] Indeed, Britain also resisted the proposed European Payments Union, which was eventually set up after months of negotiations in July 1950, with the aim of promoting European monetary cooperation.[16] Even at this early stage, the British made their preference for intergovernmental cooperation very clear and subscribed to the argument that they had three spheres of influence: Britain had an important role in Europe, a Commonwealth and a special relationship with the United States; it had to straddle all three of these and could not overemphasise one at the potential expense of others, which meant that Britain could not indulge in too close a relationship with continental Europe.

In fact, it is very striking to note that many of the arguments in the above rationale for European integration did not, or at least it could be argued that they did not, apply to Britain. Whilst the

British also clearly desired peace, prosperity and the containment of Germany, they did not feel threatened to the same extent as continental Europe; after all, Britain had not been occupied during the Second World War and emerged victorious over the Germans for the second time in 40 years. Similarly, the destruction in Britain had been comparatively less and the United States and the Soviet Union were considered on more equal terms by the British. There was a special relationship with the former and a sufficient distance from the latter, both geographically and politically, to make the Soviet threat appear much less significant in Britain. These attitudes were deeply ingrained and their historical legacy, together with a strong preference for the British version of democracy and a consequent suspicion about supranationality in Europe, do much to explain British positions towards and within the European Union to the present day. The roots of British dissent in the European camp were thus clearly there from the beginnings of the modern European movement but, whatever the merits of the British position, the case for European cooperation and integration appeared to be overwhelming to many in continental Europe.

Success and failure: the European Coal and Steel Community, the European Defence Community and the European Political Community

On 9 May 1950, Robert Schuman, the French Foreign Minister, announced a proposal to pool and administer jointly national coal and steel resources in Western Europe.[17] The Schuman Plan, drafted by Jean Monnet, was presented in such a way as to make a parting of the ways inevitable in Europe. The British were not given advance warning (unlike the West Germans and the Americans) and were certain to object to the condition that participation in the negotiations required prior acceptance of the basic principles of the Schuman Plan, including a degree of supranationality (and consequent loss of national sovereignty). They duly did so and the eventual signatories of the Treaty of Paris on 18 April 1951 were France, West Germany, Italy, Belgium, the Netherlands and Luxembourg (the 'Six'). Unlike the Treaties of Rome, the Treaty of Paris is only effective for 50 years and the arrangements for coal and steel will have to be renegotiated at the end of the century.

The central purpose of the ECSC was to set up a common market for coal and steel within which all barriers to trade were to be abolished, while a common external tariff against non-members would also be introduced. However, the ECSC marked much more than the simple creation of a sectoral common market, particularly:

- Whilst the common experience across Europe of coal shortages and an excess supply of steel did give a sound economic rationale to cooperation in these industries, the driving force was political and the ECSC was intended to be only the beginning: 'The pooling of coal and steel production should . . provide for . . a first step in the federation of Europe'.[18]
- The ECSC was a major step in Franco-German rapprochement which was essential for the future well-being of Europe. It offered an opportunity to revive the German industrial heartlands in the Ruhr in a way that made 'war between France and Germany . . . not merely unthinkable but materially impossible.'[19]
- For the first time there was an open ideological breach in Europe as Britain chose not to participate. (In fact the French insistence on acceptance of the principle of supranationality in advance of negotiations was clearly designed to prevent the British from hijacking another European organization and steering it on to firmly intergovernmental ground as it had done with the OEEC and the Council of Europe.)
- The ECSC was backed by the US, thereby confirming American support for the process of European integration in spite of potential (and eventually actual) detrimental protectionist implications for the US.
- The ECSC established the institutional structure of European integration: (supranational) Commission, Council of (national) Ministers, European Parliament and Court of Justice, although two of these had different names in the Treaty of Paris. (The Commission was the 'High Authority' and the Parliament was the 'Common Assembly', as indeed it was in the Treaty of Rome which set up the EEC, only adopting the somewhat grander 'Parliament' at a later date.)

In fact, the institutions of the ECSC were truly unique, particularly the Court of Justice and the High Authority. The former was the first international court dealing with substantial questions to have compulsory jurisdiction over a wide area, with its judgements binding upon governments, companies and the ECSC's institutions alike. The High Authority was even more innovative because it combined administrative and political (decision-making) functions. It was charged with representing the 'general interest of the Community', and it was given considerable discretion to make ECSC policy in such important areas as determining the levy on coal and steel firms which financed the ECSC, although its powers over certain matters were subscribed by the need to obtain approval from the Council of Ministers. This latter institution was not originally envisaged by Schuman and Monnet but was set up at the insistence of the Benelux countries. They wanted a body to moderate the supranationalism of the High Authority and to defend national interests, particularly of the smaller member states. Finally, the High Authority was also constrained (albeit to a minimal degree) by the Common Assembly, which was the first international assembly in Europe with legally guaranteed powers.

The record of the ECSC until it ceased to exist as a separate entity in 1967 is somewhat mixed. It did make some progress on the economic front, although its efforts to create a common market in coal and steel were considerably assisted by the earlier activities of the OEEC and the Benelux customs union. Moreover, despite some early success in its efforts to flex its muscles against governments, the High Authority was overruled by the Council during the first real crisis in 1959 (caused by the overproduction of coal) which was met by separate national measures rather than a Community-wide plan.[20] Furthermore, the ECSC did not act as an immediate catalyst for political integration and, indeed, as the European Defence and Political Communities failed, was arguably unsuccessful in political terms. However, it did initiate the process of European integration and clearly contributed to the creation of the European Economic Community (EEC) and Euratom later in the 1950s, although the element of supranationality in these organisations was rather muted compared to the ECSC.

If the ECSC represented a success then what immediately followed on was a failure. Moreover, it also seemed to undermine the functionalist theory favoured by Monnet and other federalists. The

ECSC was supposed to be only the first sector to be integrated in Europe; others were to follow, one by one, until a European political union was finally created. The key mechanism for achieving this process was 'spillover'. In one sense, spillover meant that once one economic sector was integrated the interdependence of this sector with others would force them to follow and also integrate. Another version was the concept of political spillover whereby integration in one (economic) sector causes pressure groups to operate at that (i.e. the European) political level to exert influence; in time these groups would begin to see the value of operating in this way and would support further integration in other sectors. Whilst the European Defence Community was perhaps a harsh and not entirely appropriate test of the theory, it did at least suggest that the spillover process would be much slower and more painful than the federalists had hoped.

Although there was a rather sterile discussion in various quarters about the possibility of extending integration into various sectors – particularly transport, agriculture, health, postal services and communications[21] – the next sector for debate was forced onto the agenda by events rather than choice; indeed, few would have chosen defence as an appropriate field for integration at this early stage in the process. Nevertheless, when the Americans began to press for (West) German rearmament, it was a French-sponsored proposal for a European Defence Community (EDC), based on the ECSC that emerged in Europe.[22] With the outbreak of the Korean War in 1950 and growing concern about the intentions of the Soviet Union, the US came to the view that there was a shortfall in military capability in Western Europe which they were unable and their European allies were unwilling to fill. Their solution was an integrated European force under NATO authority which would include a West German contingent.[23] The prospect of West German rearmament was unpalatable to all Europeans, especially the French who responded with a counter-proposal. The Plevin Plan followed the Schuman Plan in outline. It was essentially a proposal for a European army but also incorporated common institutions and a common budget. However, it differed from the Schuman Plan in two key respects:

- The balance of power between the supranational element (a Board of Commissioners) and the national element (Council

of Ministers) was much more in favour of the latter. This was
partly an attempt to attract British participation.

- West Germany was to play a subservient role reflecting the underlying objective of the EDC proposal (containment of West Germany). Whilst other members were to allocate only part of their
armed forces to the European army, all German forces would be
incorporated into it, thereby allowing the Germans to have no
military resources under solely national command.

The initial American reaction to the Plevin Plan was strong opposition – on the grounds that it was militarily impracticable and at
worst a French ploy to prevent German rearmament by linking it to
impossible political conditions – but this soon changed as the Six
completed the negotiation of the EDC Treaty which was signed in
May 1952.

It was immediately obvious that the EDC was incompatible with
wholly independent national foreign policies and logic implied that it
should be accompanied by a degree of political integration. Indeed,
Article 38 of the EDC Treaty made provision for such a development.
Consequently, the ECSC Assembly, together with some co-opted members from the Council of Europe, was asked to examine this possibility
and, in 1953, it duly recommended a European Political Community
(EPC). This was an ambitious proposal which would have subordinated the ECSC and EDC within a unified organisation with a single
'High Authority/Commission', Council of Ministers and Court of Justice and a two-chamber European Parliament.

However, although it had clearly much wider implications than a
mere defence community, the EPC never got further than the draft
treaty stage and it was on the success of the EDC that both Communities stood or fell. In fact, the French never really felt comfort-
able with the EDC, even though they were its initiators, for the
fundamental reason that they did not really want German rearmament in any form. Consequently, successive French governments
delayed putting the EDC before the French Assembly for over two
years (until August 1954). To no one's great surprise it was rejected
by 319 votes to 264.[24] There were also a number of more specific
reasons for the French hostility:

- Gaullist opposition to the supranational element, specifically
putting French troops under foreign control;

- Communist opposition to German rearmament under any guise;
- the lack of British involvement;
- a loss of urgency as the end of the Korean War and the death of Stalin made European defence cooperation seem less imperative.

Thus, in the early 1950s, the opportunity to move to a level of political integration beyond that envisaged by the (Maastricht) Treaty of European Union (TEU) nearly 30 years later was not taken. Instead, the British stepped in and the 1948 Brussels Treaty Organisation, a mutual defence arrangement between Britain, France and the Benelux countries was extended to include Germany (and Italy) and became the Western European Union (WEU).[25] This was a firmly intergovernmental organisation which essentially withered quietly away (until it was reactivated as the embryonic defence arm of the European Union by the TEU in 1991). For the time being, after reaching the dizzy heights of being in the process of simultaneously creating political, defence and coal and steel communities, with potentially more to follow,[26] the original Six were left with only the ECSC, in a world of intergovernmental international organisations.

From Messina to Rome

However, whilst the movement towards European integration had perhaps reached a high point that it has yet to match, the failure of the EDC and the EPC proved to be only a temporary halt; attention soon shifted to the field of economics. If external circumstances – the end of the Korean War, the death of Stalin and the French military involvement in Indochina – had worked against the EDC (and EPC), the opposite was true of the EEC and EAEC: the Suez crisis (and associated British and French embarrassment), the Soviet suppression of the Hungarian uprising and the return of the Saar to Germany (all in 1956–7) together with the swell of nationalism in Asia and Africa (which hastened the end of the colonial era) were all conducive to pushing further European integration higher up the agenda.

In 1955, building on earlier proposals by the Dutch Foreign Minister to integrate the fields of transport, oil and atomic energy and the subsequent Benelux Memorandum which went further and proposed a common market,[27] representatives of the ECSC states met at Messina on 1–2 June. They sought to 'initiate a new phase on the path of constructing Europe'[28] and agreed to pursue integration in the following areas:

- atomic energy;
- transport;
- the harmonisation of social policies;
- the establishment of an investment bank;
- the creation of common market (to be preceded by a customs union).

They further agreed to establish a committee, not simply for additional discussion, but actually to produce detailed texts to form the basis of treaties to implement the Messina Resolution. The committee created at Messina began meeting almost immediately (from July) and became known as the Spaak Committee after its chairman, the Belgian Foreign Minister. A British representative did participate but was withdrawn in November when it became clear that the Six were intending to go much further than was acceptable to Britain. Indeed, the British view subsequently hardened from 'one of indifference to one of opposition'.[29] The Spaak Committee soon chose to focus on nuclear energy and the common market proposal, although the latter eventually emerged as the centrepiece of the European Economic Community (EEC) which in fact incorporated the rest of what had been agreed at Messina. The Spaak Report was approved at a meeting of the Foreign Ministers of the Six in May 1956 and the Committee converted into a Conference and began to draft the appropriate treaties. In March 1957 two treaties were signed in Rome, one establishing the European Atomic Energy Community (EAEC or, more commonly, Euratom) and the second, the European Economic Community (EEC).[30] The treaties were ratified by national parliaments and became effective on 1 January 1958. The building of the European Union had begun in earnest and the despondency caused by the collapse of the EDC (and EPC) only four years earlier had proved to be shortlived. This was a remarkable achievement.

The Treaty of Rome (EEC) is a multifaceted document. It is extensive with 248 articles, 4 annexes, 13 protocols, 4 conventions and

9 declarations. It is wide-ranging and potentially expandable, as it includes an article (235) which essentially states that cooperation can be extended into any area provided all the member states agree. It is also permanent in that it remains in force for 'an unlimited period', in marked contrast to the ECSC Treaty of Paris which has a fixed duration of 50 years. At one level, it can be interpreted as a simple economic agreement to create a common market and some common economic policies, at another, as an innovative venture to develop a supranational community which will supersede nation states. The reality lies somewhere in between. Whilst the Treaty of Rome is virtually exclusively concerned with economic cooperation, there was (and remains) an underlying political agenda. There is no doubt that its architects saw it (and the economic integration it would bring) as another step on the road to political union.

The range of the Treaty is such as to make summarising it very difficult but, broadly speaking, it has two components: first, the creation of a common market and related measures and, second, measures to make the EEC more than a common market. Another approach which produces the same division would be to divide the contents of the Treaty into elements which are concerned with 'negative' integration (the removal of internal barriers or more simply, agreeing not to do something) and 'positive' integration (the creation of common policies requiring actual agreement to take joint action). The former group includes the following elements of the Treaty:

- the removal of tariffs and quantitative restrictions (creating a free trade area);
- the common external tariff (converting the free trade area into a customs union and constituting the first element of a common commercial policy);
- the free movement of people and capital (as well as goods, required to create the common market);
- a competition policy (to allow the internal market created by the customs union to function effectively; in fact the policy was incomplete because although it addressed restrictive practices, monopolies and oligopolies and state aids, albeit to some extent only partially, there was no merger policy).

The second, less well-specified, set of policies, involving going beyond a common market, included:

- a common agricultural policy;
- a common transport policy;
- a European Social Fund concerned with vocational training and enhancing employment opportunities;
- a European Investment Bank entrusted with providing loans to enhance economic expansion.

Beyond this, and perhaps providing a final subsection in the second group, were the various rather vague references to (implicitly long-term) objectives of more general economic integration, including the coordination of economic and monetary policies. Perhaps the flavour of these proclamations is caught by Article 2 which indicates that 'the aim of the Community, by . . . progressively approximating the economic policies of the Member States, . . . [is] . . . to promote throughout the Community a harmonious development of economic activities, a continuous and balanced expansion, an increased stability, an accelerated raising of the standard of living and closer relations between its Member States'.

The Treaty of Rome also has an external dimension consisting principally of Article 237 which allows 'any European state' to apply to join, a specification of the relationship with former colonies of member states ('Part IV Association' which was to become first the Yaoundé then the Lomé Convention), provision for 'association' of non-member states, and the common commercial policy, although this is, in some ways, an integral part of the customs union (and hence the common market). It is precise in some parts but vague, or perhaps better, lacking in detail, in many others. For example, the timetable for establishing the customs union is clear but the articles relating to the common agricultural policy (CAP) specify its objectives but not how the policy is to be implemented to achieve them. Finally, it should be observed that there were a number of 'escape clauses' triggered by economic difficulties or on the grounds of national security.

However, it was the institutional framework that aroused most interest as it was unique amongst international organisations and, indeed, remains so despite various subsequent attempts to imitate European integration in many parts of the world.[31] There were four principal institutions created:

- The European Commission, based in Brussels, had two members from each of the three larger member states and one from each of the smaller; it was the equivalent of the ECSC's High Authority. It was to represent the 'Community interest' and Commissioners had to take an oath to this effect. It had three functions: first, it was the guardian of the Treaties, ensuring that their provisions were observed; second, it was charged with implementing and administering Community policy; finally, and uniquely for a supranational body, it was to initiate policy.

- The Council of Ministers represented the interests of the member states and was the principal decision-making body, taking decisions on the basis of the Commission's proposals. It consisted of the member states' Foreign Ministers (General Council) or, if a specific policy area was being discussed then the appropriate ministers in that field – for example, the Agricultural Council consisted of the Agricultural Ministers. Most decisions were to be taken unanimously, although there was some provision for qualified majority voting[32] (and even in six very trivial cases by simple majority).

- The Parliamentary Assembly, which was to become the European Parliament, was originally not an elected body but rather its 142 members were nominated by the governments of the member states. Its principal function was to monitor the work of the Commission and Council and it had to be consulted on Commission proposals before the Council took a decision. Consequently, its powers were limited to an advisory rather than legislative role, although it was required to discharge the budget and had the rather draconian (though never used) power of dismissing the Commission (by a two-thirds majority).

- The Court of Justice, based in Luxembourg, was the unglamorous, but extremely important, fourth major institution. It had two functions: first, the provision of guidance and interpretation of the Treaties; and, second, it had to settle disputes relating to points of Community law which might involve Community institutions, member states, companies or citizens.

The key relationship was between the Commission and the Council. The clear intention of those who drafted the Treaty of Rome was that the Commission should play a pivotal role: its function as the sole initiator of all Community policies and the fact that the Council could only amend a Commission proposal by unanimous vote gave it potentially enormous powers without any checks and balances in the eyes of some observers.[33] However, it was actually the Council that took the decisions and, of course, the Commission did not devise new policies in Olympian isolation. It was to be engaged in a process of consultation with interested parties, including the Council, so that its proposals already commanded some degree of consensus by the time they reached the Council. Indeed, many who favoured integration saw this as producing a wholly novel 'Community method' of decision-making through a permanent dialogue between the Commission and the Council, a method that would oblige states increasingly to view problems within a Community, rather than a national, framework.[34]

There were also a number of more minor institutions: the European Investment Bank is a non-profit-making provider of loans (at subsidised rates) to promote the economic development of the Community; the Economic and Social Committee (ECOSOC) is an advisory body drawn from three groups (employers, trade unions and the 'general interest'); and there is a Court of Auditors which ensures the legality and sound financial management of the Community budget. There is also another quite important body which, although not actually mentioned in the Treaty, was quickly found to be necessary and so was created. This was the Committee of Permanent Representatives (Coreper) which consists of national delegations of ambassadors and civil servants and prepares the work of the Council of Ministers. In fact, it actually takes some decisions because it divides the agenda of the Council into relatively low-level issues, which are decided in Coreper and formally approved by the Council without further discussion (Agenda A), and more substantive issues which do require full discussion and decision in the Council (Agenda B).

Finally, although the principal focus of this section has quite rightly been on the EEC, it is interesting to note that, initially, the proposal for an atomic energy community was deemed the most important, particularly by Monnet and his followers, partly because a sector-by-sector approach was suggested by the concept of spillover.[35] It did also play a significant role in that there was, to some extent, a trade-off between the EEC and Euratom. The French were very keen on the latter but much less so on the former whereas the opposite was true of Germany and the others. However, Euratom was to prove to be disappointing in practice as member states continued to pursue national interests and showed little interest in cooperative projects. Its role in the process of European integration has ultimately been negligible.

The Community takes shape, 1958–1969

The 1960s were dominated by three factors: the mainly unspectacular but continuous efforts to begin the creation of the policies laid down in the Treaty of Rome; the attempts by de Gaulle to push the Community away from the model of integration set out in the Treaty; and the repeated efforts of Britain and others to join the Community. The first two of these are dealt with in this section and the third will be examined in the broader context of the creation of the European Free Trade Association (EFTA) in the next. In fact, for the first few years the Community flourished at least in part because of a favourable environment. The Six were experiencing very high rates of economic growth, linked to the massive expansion in trade, and this made it easier for the member states to indulge the ambitions of the EEC since there was more for everyone and consequently no conflict with national objectives. In a development that was to be repeated in the run up to the completion of the single market 30 years later, a major contribution was provided by the increased business activity in anticipation of the creation of a common market.[36] It is true that de Gaulle had returned to power in France but he was happy to go along with the Treaty of Rome initially as it favoured French farmers and was conducive to Franco-German rapprochement. Furthermore, he clearly did not favour the alternative, which was an industrial free trade area, probably dominated by Britain.

This harmonious atmosphere allowed the EEC to move forward quickly with establishing its most essential element, the customs union. It was agreed to accelerate the programme of tariff cuts in 1960 and the customs union was achieved on 1 July 1968, eighteen months ahead of schedule. Substantial progress was also made towards the creation of the common agricultural policy, although this was at some cost (see below) and the European Investment Bank was set up and began operations. Competition policy was a little more muted in that direct policy development was absent but much essential background work was carried out in the shape of 'investigations and surveys needed in order to obtain an overall picture of

the competition situation'.[37] However, in many spheres – particularly transport and energy – progress was slow, if not non-existent, and
was not much better in the case of social policy, a good example of
inadequate Treaty provision.[38] For example, in 1963, the attempt to
initiate a Community transport policy was described as 'a dismal
story of false starts, of politically inept Commission proposals, of
persistent Council inaction, . . . [and] . . . of divided government
views'.[39]

The initial success of the Community also gave it an immediate
international identity, role and attraction which has subsequently
been retained and extended. As a result of this:

- Many non-member states established diplomatic relations with
  the Community.
- Britain, Ireland, Denmark and Norway applied to join virtually
  immediately. In addition, Greece and Turkey negotiated association agreements, in 1961 and 1963 respectively, which were
  enhanced trade and aid agreements which included provision
  for possible eventual membership (after long transition periods).
- The Commission negotiated for the member states (under the
  direction of the Council of Ministers) in the Dillon and Kennedy Rounds of the GATT negotiations.
- As the former colonies of member states became independent
  the Commission was able to replace the Part Four Association
  arrangements of the Rome Treaty with the Yaoundé Convention.

In general, however, the progress made towards implementing the
programme laid out in the Treaty of Rome varied significantly
across policy areas and the Community's achievements were somewhat mixed during the 1960s. One of the reasons for this was the
time lost in 1965 when the Community was brought to a halt by the
French. De Gaulle had not signed the Treaty of Rome but had returned to power shortly afterwards. He had a vision of Europe based
on a longstanding preference for an intergovernmental or con-
federal framework (a 'Europe des Patries') which had some similarities but also differences with the Atlanticist version of Britain
and was completely at odds with the supranational vision of the
Commission (and many of the architects of the Treaty); he was to

clash with all of these. There were three episodes in the 1960s that arose from de Gaulle's position. The first was his unilateral rejections of Britain's applications to join the Community (in 1963 and 1967) which are taken up later; the second, and most significant, was the French walk out from the Community institutions which led to the '1965 crisis' and put a brake on the ambitions of the Commission, thereby significantly altering the course of the history of the Community; the third was the French plan for political union which appeared in 1962 and effectively gave advance warning of what was to happen in 1965.

The 'Fouchet Plan', named after the French ambassador to Denmark who chaired the committee which produced it in late 1961, can perhaps be described with some accuracy as de Gaulle's intergovernmental version of the EPC. It was actually the culmination of two years of activity during which de Gaulle had pursued his vision of political union through various channels. He had secured agreement for regular meetings of the Six's foreign ministers in late 1959 (of which there were three in 1960). He had then sought to develop his favoured method of cooperation – summitry – first, by holding bilateral summit meetings in early 1961, with Macmillan and then Adenauer; and, second, by instigating the first EC summit meetings in Paris in February 1961 and then in Bonn in July. However, it was in the Fouchet Plan that de Gaulle's design for Europe was made most explicit. This was no less than a draft treaty for a 'union of states' with five main elements:

- regular meetings of heads of state and/or foreign ministers;
- decision-making on the basis of unanimity;
- a permanent secretariat (in Paris) drawn from member states' foreign offices (and hence clearly intergovernmental and not supranational);
- permanent intergovernmental committees in the fields of: foreign affairs, defence, commerce, cultural affairs;
- a European assembly whose members would be appointed by the governments of member states which could ask questions and deliberate but played no role at all in the decision making process.

In fact, de Gaulle's brand of political union never attracted much enthusiasm outside France and the Fouchet Plan was perceived to have a number of specific flaws by the other five. In the first place, the defence arrangements did not sit well within NATO and the Atlantic Alliance and, indeed, were potentially conflictual. However, an even more fundamental objection was that the Plan appeared to challenge the supranational principles on which the ECSC, EEC and Euratom were based. More pragmatically, the British were prevented from taking part in the negotiations by the French (even though, by then, they were pursuing membership of the Community); the Belgians and the Dutch, in particular, were unhappy about this and were unwilling to sign the treaty without British participation.

The fact that these drawbacks were probably considered to be advantages by the French indicates the distance between France and its partners. Consequently, it was not surprising that, despite successive drafts of the Fouchet Plan, agreement could not be reached. Eventually subsequent events – the acrimony caused by the French veto of Britain's application for membership, the departure of Adenauer and the 1965 crisis – pushed European political union off the agenda.

The 1965 or 'empty chair' crisis exposed the rift between the French and the other five even more starkly and its outcome – the Luxembourg Compromise – marked a major turning point in the development of the European Union. In addition to the immediate cause of the crisis there was a more important underlying one: at the beginning of 1966 the Community was due, in accordance with the Rome Treaty timetable, to move from taking its decisions predominantly by unanimous agreement to taking most of them by majority voting. This change was an anathema to those with a Gaullist vision of European integration, and de Gaulle had to act to prevent it. It is therefore reasonable to suppose that the French would have made some kind of attempt to pre-empt the changes set for 1966 anyway. However, it is true that the immediate cause of the crisis would have caused problems in its own right, because it involved a set of Commission proposals which included elements that would have increased the powers of both the Commission and the Parliament. There were three parts to the 'package' proposed by the Commission.

- the completion of the financial arrangements for the CAP (which the French wanted);

- a switch in the method of financing the Community from direct national contributions to a system of 'own resources' which would deem that the bulk of the tariff revenue from the common external tariff 'belonged' to the Community (which the Commission wanted);
- an increase in the powers of the Parliament, particularly with regard to budgetary matters (which the Parliament and the Netherlands wanted).

It had become the standard practice of the Commission to try and broker 'package deals', often incorporating quite unrelated elements (although there actually were linkages in this case[40]). The objective was to encourage agreement by sugaring an unpalatable policy for any member state by offering compensation elsewhere in the 'package', and, up to 1965, this strategy largely worked. However, on this occasion the French were unwilling to compromise: they wanted the CAP financing but refused to accept the rest and they boycotted the Council for seven months and effectively brought the Community to a halt.

By early 1966 it was clear that the situation had to be resolved. Obviously the five were becoming increasingly concerned about the future viability of the Community but there were also pressures on de Gaulle. He was re-elected as President of France in late 1965 but only in the second run-off election as he did not achieve an absolute majority in the first round. He also had to face increasing hostility from French farmers who were well aware of what they stood to gain from the CAP and also the nagging worry that the other five might just decide to press on without France, and would then inevitably invite Britain to join them. However, compromise remained difficult and, at a meeting of the member states in Luxembourg in January 1966, to which the Commission was not invited, the French and the other five essentially agreed to differ. The Luxembourg Compromise stated that: 'Where, in the case of decisions which may be taken by majority vote . . . very important interests of one or more partners are at stake . . . the Council will endeavour . . . to reach solutions which can be adopted by all the members of the Council . . . the French delegation considers that where very important interests are at stake the discussion must be continued until unanimous agreement is reached.'[41] This became interpreted as giving the right of national veto to a member state if it felt that a vital national interest (never defined) was threatened. In practice, this largely amounted to a victory for France since the Commission's wings were clipped, the need for unanimity in the Council was maintained and the Community was effectively put on an basically intergovernmental track.

Britain, EFTA and the European Community

The British view of the Messina and subsequent negotiations was that the Six, particularly the French, would ultimately be unwilling to go as far as a common market and that the negotiations would collapse just as those for the EDC (and EPC) had done. On the basis of this presumption, as with defence, Britain sought to provide a watered-down, intergovernmental escape route and, working through the OEEC, proposed an industrial free trade area. In retrospect, it is clear that the British were guilty of profoundly underestimating the determination and strength of purpose of the Six. The latter were not impressed by the proposal and, despite its efforts to exert pressure on the Six, Britain was left to go its own way with the intergovernmentally inclined Scandinavian and Alpine Europeans and form the European Free Trade Association (EFTA) – the 'Outer Seven' to the Community's 'Inner Six'. This division of Europe between countries who support some degree of supranationality and those who favour cooperation on mainly intergovernmental lines continues today. It was the fundamental reason for the opt outs from the Maastricht Treaty of Britain and Denmark, both founder members of EFTA. It is why the Community of Twelve wished to get the Maastricht Treaty (and various other measures) agreed before it admitted Austria, Sweden and Finland, two founder members and one subsequent member of EFTA, respectively.

However, British reluctance to participate in the ECSC (although it did become an associate member in 1955), the EEC and Euratom stemmed not only from its ingrained suspicion of supranationalism but also its specific circumstances. As already indicated, many of the factors that drove the Six towards European integration did not apply to Britain, at least to the same extent. Consequently, whilst Britain could encourage and, indeed, play a limited role in European integration, it could not get too deeply involved. This had a certain logic but it did not prevent some from perceiving British proposals for an industrial free trade area as an attempt to gain unfair advantage: access for British manufactures to mainland Europe but a cheap food policy in Britain on the back of food imports from the Commonwealth.

Whilst British doubts about supranationalism were to continue, the two decades after the war were to provide a painful lesson: the traditional view of Britain's position in the world had now become outdated and its role and power were considerably diminished. On the economic front, continued weakness, sterling and balance of payments crises and, in the 1960s, growth rates much lower than those of the Six were indicative of the deterioration in the British economy. The political decline was in some ways steeper. The Suez debacle, the abandonment of the independent British nuclear deterrent ('Blue Streak') and the first of the two superpower summits in 1961 clearly indicated that Britain was no longer in the first rank. Moreover, the Commonwealth was rapidly becoming a source of embarrassment rather than prestige, as its members moved, frequently with some difficulty, to independence[42] and the special relationship with the Americans became a rather questionable concept as the latter increasingly exhibited a preference for a more balanced relationship with Western Europe as a whole. Finally, it became obvious that EFTA was only of limited value. In truth it had never amounted to much: the combined population of the six other members – Austria, Denmark, Norway, Portugal, Sweden and Switzerland[43] – and hence the size of the market to which Britain had free access, was little more than that of Britain by itself. An industrial free trade area was only likely to provide long-term benefits if it took in most of Western Europe; EFTA could not really 'compete' with the Community. Consequently, many began to take the view that the only means of continuing to play a significant role on the world stage was through full participation in the European Community.

Consequently, on 31 July 1961, the British Prime Minister, Harold Macmillan, announced the intention for Britain to apply for membership.[44] The first ministerial conference between Britain and the Six was in October and the negotiations were to drag on until they were halted by the French in January 1963.[45] The immediate British concerns were to become involved in the formulation of the CAP and to protect the interests of the Commonwealth. When the first of these was resolved in 1962 with no reference to Britain, the concern with agriculture continued but the focus shifted to requests for a long transition period for British agriculture and for concessions to compensate Commonwealth agricultural exporters, dependent on the British market. However, although some progress was made, the French negotiators became increasingly tough towards the end of 1962 and the Nassau Pact, by which Macmillan agreed to buy Polaris missiles from the Americans, was the immediate catalyst for de Gaulle's veto of Britain's application for membership, delivered at a press conference on 14 January 1963.

Whilst there remain some doubts as to whether the veto was inevitable,[46] the rationale for it is clear enough. De Gaulle had two concerns: that Britain did not share the objectives of the Six; and that it would act as a 'Trojan horse' for American interests in Europe. Whilst the logic of the latter is perhaps debatable, this is not true of the former: it is quite clear that the decision to apply was a defensive reaction stemming from 'a gradual official realization of the danger that the EEC might become an economic and political embarrassment to Britain.'[47] De Gaulle was thus quite right to the extent that his veto of British entry was based on a mistrust of Britain's motives and the belief that its application in no way reflected a conversion to the views of the Six. A third reason for the French action was that Britain was perceived to be a potential rival for leadership within the Community in a way that Germany, because of recent history, could not be for some time.

The effect of the veto on British entry was that the simultaneous membership bids of Denmark, Norway and Ireland[48] were withdrawn as they declined to continue without Britain; in fact, they had applied, in the wake of Britain, only because they felt compelled to do so because of their close economic ties to the latter, although the Danes were rather relieved to be able to do so as they had been torn between their two major export markets – Britain and Germany. France's five partners were basically unhappy, not so much with the veto, which was not unexpected, but with the high-handed way in which it was delivered. However, they had little option but to carry on without British participation in the Community.

In 1961–3 the Labour Party had been divided over Community membership but with a majority against. Indeed, this opposition had contributed to de Gaulle's perception of Britain still being out of step with the Six. This was reflected at the October 1962 Party

Conference where five 'safeguards' (or conditions that the Party required to be fulfilled before it could support membership) were adopted:

- a satisfactory solution for the Commonwealth;
- a satisfactory solution for remaining members of EFTA;
- guarantees for British agriculture;
- freedom to pursue an independent foreign policy;
- freedom to engage in autonomous domestic planning.

The first and last of these were particularly important to the Labour Party.

However, by 1967, after three years in government, the Party had officially changed its mind and its policy.[49] There were a number of reasons for this. In general terms, the first experience of government since 1951 had brought home to the Labour Party the extent to which Britain's position in the world had declined, and what its remaining options were. More specifically, the 'safeguards' had mostly become less relevant. The Commonwealth had become a burden and EFTA clearly had limitations and, in any case, had been shown scant regard by the new Labour Government when it had unilaterally imposed a 15 per cent import surcharge during the 1964 balance of payments crisis. Moreover, the demise of the National Plan in 1966 and the realisation that an independent defence policy was something that Britain could not afford, made autonomous domestic planning and an independent foreign policy, respectively, unrealistic aspirations. There was also a strong economic impetus towards Community membership in the shape of the parlous state of the economy, typified by successive sterling crises, comparatively low rates of economic growth and the realisation that Britain's economic prosperity was beginning to lag behind France and Germany in absolute terms.

On 11 May 1967 Britain applied for membership of the Community for the second time and Denmark, Norway and Ireland followed again. This time the background and the approach were radically different. There was little domestic opposition and few conditions were imposed. A systematic attempt was made to win over the five and pressurize de Gaulle and the British contribution to science and technology was emphasised; in fact, there was talk of a European Technological Community which would help Europe compete with the Americans. The Commission produced a favourable 'opinion' on the British application in September but on 22 November, superficially prompted by the sterling crisis and the devaluation of the pound (with the implication of a weak British economy), de Gaulle delivered his second veto, at a press conference, for much the same reasons as the first and with much the same effect. On this occasion the British (and other) applications remained on the table, although it was clear that their acceptance would have to wait for the demise of de Gaulle. They did not have to wait too long.

The end of the 1960s and the Hague summit: taking stock and setting the agenda

As the 1960s drew to a close there were three other significant events in the Community. The first of these was that the three communities created in the 1950s – the ECSC, EEC and Euratom – were merged in July 1967 to form the 'European Communities' which became commonly referred to in the singular.[50] The three had always shared the Assembly/Parliament and the Court of Justice but, from mid-1967, they also had a common Council of Ministers and Commission (/High Authority). The second was the very first attempt to reform the CAP in the shape of the Mansholt Plan, named after the then Agricultural Commissioner, which appeared in 1968.[51] This sought to address the rising cost of the CAP through increasing farm incomes by structural reform of the agricultural sector. There were too many small inefficient farms and too much disguised unemployment in agriculture; rationalisation was required on a massive scale to create farms of an economically viable size. The Mansholt Plan would have substantially reduced the amount of land under cultivation and halved the numbers working in agriculture by 1980. Not surprisingly, it was far more than the member states could take; it earned Mansholt the nickname, 'peasant killer', and led to very little, although some half-hearted, minor structural reforms were introduced in the early 1970s. Effectively, however, the Mansholt Plan was ignored.[52]

The third major event was the Hague summit at the very end of the decade in December 1969. Shortly after his veto of the second British application to join the Community, the tide began to turn against de Gaulle domestically and he fell from power in 1968. His successor, Pompidou, although he too had a strong preference for intergovernmentalism over supranationality,[53] proved to be much more amenable to developing the Community further. Indeed, it was the French who proposed that a meeting of heads of state should be convened and the ensuing summit was to mark a turning point in the history of the European Union and a renewal of the 'Community spirit'. The Hague summit was concerned with the completion, deepening and enlargement of the Community and, specifically, agreed (or set in motion steps that led to agreement of) the following:

- the financing of the CAP;
- the reactivation of applications for membership of Britain, Ireland, Denmark and Norway;
- the objective of economic and monetary union;
- the establishment of regular discussions between foreign ministers;
- measures relating to a whole range of minor issues, including technological cooperation, development aid, social policy and the creation of a European university.

This agenda – particularly enlargement, EMU and political cooperation – was to preoccupy the Community for much longer than the immediate future.

7 The European Union, 1970–1985: Turbulence, Europessimism and Euroscelerosis

Introduction

During the 15 years after the Hague summit the Community, like much of the rest of the world, suffered from economic recession. The dreams of continuous economic growth which had sustained it through the trials and tribulations of its first decade were shattered. Negotiating the sharing out of the fruits of economic growth was clearly much easier than distributing the cutbacks and losses during recession. It is true that the Community continued to move forward on a significant number of fronts but, where progress was made, it was not easily achieved. Thus the overall characterisation of the Community in this period is one of failure leading to pessimism, economic paralysis and, above all, disagreement, lack of cooperation and turbulence. This culminated in a total loss of direction in the early 1980s when the Community virtually ground to a halt in the face of (related) disputes over its budget and the CAP. In short, the shared vision of a unified European which had sustained the movement towards European integration in the 1950s appeared to have dissipated.

In many ways this period was typified by the 1973 oil crisis and the reaction of the members of the Community: the combination of adverse external circumstances, economic gloom and unilateral national responses was to set the tone of the 1970s and early 1980s. The Community had been moving (very) gradually towards some kind of energy policy with security of supplies before 1973 and the OPEC decision to raise prices in late 1973 might have been expected to act as a catalyst for the policy. After all, here was an enormous common challenge that no member state could hope to meet alone and which, therefore, surely demanded a common response. In fact, there was disarray in the Community and little solidarity.

The British and French sought bilateral arrangements with Iran and Saudi Arabia respectively and the Netherlands found its supplies completely cut off by OPEC. The cooperation that did occur was through the International Energy Agency and not the Community. Indeed, the Community has struggled, with very limited success, to create an energy policy ever since.

The first enlargement: Britain, Ireland and Denmark

The first major challenge facing the Community in the 1970s was the accession negotiations with Britain, Ireland, Denmark and Norway. To a large extent the entry bids of the three smaller countries stood or fell with that of Britain, since they were largely following Britain because of strong economic linkages with the British market. Indeed, they pursued Community membership with varying degrees of underlying enthusiasm ranging from the Irish who saw it as means of diversifying their trade partners through the doubtful Danes to the increasingly (and, ultimately, too) sceptical Norwegians. The French remained far from enthusiastic about British accession, with Pompidou harbouring similar doubts to de Gaulle. However, in the face of an increasingly assertive and confident (West) Germany, France began to perceive Britain as a potential ally. More pragmatically, the French saw withdrawing their opposition to British membership of the EC as a bankable concession that could be traded off for the agreement of a new system of financing the CAP. Finally, the obvious Europeanism of Edward Heath and the fact that he was even prepared to distance himself from the US[1] were clearly helpful.

It was perhaps fitting that Britain should finally progress to EC membership in January 1973 under the government of Heath,[2] although support of the general public was far from certain with an April 1970 Gallup poll indicating that nearly three-fifths of the electorate did not even approve of the application for membership.[3] It was not surprising, therefore, that the negotiations, which began in mid-1970 and lasted for almost exactly a year, required a Heath–Pompidou summit in May 1971[4] to regenerate momentum – the acquiescence of the French remained critical – and had to deal with a number of contentious issues, most notably:[5]

- The length of the transition period: eventually it was agreed that it should be five years for both agricultural and industrial goods.
- Agriculture: essentially the Heath government accepted that higher food prices were an unavoidable cost of EC entry but sought to minimise the impact, in the short term, by phasing in the CAP as slowly as possible, and, in the long term, by negotiating a satisfactory budgetary arrangement.
- The UK contribution to the Community budget: the agreement for the transitional period was that Britain should pay 8.64 per cent of the EC budget in 1973 rising to 18.92 per cent in 1977 with limits on further increases in 1978 and 1979; this fell somewhere between the British proposal of a maximum of 15 per cent and the Commission's two scenarios (21.5 per cent and 20–25 per cent). However, there was no agreement about the permanent arrangement to apply from 1980 and so, implicitly, this meant that the Community's recently agreed 'own resource' system (see below) would apply.[6]
- Exports of Caribbean sugar and New Zealand diary produce to the British market: these were accommodated by special arrangements.
- General problems of the Commonwealth countries: a variety of arrangements were offered depending on the precise situation of each country, including membership of the Yaoundé Convention (which soon became the Lomé Convention), other forms of association, commercial agreements and inclusion in the Community's GSP (Generalised System of Preferences).
- Sterling: this particularly concerned the French who, on the one hand, saw sterling's international role as potentially a burden that might have to be shared by France and the rest of the Community in the event of a run on sterling;[7] however, somewhat contradictorily, they also saw it as a source of advantage to the British who could finance balance of payments deficits by simply issuing more sterling (which, of course, potentially exacerbated the first problem). For a while, it seemed that the French were, once again, set to throw a spanner in the works, but the matter was resolved amicably at the Heath–Pompidou summit and effectively disappeared off the agenda. At a subsequent meeting of Britain with the Six, the French simply accepted the British assurances that sterling

would be dealt with (which was no more than the British had said at earlier meetings).

- Fisheries: at the very same time as they were negotiating the first enlargement, the existing EC members agreed a common fisheries policy which included free and equal access to each others' waters. This was widely perceived as a cynical attempt to gain advantage over the four applicant countries which all had extensive fishing industries. It was not acceptable and special arrangements had to be made for the three countries that eventually joined and, indeed, the fisheries issue was an important one in the Norwegian decision not to join.

All these issues related to the EEC (since membership of the ECSC and Euratom raised only minor problems) and, although they were resolved, in some cases the resolution was superficial and the issues subsequently re-emerged as major problems. Indeed, it was the economic aspects of EC entry that dominated the debate in the UK[8] and the rather lofty political aspirations that had inspired the European integration movement in the 1950s barely featured at all.

Formal political positions in the House of Commons took the traditional line. Notwithstanding that it was formally the (reactivated) 1967 application of the then Labour government on which the negotiations were based, the Labour Party in opposition opposed the terms of entry (and actually voted against accession).[9] Moreover, in its manifesto for the October 1974 election, it pledged to 'renegotiate' membership. In the event this proved to be a rather perfunctory re-examination of the main points of contention of the British membership bid. Few concessions of real substance were obtained and, in particular, the agreement for budget rebates agreed at Dublin in 1975 was wholly inadequate, as subsequent events in the early 1980s were to show.[10] Indeed, the Labour Party's volte-face was largely due to the realisation that many of its concerns were unfounded. The manifesto listed objectives in the following seven areas:[11]

- agriculture;
- the Community budget;
- economic and monetary union;
- regional, industrial and fiscal policies;
- capital movements;

- the economic interests of the Commonwealth and developing countries;
- the harmonisation of VAT.

On the basis of this 'renegotiation' the government recommended the continuation of British membership of the Community, even though the cabinet was split and could only vote 16–7 in favour.

The House of Commons vote was of similar proportions (396 votes to 170[12]) as was the popular vote in the referendum with 67.2 per cent voting in favour of membership. To what extent this reflected a underlying belief in the value of continued EC membership and to what extent it reflected the impact of a well orchestrated and much better funded 'yes' campaign is perhaps debatable. Moreover, despite this apparently definitive majority in favour, a substantial hard core of 'anti-marketeers' have continued to oppose EC membership (and/or further integration within the Community) to the present day. This has been particularly true of the left wing of the Labour Party which even managed to get a commitment to withdraw from the Community incorporated into the Labour Party programme for a time in the early 1980s. However, there is also a significant element of the Conservative Party which is sceptical about the value of membership and which was causing more than embarrassment to the Major government in early 1995.[13]

Meanwhile, Ireland and Denmark had also joined the EC in 1973. Their negotiations had proceeded in parallel with those of Britain. For the Irish, despite the constraint of neutrality, there was little option but to follow the British; some 70 per cent of Irish exports were to Britain and EC membership was not only essential but also desirable because it provided an excellent opportunity to reduce this dependence on Britain. In the referendum in 1972, 83 per cent voted in favour of joining the Community. The passage to EC membership proved more difficult for the Danes. The economic logic of membership was inescapable: Denmark had a substantial agricultural sector that would clearly benefit from the CAP and, with one of the two main Danish export markets (Germany) already within the Community and the other (Britain) about to join, remaining outside could have been economically catastrophic; but there were other considerations. In particular there were Denmark's Nordic ties and its preference for intergovernmental rather than supranational cooperation. Also, the Norwegian 'no' which was delivered the week before the Danish referendum was not encouraging. In the end, however, economic logic won the day and there was a clear majority in favour of accession in the Danish referendum although, at 63 per cent, the vote was not as overwhelming as in Ireland.

Norway proved to be even more difficult with 53 per cent eventually voting against accession in the referendum. In a configuration that was to repeat itself 23 years later, concerns about agriculture, fisheries and the (then fledgling) oil industry swung the balance against EC entry. Moreover, the preceding campaign[14] tore the country apart and effectively made EC membership a taboo subject in political circles for 15 years. Two governments fell, old parties divided and new ones were created. Norway, like the remainder of EFTA, was eventually content with an agreement to create an industrial free trade area to cover the 16 countries of the EC and EFTA.

Economic and monetary union: the snake, the tunnel and the European Monetary System

Whilst the decision to 'widen' the Community through enlargement was largely successful, the main plank of the other decision (taken at the Hague) to 'deepen' the Community – economic and monetary union – fell by the wayside, although it was reactivated in a less ambitious form at the end of the 1970s. The origins of the European Union's efforts to create economic and monetary union actually go back to the late 1960s. Until then the Community already had one of the main components of monetary unions – fixed exchange rates – through participation in the IMF system. However, in 1969 the French were forced to devalue and the Germans to revalue. This created immediate problems because it led to arbitrary changes in French and German agricultural prices and, in fact, led to the creation of monetary compensation amounts and hence the green currency system. However, it was also indicative of the wider malaise in the IMF system which was to cause its temporary (in 1971) and eventually permanent collapse (in 1973). The effect of the problems in 1969 was, therefore, to push monetary union on to the Community's agenda. A formal commitment at the Hague summit was followed by the creation of the Werner Committee.

The Werner Report advocated economic and monetary union (EMU) by 1980 to be achieved in three stages although only the first of these, the 'snake' (in the tunnel), was outlined in detail. The vagueness about the subsequent stages reflected an internal disagreement which still persists in current debates. The 'monetarists' (France, Belgium, Luxembourg and the Commission) argued that EMU could best be achieved by fixing exchange rates (and thereby completing monetary union) as soon as possible since this would force member states to pursue complementary macroeconomic policies and hence move quickly towards economic union. The 'economists' (Germany and the Netherlands) asserted that some degree of movement towards economic union (economic convergence) should be pursued first as, without it, any attempt to secure monetary union was doomed to failure. In the event, the 'monetarists' won the argument to the extent that it was principally the 'monetarist' elements of the Werner Report that were eventually adopted. However, subsequent events tended to support the view of the 'economists'.

The first stage involved the narrowing of permitted intra-Community exchange rate fluctuations and the establishment of medium-term financial assistance (to help those countries with weaker currencies to stay in the system). The reduced exchange rate fluctuation was to take the form of an agreement to limit the degree of fluctuation between Community currencies to a band of 1.2 per cent of their central parities (the 'snake') which was to operate within the wider band of 1.5 ($\pm$ 0.75) per cent against the US dollar (the 'tunnel').[15] Unfortunately, an international monetary crisis arose before the system could begin. A feature of this was a loss of confidence in the dollar and a consequent flow of funds into Europe; but this was a flow mainly into the deutschmark (and, to some extent, the guilder) which put severe pressure on intra-Community exchange rates and forced those two currencies to revalue. EMU had to be temporarily abandoned. The essential problem was that the worldwide system of fixed exchange rates established after 1945 was entering its death throes.

Following the Smithsonian Agreement which restored the IMF system with revised central rates for the major currencies and wider bands (the revised 'tunnel') around the central parity – 4.5 ($\pm$ 2.25) per cent – the 'snake' was finally launched on 24 April 1972, also with a wider band of 2.25 per cent. The 'snake' initially contained only the six EC member states but the three applicant countries joined after a week. Sterling came under strong pressure very quickly and Britain and Ireland[16] were forced to leave the system within eight weeks. The Danes also left in June although they rejoined in October. The Italian lira departed in February 1973 and then in March the IMF system of fixed exchange rates collapsed completely. This meant that the tunnel disappeared. However, the 'snake' continued but with some flexibility which allowed the Germans to revalue; the 'snake' also admitted two associate members (Norway and Sweden).

The 'snake' had thus weathered the storm of this international monetary crisis but within its first year had been reduced to a membership of two-thirds of EC member states, included two non-EC members and did not include the currencies of two of the 'big four' countries of the Community. The system did not look like the first stage of economic and monetary union. This was effectively recognised at the December 1974 Paris summit by which time the franc had also left (January 1974) and the currencies of the Netherlands, Norway and Germany (again) had been revalued.[17] The system did carry on and, indeed, the French did rejoin (at the old parity) in 1975, only to leave again in 1976. However, adjustments of central rates became commonplace and the 'snake' degenerated into a mere deutschmark bloc or zone. Thus its membership consisted of the deutschmark and the currencies of a number of smaller countries which found it desirable to be linked to the German currency, mainly because of trade links with Germany.

The attraction of the 'snake' was clearly the link with Germany and not EMU. The 'snake' had failed completely and the aspirations of achieving EMU in Europe had faded with it. There were a number of reasons for this but essentially they fall into two categories: internal and external. The latter were largely beyond the EC's control (although not the former) and the principal factor was the collapse of the international system of fixed exchange rates. The situation was aggravated by the emergence of high and divergent inflation rates[18] in the early 1970s and the oil crisis from late 1973. The early to mid 1970s was a wholly inauspicious period in which to attempt a narrowing of exchange rate fluctuations. However, it was not merely these external factors but also the inadequate response of the Community in dealing with them which led to the demise of the 'snake'. Arguably the fundamental deficiency was the lack of (internal) political will to pursue EMU. Whenever short-term national interests clashed with the pursuit of EMU, member state governments favoured the former. The French were typical – into EMU (1972) and out (1974), in again (1975) and out again (1976) – treating membership of the 'snake' as an optional addition to its national policy; there was never any question of giving EMU priority.

In the face of such abject failure it is perhaps surprising that EMU did not disappear from the agenda completely in the late 1970s. In fact, not only did it not disappear but the 'snake' was replaced by a successor: the European Monetary System. The full story of its creation has been told elsewhere[19] but several factors might be highlighted here:

- The arguments for (and the proponents of) economic and monetary union had not disappeared; they remained much the same as before, as did the belief that EMU was an inevitable staging post on the road to a fully integrated Europe and, therefore, the sooner it was reached the better.
- The experience of the 1970s could, if anything, be interpreted as strengthening the case for EMU. The 'snake' had failed as a first stage of EMU but much had been learnt about the practicalities of narrowing exchange rate fluctuations and the difficulties; furthermore any naïvety had been brushed aside and the commitments needed to achieve EMU were painfully clear. Perhaps even more important, the collapse of the international system of exchange rates and the ensuing experience of worldwide floating exchange rates had made many uncomfortable and encouraged the belief that fixed exchange rates within the EC had become even more essential in the absence of an international 'safety net'.
- A consequence of this, but important in its own right, was the fact that EMS was much less ambitious (and therefore more realistic) than the grand design of which the 'snake' had comprised the first stage. The immediate objective was not EMU, or even a stage on that road, but rather a 'zone of monetary stability' (against what was perceived as a turbulent international monetary backdrop).
- The external situation, although far from calm with floating exchange rates and another oil shock in 1979, was still more

propitious than it had been in the early 1970s when just about the worse possible configuration of external economic circumstances occurred.

- Internal circumstances were also better to the extent that there was a sense in which EMS represented a modest and attainable objective with a degree of clear internal political backing. Credit is frequently given to the then Commission President, Roy Jenkins,[20] for relaunching economic and monetary integration but, in fact, it was reconstructed firmly on the back of the Franco-German understanding between Giscard d'Estaing and Schmidt; consequently, it was much more likely to be backed by a strong internal political will to succeed. Moreover, the absence of Britain from the exchange rate mechanism (ERM) was quite probably helpful in this respect.

The European Monetary System was agreed at the Bremen and Brussels summits in 1978 and came into effect on 13 March 1979. It had five main elements:

- The European Currency Unit. This is a basket currency and is built up of snippets of each EC member state currency. It serves as a means of settlement between Community monetary authorities and as a divergency indicator.[21]
- The Exchange Rate Mechanism (ERM). If a country's currency deviates by more than three-quarters[22] of its permitted (± 2.25 per cent) margin of fluctuation against the ECU then it is deemed to have crossed its divergency indicator and there is a presumption that some corrective action will be taken. However, as was the case with the 'snake' it is the bilateral parity grid that really matters: every EMS currency has a central rate against every other and can only fluctuate ± 2.25 per cent[23] around this; if it goes beyond this then it must be brought back within the proscribed limits, otherwise it drops out of the system.
- The European Monetary Fund which was supposed to be created after two years. In fact, this did not happen, and the European Monetary Cooperation Fund carried on with a somewhat extended role.
- Credit facilities to assist currencies with temporary problems and to discourage speculation.

- Special measures to help less prosperous members – that is Italy and Ireland (and Britain, had it joined) in the form of cheap loans.

Although it became a member of the EMS (like all EC member states), Britain did not join the exchange rate mechanism (ERM). This was essentially because of the implied loss of sovereignty and, specifically, a reluctance to accept externally imposed discipline on economic policy, although the precise nature of the argument differed according to the political party in power. The Labour government, in place at the time of the inception of EMS, was concerned with the UK's tendency to relatively high inflation and was unwilling to accept the prospect that it might have to deflate the economy, thereby aggravating unemployment, in order to stay within the ERM or, alternatively, accept a decline in competitiveness which would ultimately have the same effect. The Conservative government, which replaced it in 1979, wished to pursue control of the money supply as the centrepiece of its economic policy, and targeting the money supply was incompatible with an exchange rate target. In the event, membership of the ERM proved to be relatively flexible in the first five years as there were a number of changes in central rates and the system was very much an adjustable (or, for some currencies, even a crawling) peg rather than a fixed system.[24]

Political cooperation and decision-making

Whilst progress towards the principal economic objectives of the 1970s was very limited, some modest developments occurred on the political front although it is not clear that the adoption of a formal role for EC summits was in line with the supranational, and clearly federal, aspirations of many of the founders of the Community and the practice of political cooperation proved to be rather more difficult than the theory. However, whilst the major developments were pragmatic, there were continued discussions on a somewhat higher plane. In particular, two documents appeared in this period which were indicative of and, indeed, ultimately influenced some of the thinking about the future course that European integration should take.

The Tindemans Report on European Union was commissioned by the December 1974 Paris summit and appeared in early 1976.[25] It was a combination of an elaboration of the general framework for integration and specific proposals. The latter included a common foreign and defence policy, the relaunch of EMU, and more European social, regional and industrial policies. However, there were two radical proposals: firstly, a clearly federal institutional framework with a supranational executive independent of national governments, accountable to an elected and bicameral parliament; secondly, the report raised the possibility of a two-tier Community to encourage movement towards European Union at the speed of the fastest rather than the slowest in the 'convoy'. In the event, the Tindemans Report was never really seriously discussed,[26] although it appeared on the agenda of several summits; it proved to be too bold and too federal a blueprint for the times and, more practically, it did not offer a timetable for achieving Union. However, many of its ideas were eventually taken up and, in fact, the 1991 Intergovernmental Conference covered much the same ground.

The Draft Treaty of European Union was prepared by a parliamentary committee under the chairmanship of Altiero Spinelli and was overwhelmingly approved by the European Parliament in February 1984. In essence the Draft Treaty sought to reverse the drift towards intergovernmentalism by increasing the powers of the Commission and the Parliament and reducing those of the Council. However, the Draft Treaty was never going to be taken up by the member states and, ultimately, amounted to no more than a contribution to the debate.

The problem for the authors and advocates of the ideas of the Tindemans report and the Parliament's Draft Treaty was that, on balance, the EC was moving in the opposite direction. Despite the provisions of the Rome Treaty, it was the Luxembourg Compromise that prevailed in the 1970s and early 1980s and majority voting was rarely used. It is true that the Paris 1974 summit drew attention in its communiqué to the need to abandon the practice of unanimity and that majority voting was eventually used – in 1982, on farm price increases despite a British 'veto'. Nevertheless, even the Commission was well aware that this remained the exception rather than the rule as indicated by its observation that there was 'not likely to be any sudden change from former practice'.[27] Furthermore, the most significant institutional development in this period was the formal recognition of the role of the summit meetings of heads of state – the creation of the 'European Council'; this was clearly a step towards intergovernmentalism.

Despite some scepticism, the decision was taken at the Paris summit in December 1974 to have regular summits three times a year, reduced to two in 1985. In essence, two roles have emerged for summits; firstly (and their preferred role), is to set the agenda and direction of the Community; secondly (and largely by default), summits are the fora which settle those disagreements which are so politically sensitive that they cannot be agreed at lower levels – for example the British budgetary dispute (see below).[28] To a significant degree, the European Council usurped the role of the Commission as the initiator of EC policy and, at the very least, its emergence pointed the Community in a firmly intergovernmental direction.

The other principal institutional development was the first direct election of the European Parliament in 1979. On the face of it this marked a significant step forward as the Parliament of appointed part-time members metamorphosed into one of directly elected full-time members. However, the turnout in the elections was disappointing in some countries and the French and Danish national parliaments made it clear that there was no presumption that direct elections implied an extension of the European Parliament's powers. Indeed, with the exception of budgetary matters (see below), business carried on much as it had done before direct elections and the Parliament had to wait until the Single European Act before its powers were significantly enhanced.

The other notable advance in political integration was the establishment of the European Political Cooperation (EPC) procedure, although this was a mixed blessing for proponents of federal-style integration. It did clearly mark a step forward but had limited success and was intergovernmental and actually took place outside the treaties of the ECs, although the Commission was eventually allowed to attend meetings from 1974. Indeed, in many ways, it was reminiscent of de Gaulle's Fouchet Plan, the ideas of which had become more acceptable to France's original five partners because of the participation of Britain. EPC was successful in a number of areas in the 1970–85 period, notably:[29]

- the EC was able to exert more influence at the 1975 Helsinki Conference on Security and Cooperation in Europe through acting jointly;

- more generally, the coordination of member states' positions in the UN enabled the EC to play an enhanced role;
- the imposition of economic sanctions on Rhodesia (after 1975), Iran (1980) and the Soviet Union and Poland (1981);
- some progress was made in the Euro-Arab dialogue;
- speaking with one voice allowed the EC to pursue a policy towards Latin America which was independent of the US.

However, in some cases EPC proved more difficult and only rather strained and limited joint responses could be agreed. There were two cases in 1982 involving the imposition of economic sanctions on Argentina and Israel, after their respective invasions of the Falklands and the Lebanon. Two further instances arose in 1986, relating to sanctions on South Africa and on Syria in reaction to its alleged involvement in terrorism. More generally, the EC member states only managed to vote as a bloc in the UN about 50 per cent of the time. Moreover, there were a number of occasions on which EPC clearly failed, particularly:[30]

- the 1974 Cyprus crisis following the Turkish invasion(s); this was the first real test of the EPC procedure and, after some initial promise, the EC failed to establish a common position and, essentially, it just fell in line behind the US and the UN;[31]
- the very long delay in reacting to the Russian invasion of Afghanistan (in 1980);
- the very limited response to the shooting down of a South Korean airplane by the Russians in 1983.

It is clear from the above catalogue that EPC had a somewhat chequered history in its initial 15 years. Nevertheless, there were some successes and, to that extent, it could be interpreted as marking the first tentative steps towards political integration (although some member states would question this and see it as no more than mutually advantageous intergovernmental political cooperation between economic partners).

Thus, in spite of the economic difficulties experienced in the 1970–85 period, there were a number of positive developments in political integration. However, on balance, these were at the expense of the Commission and supranationality, and biased towards intergovernmentalism. Indeed, in some ways, it is the reinforce-

ment of the Franco-German alliance and its centrality to the process of European integration[32] that is most striking (along with the
unwillingness, or perhaps inability, of the British to participate constructively in the debate). Ultimately, therefore, a degree of
momentum, which was clearly absent in the economic sphere, was
apparent in political integration, although perhaps not in the direction that the fathers of the Treaty of Rome would have preferred.

Building during adversity: some positive developments in 1970–1985

Although the primary objectives of the Hague summit were either
fraught with difficulty (enlargement and EMU) or had a rather
mixed outcome (EPC), it would be wrong to characterise this period as one of total failure. Indeed, positive steps were taken in a
number of areas which marked the beginnings of significant policy
developments. The first of these was regional policy and advance-
ment here was related directly to the accession of Britain. The decision at the Hague in 1969 to press forward with EMU created a need
for some kind of regional fund to cushion its effects on less prosperous regions and, indeed, this was recognised in the Werner Report.
The final push which led to the establishment of the European Regional Development Fund (ERDF) was provided by the British[33]
who saw such a fund as a means of compensating them for their
relatively small share of agricultural expenditure. In fact they were
allocated 28 per cent of the ERDF but the fund amounted to only
1.3 billion units of account over its first three years (1975–7) – the
British had wanted 3 billion; this was only 5 per cent of the total
budget compared to the more than 70 per cent allocated to CAP
spending over the same period.

   However, the initially temporary ERDF became permanent and
progressively larger, although the British share declined after the
Mediterranean enlargement in the 1980s. At the same time as one
of what were to become the two major structural funds was being
created, the other was being recast. The European Social Fund was
established by the Treaty of Rome but was primarily concerned with
providing retrospective financial assistance to migrant workers until
1971. Then it was radically reformed to become larger and more
proactive; in addition, its scope was widened to address vocational

training more specifically and to assist a broader range of disadvantaged groups. Thus the 1970s saw modest advances in regional and social policy which prepared the ground for the subsequent development of a substantial structural policy.

A second major development – the Lomé Convention – was also directly related to Britain joining the Community. British accession raised the problem of how to accommodate the former British colonies; indeed, a satisfactory arrangement for the Commonwealth was one of the conditions set by Britain in its accession negotiations. The original EC6 already had an arrangement with their former colonies – the Yaoundé Agreement – which was due to expire in 1975. It was decided that its successor should also include appropriate members of the British Commonwealth. The resulting Lomé Convention covered 46 countries – known collectively as the ACP (African, Caribbean and Pacific) countries – and was hailed as a breakthrough in North–South relations, replacing a colonial relationship with partnership. It was innovative in a number of ways, most notably, through the creation of a stabilisation fund ('STABEX') which sought to compensate ACP countries for unanticipated falls in export earnings. The reality of Lomé has fallen well short of its aspirations[34] but it has to be conceded that, not only has the 'membership' of the ACP grown to more than 70, but the relationship still continues, not least because of the wishes of the ACP.

A third area of significant EC activity was industrial policy. This initially seemed an unlikely area for meaningful progress. The Colonna Report[35] in 1970 tried to establish a very broad framework for industrial policy but was essentially ignored by the member states. However, drawing on its wider powers with respect to the steel industry,[36] the Commission was able to develop the much narrower role of mitigating the effects of the decline of the 'traditional' industries within Europe, not only steel but also, to a lesser extent, textiles and shipbuilding. Having established its credentials, it then sought to make a more positive contribution by championing the cause of new 'high technology' industries. Following the success of 'Eureka' and, particularly, 'ESPRIT', which dealt with new, high technology products in general and information technology, respectively, the EC was able to move to a genuine industrial policy. This consisted of the 'First Framework Programme' (1984–7) which sought to integrate all Community assistance for research and development into a single coherent system. The current 'Framework

Programme' accounts for nearly 4 per cent of the total EC budget (more than half the expenditure on 'Internal Policies').

After a difficult start in the early 1970s the Common Fisheries Policy (CFP) was also created in this period. This had been a major point of contention between the original Six and the three new members who joined in 1973 (and Norway). The latter, with much more substantial fishing interests (and waters) than the Six felt that the agreement immediately before they joined of a CFP which embodied the principle of free and equal access to each others' fishing grounds was unacceptable. The disagreement was resolved by the granting of a variety of exclusions and exceptions to the new members for a ten-year period. This meant that the CFP had to be renegotiated in 1983. The need to do so was made even greater by the adoption by all major fishing nations in the mid-1970s of much extended fishing limits off their coasts of up to 200 miles. This created vast tracts of fishing waters 'belonging' to EC member states, notably the 'Community fishpond' consisting of most of the North Sea. These had to be managed and the need for a coherent CFP became critical. The debate and negotiations were protracted and acrimonious but eventually a new (20-year) CFP emerged in 1983 which consisted of:

- the principle of free access for all EC fishermen to all EC waters but with some exceptions;
- a modified version of the marketing measures of the original CFP;
- a system of conservation and management of stocks, notably the establishment of scientifically determined, annual total allowable catches (TACs) which are then divided into national quotas;
- structural policies to assist regions highly dependent on the fisheries industry;
- various agreements with third countries, negotiated at Community level.

The CFP has continued to have a somewhat chequered history with a variety of internal disagreements and disputes with third countries. However, in some ways it is a model policy, which shows how common problems can be addressed to the potential advantage of all, and at a relatively low cost.[37]

Whilst the above – the beginnings of regional, industrial and fish-eries policies and the Lomé Convention – mark the major (though not only) policy advances besides the EMS in 1970–85, there were two other developments in this period which could be construed as important steps forward. The first of these was the first phase of the second (Mediterranean) enlargement of the EC, with the accession of Greece in 1981, although this has been widely interpreted as a mixed blessing on both the economic and political fronts. Unique-ly, a broadly negative Commission opinion[38] on the Greek member-ship bid was overturned in the Council of Ministers for political reasons: the need to provide support for (restored) democracy in Greece was judged to override all other considerations. Neverthe-less, the Commission's misgivings were soon proved to be well-founded as the Greeks effectively sought to renegotiate the economic conditions of their accession in 1982[39] and went on to play a frequently rather maverick role in the EPC procedure. In-deed, the Greeks, along with the British and the Danes, have become widely regarded as among the least enthusiastic EC mem-bers and those most likely to cause 'difficulties' for the process of European integration.

The other significant step forward concerned changes in the budgetary arrangements of the Community. The Community was originally financed by direct contributions from member states but it was always envisaged – in Article 201 of the Treaty of Rome (EEC) – that it would eventually be funded by its 'own resources'. In part this intention reflected a desire to extend integration further but it also had a certain logic since it was difficult to assign the proceeds of the common external tariff accurately; for example, duties on goods entering the Community through Rotterdam but bound ultimately for Germany would be collected by the Dutch authorities. It was eventually agreed to adopt the 'own resource' system in 1970 but it was not fully implemented until 1980. At this stage, there were three 'own resources':

- the proceeds of the common external tariff (customs duties);
- agricultural levies, consisting primarily of the (variable) import duties levied on agricultural imports but also including sugar and isoglucose levies which are a kind of production tax on EC sugar producers to contribute to the cost of the EC sugar regime;

- up to 1 per cent of VAT levied on the common assessment base.[40]

However, whilst the 'own resource' system was clearly perceived as an essential step forward on the path to fuller European integration, its financial implications for Britain were such as to make it appear a retrograde rather than a progressive development; this matter is taken up in the next section.

Budgetary crisis in the Community: problems and reform of the Common Agricultural Policy

In the early 1980s the Community entered a period of paralysis which was essentially due to two related issues: a range of budgetary difficulties and an unreformed common agricultural policy (CAP). There is insufficient space to dwell too much on the latter here but the deficiencies of the CAP have been extensively catalogued elsewhere.[41] The main points relate to EC prices set well above world levels which led, not only to dear food for EC consumers, but also to excessive food production, creating surpluses which were expensive to store and to dispose of, leading to a situation in which two-thirds of the EC budget was spent on agricultural price support. The issues of CAP reform and budgetary problems were thus inextricably linked. Indeed, the need for the reform of the CAP was recognised virtually from its inception and the unsuccessful Mansholt Plan has already been described in the previous chapter. The Commission subsequently went on to produce a whole range of documents which had no more effect than the Mansholt Plan, including *The 1975 Stocktaking, The 1978 Reflections, Reflections on the CAP* (1980), *The Report on the Mandate* (1981) and *Guidelines for European Agriculture* (1982).

However, it was not until the budgetary pressures became uncontainable that serious CAP reform could begin; indeed, this has been a general feature of CAP reform. There were actually three serious budgetary problems that emerged in the early 1980s:

- intra-EC institutional disputes over the control of the budget (principally between the Council and the Parliament);
- the issue of budgetary imbalances (particularly the net contribution of Britain);

- the tendencies of EC expenditure (mainly on the CAP) to exceed EC revenue, thereby effectively causing the EC to run out of resources.

The difficulties began in December 1979 when the European Parliament chose to assert its new, directly elected status by rejecting the 1980 budget because it was unhappy with the way the Council had ignored its efforts to reduce agricultural expenditure and increase spending on the ERDF and elsewhere. The 'twelfths' rule had to come into effect, whereby in each month the Community could only spend up to one twelfth of its total budget in the previous year, until the budget was finally adopted in July 1980 (after the Council had made some concessions). In 1982 there were disputes between the Council and the Parliament over both the general and a supplementary budget. A shortfall in the 1983 budget was averted only by the device of suspending (and thereby postponing) some agricultural payments. By mid-1984 EC budgetary arrangements were on the verge of chaos with the 1983, 1984 and 1985 budgets all causing problems: the Parliament was blocking Britain's 1983 rebate in an attempt to force budgetary reform, most member states were opposing the Commission's request for a loan to cover the imminent shortfall in the 1984 budget and the Commission's preliminary draft budget for 1985 actually anticipated an (illegal) deficit. These difficulties led to the first major budgetary reforms agreed at the Fontainebleau summit in June 1984 (and discussed below).

Underlying this rather sorry saga were the three recurring themes listed above. The intra-EC institutionary struggle to control the Community purse strings (principally between the Council and the Parliament) is well illustrated by the events described above and dates back to 1975 when the Parliament was given the last word on non-compulsory EC expenditure, that is, expenditure not covered by the Treaty of Rome. This prepared the ground for a long power struggle as the Parliament sought to increase its budgetary powers, usually by trying to shift the balance of EC spending away from compulsory (agricultural) to non-compulsory (particularly the Regional and Social Funds) expenditure. This led to a spate of European Court cases. The Joint Declaration (of the Commission, Council and Parliament) in June 1982 sought to restore harmony by clarifying certain ambiguities and setting up a conciliation procedure within which disputes can be resolved. However, the disagreements continued throughout much of the 1980s.

The second problem – budgetary imbalances – was the one of greatest concern in Britain. The problem was not unanticipated and stems from the original accession terms in 1973 and the total inadequacy of the 'Dublin Amendment', agreed as part of the Labour government's 'renegotiation', which was supposed to have addressed the problem. At the end of the 1970s Britain came to the end of its transition period, began to pay its full share of the EC's budget and its sorry position was fully revealed. The problem was not so much that it was paying too much into the EC budget since its contributions were not radically out of line with its share of the total EC GDP [42] but, rather, that it was receiving a disproportionately low share of EC expenditures; this essentially came down to the fact that Britain received a relatively small share of CAP spending – the largest category of EC spending by far – because it had a relatively small agricultural sector. For the British, reducing their net contribution to the budget and reforming the CAP went hand in hand. Thus in 1979, Britain, one of the poorest EC members, was one of only two (very substantial) net contributors along with (West) Germany.

It should have therefore come as no surprise to Britain's partners when, at the 1979 Dublin summit, Mrs Thatcher demanded a £1 billion refund, thereby setting the scene for five years of bitter wrangles (and, indeed, the tone of British relations with the rest of the Community for some years). It was clearly unfair that Britain should be so substantial a net contributor, although the Thatcher style of putting this across was perhaps unfortunate in some ways. Consequently, the principle that Britain was paying too much was only grudgingly conceded. Nevertheless, a series of ad hoc settlements followed for 1980–3 during which Britain actually did rather well (achieving a near-zero contribution in 1981), although this was mainly paid in the form of additional expenditure in the UK rather than a rebate as such. Britain had to wait until 1984 when its rebate was formalised as part of a package of budget reforms.

The third and, from a Community point of view, arguably the major problem of the budget in the early 1980s, was the spectre of running out of funds which stemmed from the inadequacy of its resources. The obvious means of dealing with this was to reduce expenditure but this proved impossible for two main reasons.

Prolonged efforts to reform the CAP and reduce agricultural expenditure continued to be unsuccessful and, in any case, it was becoming increasingly clear that this alone would not be sufficient anyway because of the second reason: the Community was increasing the scope and the range of its non-agricultural activities and this expansion required additional resources. The final pressure which made increasing Community revenue the more realistic option came from the erosion of the revenue generated by traditional 'own resources': growing intra-EC trade and GATT-negotiated reductions in tariffs had reduced customs duties and increasing self-sufficiency in agricultural production reduced agricultural levies; this shifted the burden on to VAT receipts but these also stagnated as the overall VAT base (the share of GNP accounted for by consumption) of the EC economy decreased in size.

The EC ran out of funds in 1983 when it had to suspend (and postpone) some agricultural payments to balance the budget. This brought the crisis to a head and led to the first major attempt at reform at the Fontainebleau summit in June 1984 where the following was agreed:

- the ceiling on VAT contributions was raised from 1 to 1.4 per cent from 1986 (with the prospect of a further rise to 1.6 per cent at a later date);
- the British rebate was set at two-thirds of the difference between its VAT payments to the Community and its share of expenditure (to be paid by an automatic downward adjustment in its VAT payments the following year);
- one-off measures were agreed to deal with the shortfalls in the 1984 and 1985 budgets;
- the agreement at the preceding (March 1984) summit on financial discipline was confirmed; this included the requirement that CAP expenditure should grow at a slower rate than the 'own resource' base, which implied a declining share of total expenditure on agriculture.

The summit had been preceded by a decision to introduce a quota system for milk production. Although the level of quotas was generously set, for the first time guaranteed prices were only to be paid up to a limit and open-ended price support for milk came to an end. All this marked the first step towards genuine reform of the

CAP and a resolution of the budgetary crises and, retrospectively, it is clear that it amounted to a turning of the tide. Nevertheless, a comprehensive solution could only be achieved in the glow of the aftermath of the Single European Act and the launch of the single market programme in the mid-1980s. The pessimism and Euro-sclerosis of the first half of the 1980s were then to change quite dramatically into optimism and dynamism in the second half of the decade. This is the subject matter of the next chapter.

8 The European Union, 1985–1995: the Relance: from the Single European Act to the Maastricht Treaty and European Union

Introduction

There was a remarkable transformation in the European Community in the mid-1980s. It is not clear exactly why this rediscovery of the ideas and objectives of the architects of the Treaty of Rome took place; this 'relance' had the air of an addict at his nadir, deciding that he had had enough, renouncing his vice and returning to the straight and narrow by sheer strength of will. Perhaps the answer lies in a combination of political and economic factors:[1]

- On the political side there was unease about the attitudes and policies of the Americans. Initially, in the 1980s, this stemmed from Reagan's rather aggressive style of diplomacy which led to fears of an arms race and renewed cold war between the two superpowers. When the Soviet Union collapsed at the end of the decade, European integration was further fuelled, somewhat ironically, by the fears of US troop withdrawals.
- More importantly, on the economic side, the deep recession of the early 1980s, the comparative economic decline of Europe, its failure to create jobs at the rate the US seemed able to do, renewed fears about technological backwardness and dependency in Europe, all combined to concentrate European (Community) minds. European industry began to adopt an increasingly European perception and strategy[2] and began to see the fragmentation of the European economy as a major problem. There was also a growing consensus in favour of supply-side policies, economic deregulation and budgetary discipline. The combination of all these factors created an irresistible pressure for change and led to two major steps forward in the

field of industrial policy: the establishment of the first Framework Programme for EC research and development policies and the single market programme (SMP); the latter was to be seized upon, by proponents of European integration in general, as a flagship for their cause and was, therefore, to develop into much more than a mere component of industrial policy.

The clarion call for this renewed ambition was '1992' which was technically no more than the date – to be precise, 31 December 1992 – by which the EC was to have achieved the completion of its internal market. However, '1992' became about much more than the single European market (SEM). It was about relaunching the idea of European integration after 15 years of virtual stagnation and it was about reviving the economic fortunes of Europe in a much broader sense, through the artifice of further integration. The single market programme – '1992' – became a target, a symbol and, indeed, an advertisement (almost to the point of being a vehicle of propaganda) for the Community. The adoption of the SMP was a catalyst for a new phase of European integration which was, together with the collapse of the Soviet empire, to transform the agenda of the Community and of the wider Europe. Whatever the outcome of the 1996 intergovernmental conference, the ten years preceding it will arguably have marked the most significant period for European integration since the ten years preceding the signing of the Treaty of Rome.

Unfinished business: reforming the budget and the Common Agricultural Policy

A side effect or perhaps necessary requirement for the SMP (or perhaps both) was the resolution of the two related problems that had been the source of so much internal EC conflict in the early 1980s – the budget disputes and the reform of the CAP. As suggested in the previous chapter, the reforms agreed at Fontainebleau provided only a temporary respite. Budgetary shortfalls continued in 1985 and 1986 and had to be made up by additional contributions while agricultural surpluses continued to mount. An anticipated deficit of ECU 6 billion in 1987 concentrated minds and a Commission plan

– what became known as the 'Delors I' package – was put forward and formed the basis of discussion (and, ultimately, agreement). However, the debate dragged on and agreement could not be reached even at the Copenhagen summit in December and the 1987 shortfall had to be filled by various technical devices, notably by switching the basis of certain agricultural payments so they were paid in arrears rather than in advance. Finally, after more protracted and difficult negotiations, agreement was reached on reform of the CAP and the future financing of the EC – the one could not be agreed without the other – at a special EC summit in Brussels in February 1988. The main elements of the budget deal were as follows:

- a five year (1988–92) 'financial perspective' which set out guidelines for the total budget and its main subcategories for each of the five years;
- an overall ceiling for expenditure progressively rising from 1.15 per cent of Community GNP in 1988 to 1.2 per cent in 1992;
- a shift in the composition of expenditure away from the CAP – the growth of spending on agriculture was limited to a maximum of 74 per cent of the growth rate of the EC's GNP – to the structural funds (principally the Regional and Social Funds) which were to double in size by 1993 and thereby increase their share of the budget to 30 per cent;
- a fourth 'own resource' was added in the shape of a percentage of each country's share of the EC's GNP – the remaining three sources of revenue (agricultural levies, customs duties and VAT) were to continue as before with the VAT contribution to remain at a maximum of 1.4 per cent;
- the British rebate was to continue in a slightly modified form to that agreed at Fontainebleau.

Shortly after the Brussels summit, an Interinstitutional Agreement was reached between the Commission, Council and Parliament, designed to facilitate improvements in budgetary procedures.

The overall package was a major step forward. At a stroke it pre-empted further disagreement amongst EC institutions since the size of the overall budget and its main constituents became pre-determined, the shortfall in revenue was made good and the British budgetary rebate was renewed on a permanent, mutually acceptable basis. The most fundamental effect of the reform was that it freed the Community to focus on new initiatives. The other main consequence was allied to this last point: the introduction of the fourth 'own resource' based on GNP created a degree of progressivity into the EC budget. There still remained the same random distributional effects on the expenditure side, which were as likely to be regressive as progressive (as the British had found out to their cost), but these too were being mitigated by the shift away from agricultural spending to the structural funds. The budget was thus redesigned so as to be more likely to cause redistribution from the richer to the poorer member states. Indeed, the three poorest members – Greece, Ireland and Portugal – are the major beneficiaries (in terms of net receipts as a percentage of GNP) but anomalies remain: the extent to which the net contributions of the two major contributors (Germany and Britain) exceed those of the rest is too large and it is inequitable that relatively rich countries like Denmark and the Netherlands should be net beneficiaries. Finally, there is one other positive point: the GNP-based resource introduced an element of flexibility into the budget which would allow a technically (if not always politically) easy solution to any problem of future shortfalls.

At the same summit in Brussels in 1988, after the modest start made with dairy quotas in 1984, the reform of the CAP began in earnest. The limitation on agriculture's share of the budget has already been mentioned but this was allied with the introduction of 'stabilisers'. Their adoption brought to a halt the system of open-ended price support which had been a central feature of the CAP since its creation. From now on full price support would only be provided up to a certain level of production; 'stabilisers' amounted to production quotas and the CAP had finally been capped. The other element of the reform was the introduction of a Community funded set-aside scheme whereby farmers would be encouraged to take some of their land out of production. It is, of course, important to set the 1988 package in context because both the size of the 'quotas' and the levels of guaranteed prices remained generously high but a real start had finally been made.

The very success of the Delors I package meant that there was less pressure to negotiate a successor because budget crises had been effectively kept off the agenda. Nevertheless, the ambitious Maastricht agenda (discussed below) arguably meant that the absence of disputes over the budget had become even more critical in the 1990s. Eventually, agreement on a successor – Delors II – was reached at the Edinburgh summit; its main elements were:[3]

- a seven-year financial perspective (1993–99) with guidelines as before;
- an overall ceiling for expenditure progressively rising from 1.2 per cent of Community GNP in 1993 to 1.27 per cent in 1999;
- a further shift in the composition of expenditure along the same lines as Delors I with agriculture set to fall to 46 per cent of the total budget in 1999 and structural operations to increase to 35 per cent;
- a continuation of the British rebate;
- the same four 'own resources' but with the VAT rate to be reduced from 1.4 to 1 per cent by 1999.

Thus, in general, Delors II was similar to Delors I: it may well free the EC from budgetary disputes, it continued the shift of expenditure from the CAP to structural operations and, once again, introduced greater equity: the shift away from the regressive VAT and the implied increase in the GNP-based resource adds a further element of progressivity.

As in 1988, the CAP was also further reformed, although agreement was not reached easily – it took five drafts by the Portuguese presidency alone, before the reform was agreed in mid-1992. The main elements were as follows:

- a 29 per cent decrease in the price of cereals over three years;
- a 5 per cent decrease in the price of butter over two years (the price of skimmed milk powder remains unchanged); the quota system will continue until the year 2000 but there will be no immediate cuts in diary quotas;
- a 15 per cent decrease in the price of beef over three years;
- various accompanying measures to promote environmental protection, afforestation of agricultural land and early retirement for older farmers.

In general, prices are being moved much closer to world levels and this should result in export subsidies virtually disappearing and agricultural expenditure stabilising by 1996/97. Moreover, although they may not go as far as the Commission's original proposals, these reforms are radically different from earlier efforts: the large price cuts and the shift in emphasis from price support to direct income supplements lays the ground for transforming the CAP into a much improved policy.

Relaunching the Community: the Single European Act and the Single European Market

With substantial progress being made to address its budgetary and agricultural blight, the Community was freed from its paralysis and in a position to revive its integrationist aspirations. The beginnings of this revival were rather muted and are to be found in the agreement at the Fontainebleau summit to set up an ad hoc committee of 'personal representatives' of government heads under the chairmanship of James Dooge, leader of the Irish Senate. (The Irish assumed the EC presidency in the second half of 1984.) The Dooge Committee eventually reported to the Milan summit in June 1985 and made a number of rather familiar proposals to reform the EC's institutional structure. At this stage, it seemed quite probable that the Dooge Report would go the same way as the Tindemans Report on European Union and the Draft Treaty of European Union approved by the European Parliament in 1984. However, one proposal – for an intergovernmental conference (IGC) to discuss the next stage – was put to a vote and, despite opposition from Britain, Denmark and Greece, it was decided to pursue this.

In spite of their position, the three dissenting members felt compelled to take part in the IGC, reassured by the knowledge that any decisions had to be taken unanimously. The document that was agreed – the Single European Act (SEA) – fell far short of the aspirations of even the Dooge Report but it did contain something for everyone (which was why it was acceptable).[4] On the face of it, it did little more than put the Community back on the track of the Treaty of Rome, particularly as, ostensibly, its main element was the completion of the single (common) market (which appealed to the British and the Danes and won their support). However, it had much potential for extension, a point to which those countries with a minimalist approach to integration, who had opposed the IGC, seemed blind. More specifically, the institutional reforms clearly took the EC nearer to the edge of the slippery slope of federalism and, although economic and monetary union was largely excluded (despite Delors' best efforts), it was the logical next step after the completion of the single market and did not stay off the agenda for long.

Four countries had difficulties with ratifying the SEA. Initially, the Italians held out because they thought it did not go far enough, the Greeks in symbolic support of the Danes and probably because of various concerns about loss of sovereignty, and the Danes because of the well known Danish popular doubts about any further integration; eventually, a referendum was held (which effectively became a vote on Danish membership of the EC) and the SEA was narrowly approved. Then, shortly before the SEA was to come into force at the beginning of 1987, the Irish government had to bow to a court ruling and hold a referendum. The problem was the reference to security in the SEA which conflicted with the Irish constitution which required it to be amended. Approval for the change was duly sought and given, and the SEA came into force in July 1987.

Ultimately, it was a rather modest document although it still represented a major achievement in the light of the state of the Community in the early 1980s. It lacked a dominant central focus but rather was something of a *pot pourri* which sought to tidy up the Treaty basis of the Community by putting a number of EC activities on a more formal basis and to press forward by initiating progress in an number of new areas and modifying the decision-making process to facilitate this. More specifically:

- the completion of the internal market (see below) was formally adopted as an objective and became Article 8A of a revised Treaty of Rome (EEC);
- a number of areas in which the EC was already active – the environment, research and development and regional policy – were formally incorporated into the EEC Treaty;
- the EPC procedure and the European Council (summits) which had always operated outside the Treaties were given a legal basis (although not by Treaty incorporation);
- a new means of legislating was established for ten areas (which were mainly concerned with the creation of the single market) whereby the single reading of legislative proposals by the Parliament and Council of Ministers was replaced by two readings; the Parliament's powers were then marginally enhanced by

only allowing the Council to overturn Parliamentary amendments at its second reading by a unanimous vote;
- the Parliament's role was further enhanced by the introduction of the 'assent procedure' which required its approval (by
an absolute majority) of the accession of new members to the
EC and association agreements with third countries;
- the use of (qualified) majority voting in the Council was extended
to cover two-thirds of the single market measures (although
unanimity was still required for the more contentious areas,
notably taxation, free movement of people and employees'
rights and interests);
- the workload of the Court of Justice was eased with the creation
of a junior appendage – the Court of First Instance – to deal
with cases in a few specific areas.

Thus the SEA was rather constrained by the need to secure the acquiescence of those member states with rather minimalist objectives and, indeed, was consequently disappointing for many
proponents of further European integration. However, it sowed the
seeds for much more than its somewhat meagre contents suggested.

The flagship of the SEA, and indeed of the EC, soon became the
single market programme (SMP). The immediate source of the
SMP was the Cockfield White Paper[5] which appeared in mid-1985.
However, in reality its origins lay in the Treaty of Rome. The fundamental core of the EEC had been a customs union to be
extended into a common market by the free movement of factors
of production. However, whilst tariff barriers had been removed,
the development of non-tariff barriers meant that trade was still im-
peded, whilst the majority of the measures required to establish the
common market had simply not been taken. The White Paper
sought to complete this original task and create a single market
within which the four freedoms (of movement) – of goods, services,
capital and people – would apply. Three types of non-tariff barriers
were identified:

- Physical barriers: these exist at customs posts and relate to
goods (import controls and documentation, veterinary and
plant health controls, etc.) and people (passports, immigration controls, baggage searches, etc); clearly, with regard to the
latter, there is an important issue concerning the need for

alternative measures to facilitate asylum and immigration policy and the suppression of international terrorism and drug
trafficking.
- Technical barriers: these impede all four freedoms. The essential element for goods is the differing technical standards
which prevailed in different member states. Previous EC practice had been to try and negotiate European standards but this
had proved to be time-consuming and not very successful. As
part of the SMP, this was largely replaced by a system where
only essential requirements had to be agreed collectively and
anything beyond this is subject to the principle of mutual recognition – thus if a product is acceptable in Germany or Spain
or any other EC member state then it is also acceptable in
Greece or Ireland or any other part of the EC. This speeded
progress up considerably. Other areas covered related to free
movement of labour and the professions, a common market
for services (particularly transport and financial services), the
liberalisation of capital movements, harmonisation of company law and rules on intellectual and industrial property
rights and public procurement (the purchase of good and services by governments and the public sector); the latter was particularly important as it accounts for about 15 per cent of
Community GDP.
- Fiscal barriers; indirect taxation obviously creates significant dis-
tortions. Consequently, the approximation of VAT rates and ex-
cise duties was considered an essential component of the SMP.

In many ways, the White Paper was a remarkable document because not only did it describe some 300 measures that were necessary to complete the single market but, in an annex, it laid out a
detailed timetable indicating the dates by which each of the
measures should be proposed by the Commission and adopted by
the Council; the target date for completion was 31 December 1992.
It was the adoption of the White Paper with its target date which
gave the SMP its impetus: the '1992 programme' (or more correctly
'1993 programme') was born and a new piece of European Community jargon came into existence.

In general, the benefits to be had from creating a single market
are indicated in the standard theory of customs union.[6] However,
the Commission felt it necessary to produce a rationale specifically

for the SMP. A series of studies were therefore commissioned and the results were summarised in the Cecchini Report.[7] This is a very upbeat estimate of the effects of the SMP – indeed, it does much to undermine the assertion that economics is the 'dismal science'! The Cecchini Report is in two parts: the first identifies the costs of not having a single market (the costs of 'non-Europe') and the second tries to estimate the benefits of its creation. This section is also divided into two, reflecting the two different kinds of techniques that were used:

- The microeconomic estimates consider the impact of removing non-tariff barriers on individual actors in the EC economy, that is consumers, companies and governments. The end results are welfare gains of 4.3–6.4 per cent of (1988) EC GDP and the Report focuses on the mid-point – 5.3 per cent or over ECU 200 billion – as an appropriate summary statistic.[8]
- The macroeconomic estimates make use of macroeconomic models – specifically those of the OECD (INTERLINK) and the Commission itself (HERMES) – and come up with an average gain of 4.5 per cent of Community GDP over the medium term.[9]

The obvious point to make is that both the micro- and macro-economic estimates are of the same order, which implies that some kind of confidence can be attached to them. A second point is that the gains could be even greater because these are what Cecchini calls the 'raw' benefits which can be improved by 'accompanying measures'. Essentially, one effect of the 'raw' benefits is to improve the public budgetary balance by a value of 2.2 per cent of Community GDP. The Cecchini Report postulates that this can be used to stimulate the economy further and after exploring various scenarios settles on the most 'plausible' which indicates an improvement of 7 per cent in the EC's GDP and the creation of 5 million jobs in the medium term.[10]

At first glance this seems to be very good news but even setting aside the criticisms of the Cecchini Report (see below) Cecchini himself identifies a number of 'conditions' that need to be fulfilled for the benefits to come through:[11]

- the strategic response to '1992' had to be positive – companies had to grasp the new opportunities;

- a firm and watchful EC competition policy was required to ensure that non-tariff barriers were not simply replaced by collusive behaviour amongst firms, effectively causing the single market to be still-born;
- the benefits of the SMP had to be shared across the whole Community otherwise individual governments or actors might be pushed into undertaking covert protectionist action;
- convergent and prudent (non-inflationary) policies still had to be followed by the member states;
- EC governments had to be seen to be enacting the SMP efficiently and irreversibly in order to ensure its credibility.

This last point was critical.[12] Member states not only had to agree the single market rules in the Council of Ministers but had to implement them to the letter (and the spirit) of the law. Indeed, delays in transposing single market measures into national law became a significant problem in some countries and a cause of tension within the Community. Moreover, the Cecchini Report attracted a number of criticisms[13] which implied that it might be overstating the benefits, notably:

- the programme is incomplete and inadequate and, in any case, it was extremely optimistic to assume that it would be completed by the end of 1992 even as it stands;
- a large proportion of the benefits stem from economies of scale (the cost savings to be generated by larger production runs) implying that European firms are too small but many economists would dispute this; they would argue that most economies of scale are already being secured and, moreover, in many markets differences in national tastes are such that a European market which could be served by a single homogeneous product does not exist;
- the redistributive effects of the SMP are largely ignored and, implicitly, the transitional costs (such as unemployment) are assumed to be negligible; clearly the rationalisation of production patterns required for the benefits of the SMP to come through will have differential regional effects and will leave some regions and, indeed, countries worse off either temporarily or permanently; at best this implies a need for financial transfers through regional policy, at worse it implies that some

countries will be unwilling to implement the SMP, thereby reducing the overall benefits to the Community;

- allied to this is the argument that the SMP (and the Cecchini Report) neglected the 'social dimension' (which had to be subsequently created) and was for business and not for people;
- the external impact of the SMP is ignored and, in fact, there is only one, rather threatening reference to this in the entire single market;[14] one important implication of the external effect is that if a 'Fortress Europe' is created, or even perceived to be, then it might lead to retaliation which would undermine the benefits of the SMP.

At this point it is only fair to observe that one study[15] actually found much greater benefits – of up to 35 per cent of GDP – but this was based on a theoretical basis that few economists would find acceptable and is not supported by any other estimates. Consequently, there remains a strong case for arguing that the benefits as calculated by the Cecchini Report were overstated. The obvious question then becomes why was so much fuss made about '1992'? The answer is probably twofold: firstly, the effects were still positive and non-negligible (if smaller than the official estimates); secondly, the real importance of the SMP was its psychological effect – it reinvented the Community and set it on an upswing, the like of which had not been seen since the 1950s. The importance of the SMP was not so much in itself but in the way that it prepared the ground for something much greater: the (Maastricht) Treaty of European Union.

The Maastricht Treaty and European Union

Thus there were two internally generated forces driving the European Community towards further integration in the late 1980s: the SEA, with its inbuilt dynamic which encouraged further development, and the SMP, which highlighted the absence of (and therefore the need for) accompanying monetary and social measures. To these should be added a potent external factor which Jacques Delors has called 'the acceleration of history'[16] – that is the events in eastern Europe since 1988: the 1989 revolutions which led to the collapse of communism, the reunification of Germany in 1990 and the collapse of the Soviet Union in 1991. This created pressures for further development of the EC through a number of channels:

- most simply the Community had to respond and, equally important, had to have the structures to respond to events in eastern Europe;
- reunification reawakened old fears about Germany and many saw reinforcement of the Community as the best way of coping with the new Germany;
- the switch from an East–West focus to new security concerns in south-eastern Europe and the Gulf revealed deficiencies in the Community's ability to respond and laid bare the inadequacy of its procedures for political cooperation;
- finally, dramatic change in Europe became almost normal for a few years, and this created pressure for change in the Community and also a climate in which even quite ambitious development of the EC did not seem extraordinary.

The eventual outcome of all this renewed momentum was two intergovernmental conferences (IGCs) on economic union and political union which were initiated at the Strasbourg (December 1989) and Dublin (June 1990) summits, respectively. The IGCs revealed the wide range of opinion across member states ranging from the ultrasupranational and federal Italians whose main fear (along with the Spanish) was relegation to the second division of economic and monetary union (EMU) to the minimalist British with their (ultimately successful) obsession with avoiding the 'F-word' (federalism). The French with their reservations about political union and the Germans with a very fixed view of EMU (involving an independent European central bank charged with maintaining price stability) were somewhere in between. The smaller countries, though less influential, shared various combinations of the concerns of the larger countries.

There was an early debate about the form the final outcome should take: on the one hand, there was the 'tree with branches' model favoured by the more federal elements whilst, on the other, there was the 'three pillars' approach which gave some scope for intergovernmentalism; ultimately, pragmatism won the day and the latter prevailed. The negotiations[17] dragged on throughout 1991 but proceedings were eventually brought to a successful conclusion when the Treaty of European Union (TEU) was signed at Maastricht in December. Ultimately the agreement owed much to the negotiating skills of the Dutch presidency and, more fundamentally, to the fact that all the member states and, indeed, the EC institutions (the Parliament rather more so than the Commission) were able to claim victory on some issues. Thus, in the usual way, heads of state were able to return to the electorates and put their own nationalistic and self-serving gloss on the outcome of the summit. The TEU which they agreed has three main elements or 'pillars':

- the new European Community which builds on existing EC treaties (the ECSC, EEC, and Euratom Treaties and the SEA) and includes economic and monetary union;
- foreign policy and defence cooperation which will essentially develop the European Political Cooperation (EPC) procedure and will remain intergovernmental;
- the justice and home affairs pillar which covers police and judicial cooperation, immigration policy and asylum and is also intergovernmental.

Together these three components constitute the 'European Union'.

There is one final feature of importance – the British 'opt outs'. The first of these gives Britain the right to determine if and when it will join the third stage of economic and monetary union (see below). It is thus more properly described as the right to opt out or in. However, the second opt out is precisely that: Britain has chosen not to participate in the social chapter of the TEU and the enhancement of the EC's social policy (to which the other eleven are party) is attached to the Treaty as a separate agreement.

Within this overall framework there are a number of elements that require further elaboration. Economic and monetary union is taken up in the next section and so the focus here will be on the other important aspects of the TEU. A Common Foreign and Security Policy (CFSP) is to be developed and will take the form of 'common positions' and 'joint actions'. It shall include 'all questions relating to the security of the Union, including the eventual framing of a common defence policy, which might in time lead to a common defence.'[18] The elaboration and implementation of any actions with defence implications are to be undertaken by the (revitalised) Western European Union (WEU). In the Social Protocol, the Eleven (excluding Britain) commit themselves to 'the promotion of employment, improved living and working conditions, proper social protection, dialogue between management and labour, the development of human resources with a view to lasting high employment and the combating of exclusion'.[19] This did not actually add much to the SEA provisions for social policy. However, it does raise various issues concerning the practicability of Britain's opting out, including the possibility of Britain being accused of 'social dumping' (using its lower social provisions to reduce labour costs and attract investment and jobs from its European partners with higher standards).

There was a range of institutional reforms in the TEU. In the first place, various reforms introduced by the SEA were extended, notably the use of qualified majority voting in the Council, the areas covered by the cooperation procedure (whereby the Parliament has two readings and the right to table amendments in some of the areas where the Council takes decisions by majority vote) and the assent procedure (whereby an absolute majority in a Parliamentary vote is required before a measure is finally approved). Secondly, the Parliament's powers were extended in a number of relatively minor ways. It now formally has the right to set up committees of enquiry, appoints an ombudsman and is consulted on the appointment of the Commission, which is then subject to a vote of confidence in the Parliament. Thirdly, a new procedure – co-decision-making – was introduced in a limited number of fields.[20] This is identical to the cooperation procedure except whereas under the latter the Parliament's amendments at second reading can be rejected by the Council if unanimous, under co-decision a conciliation committee has to be convened and if a compromise does not emerge then the Parliament can, as a last resort, reject the legislation. This is clearly a negative power and, indeed, the British government referred to it as the 'negative assent procedure' (finding the term 'co-decision' distasteful). Nevertheless, it does represent a new departure in EC decision-making procedures.

Finally, there are four other elements of the TEU that merit attention:

- The establishment of a Committee of the Regions 'with advisory status'.[21] This creates a direct channel through which regional representatives can participate in the EU's decision-making process. Although it is rather like the ineffective Economic and Social Committee (ECOSOC) and, indeed, shares its administrative machinery, it has a much more focused constituency and hence much greater potential than the latter.

- The creation of a new Cohesion Fund to fund 'projects in the fields of environment and trans-European networks in the area of transport infrastructure.'[22] This is a substantial source of funds rising from ECU 1.5 to 2.6 billion during the 1993–9 financial perspective. It is clearly geared to compensating the poorer regions from the inevitable worsening of regional imbalances the EMU would entail.

- The concept of common citizenship of the European Union.[23] This is modest in content, involving extensions of electoral rights throughout the Union, the sharing of consular services outside the EU and so on, but is highly symbolic.

- The principle of subsidiarity is enshrined in the TEU.[24] In general this requires policy decisions to be taken at the appropriate level, be it local, regional, national or European. However, there are differing interpretations of its impact and purpose, with the British seeing it as a way of restricting the powers of the Commission whilst the Germans view it as a means of protecting the constitutional position of the Länder. Whilst the Commission has become more circumspect in its policy proposals, subsidiarity can obviously work both ways and will, in some circumstances, actually strengthen the argument for taking decisions at European (Union) level.

The Treaty of European Union is thus a complex document and the member state governments completed the negotiations with some relief. However, the actual negotiations of the TEU proved to be only half the story as the Treaty now had to be ratified by each member. Unfortunately, in the face of economic downturn, the mood changed in the EU in 1992 and it became clear that the enthusiasm of governments for extending European integration was running a considerable way ahead of popular opinion. The result was that several countries had difficulties in ratifying the TEU[25] and the Treaty did not come into effect until November 1993, eleven months late.

The French only managed to vote narrowly in favour after their referendum degenerated into a vote of confidence in Mitterand. The British Conservative government found its small majority squeezed by its own 'Euro-sceptics' and a Labour opposition highly critical of the opt out of the Social Chapter. The German government faced a certain amount of popular hostility to the possibility that the deutschmark might be replaced by the ECU. More importantly, it had to await the outcome (and ultimate defeat) of a case in the Constitutional Court brought by several prominent figures who argued that ratifying the TEU would infringe the German Basic Law.[26] However, the real problem was Denmark. The (narrow) vote against the TEU in the Danish referendum on 2 June 1992 was all the more traumatic for the EU in general as Denmark was the first member state in which the Treaty had been put to the test of public opinion. The campaign exposed the deep divisions over European integration in Denmark and the opposition to any further loss of sovereignty and the fears about the possible effects on the high Danish social and environmental standards. Ultimately, the Danes were offered two opt outs – of the third stage of EMU and of deliberations and actions under the CFSP which have defence implications; some assurances were also given that the concept of European citizenship did not threaten that of national citizenship. This proved sufficient and, in a second referendum in May 1993, the Danes were able to approve the TEU.

The TEU could then come into effect, albeit belatedly. It is obviously the most important document in the history of European integration since the Treaty of Rome (EEC). It is very complex and, although it lacks the 'F-word' it contains much to please those of a federalist persuasion; on the other hand, major parts of it are clearly intergovernmental. It is thus not clear that the euphoria that surrounded this 'historic' agreement is fully justified. The TEU does take some decisions but is, in many ways, better considered as an agenda or framework. A great deal is yet to be determined and, indeed, much of the Maastricht agenda will be reconsidered at the 1996 intergovernmental conference. For example, it is not clear who will be in the first wave of EMU, particularly given the problems that the EMS has experienced, and the EU has trodden this path before and not reached the end. Moreover, many elements – such as the CFSP – have only principles and procedures and need to be fleshed out by practice and, furthermore, there have already been various problems which have slowed down progress in key areas like justice and home affairs. However, one (probably unintended) effect of the TEU is clear: it has moved Europe closer towards a multi-speed EU. Such an arrangement is incorporated into the Treaty through only partial membership of EMU and the British and Danish opt outs.[27] The TEU may eventually be regarded as a significant turning point, although perhaps not quite in the way that its more enthusiastically federalist architects would have wished.

From EMS to economic and monetary union

The centrepiece of the first pillar – the new European Community – of the TEU was undoubtedly economic and monetary union (EMU). Of course, this is by no means a new ambition and the previous chapter described the unsuccessful effort to achieve this in the 1970s. It is perhaps useful to define what precisely EMU is, which turns out to be rather more straightforward for monetary than for economic union. There is common agreement that the former consists of a single currency or permanently and irrevocably fixed exchange rates,[28] a European central bank implementing a common European monetary policy, the pooling of reserves and free capital movement. Economic union is more controversial: at one extreme lies the view of economic liberals who would see it as little more than a single market with market forces essentially left to get on with it; at the other end of the spectrum, there are those who are committed to strongly interventionist government policies who would regard economic union as being much more and requiring a whole range of common policies. The version of EMU espoused by the TEU lies somewhere in between, and a reasonable approximation is provided by the Delors Report which describes economic union in terms of four basic elements: the single market, competition policy, structural and regional policies, and macroeconomic policy coordination (including budgetary matters).[29] However, this issue of definition is rarely explicitly addressed even in the academic literature. The tendency is to refer to economic and monetary union but actually to focus much more on monetary than economic union and what follows here will reflect that practice.

The EMU provisions grew out of the EMS which was the much more modest successor – seeking merely to create 'a zone of monetary stability' – that emerged from the ashes of the rather grandiose EMU 1980 project. EMS operations began in 1979 and had been progressively more stable, culminating in effectively fixed exchange rates in the five years preceding the crisis in September 1992. Indeed, to the surprise of many, in the period 1979–92, the EMS was generally considered a success (with some qualifications). In particular:

- Currencies in the exchange rate mechanism (ERM) were more stable than they had been before 1979 and compared to non-ERM currencies since 1979.[30] Moreover, realignments had been carried out promptly and efficiently so as to be largely free of speculation.
- EMS has provided a more efficient framework for reducing inflationary expectations (because of the linkage with Germany) and hence for counter-inflationary policies. This is a more controversial claim although there is no doubt that many countries have tried to use the EMS for this purpose.
- Not only nominal but also real exchange rates (the nominal rate corrected for relative prices), which are a measure of competitiveness, have been more stable within the ERM.

It was partly on the back of this success that the Committee on Monetary Union was established at the Hanover summit, under the chairmanship of Jacques Delors, to draw up a plan for economic and monetary union. The seeds of this had been effectively sowed by the SEA, particularly its references to economic cohesion and the adoption of the SMP; indeed, many regarded a single currency as a logical consequence of a single market.[31] The resulting Delors Report,[32] echoing the strategy of the 1970s, proposed a three-stage approach to EMU: in Stage I all member states would join the ERM; Stage II would involve the creation of a European Central Bank and its gradual acquisition of monetary competencies; and Stage III would see the transfer of full economic and monetary authority to the EC and the irrevocable fixing of exchange rates (and subsequently a single currency).

At the Madrid summit in June 1989 it was agreed to proceed to the first stage of EMU on 1 July 1990 but it was decided that the subsequent stages needed further consideration and the IGC on EMU was set up at the Strasbourg December 1989 summit. The

EMU section of the TEU that emerged was essentially based on German conditions and a French timetable. There were five convergence criteria that member states had to fulfil before they could participate in the third and final stage:

- price stability: the inflation rate should be no more than 1.5 per cent above the average of the three EC countries with the lowest price rises;
- interest rates: long-term interest rates should be no more than 2 per cent above the average of the three EC countries with the lowest rates;
- deficits: national budget deficits should be less than 3 per cent of GDP;
- debts: the public debt ratio must not exceed 60 per cent of GDP;
- currency stability: a national currency must not have devalued within the previous two years and must have remained within the 'normal fluctuation margins'[33] of the ERM during the same period.

Stage II of EMU began on 1 January 1994 with the creation of the European Monetary Institute (EMI), sited in Frankfurt, which is to pave the way for the final stage. Also during Stage II national central banks are to be granted their independence and governments are to avoid excessive budgetary deficits. Finally, if a majority of member states fulfil the convergence criteria then a special Council, meeting before the end of 1996, can agree to move to Stage III on 1 January 1997 (with only those states participating). If no majority exists then Stage III will begin with those states that are ready (even if they comprise a minority) on 1 January 1999.[34]

Thus the EC seemed at last to be set fair on a course to economic and monetary union. The only concern was that one of the great ironies of the TEU was that, at the time of the Maastricht summit, only two member states fulfilled all five conditions for participation in the final stage of EMU and this 'group' did not include Germany (because of the inflationary and budgetary impacts of reunification). However, things were to get even worse as the ERM all but collapsed in 1992–3. There was a lull before this storm when the first stage of EMU seemed to be moving towards completion as first Spain (June 1989), then Britain (October 1990) and finally Portugal

(April 1992) joined the ERM. (This left only Greece – which was not expected by anyone to be in an economic position to participate for some time – outside the ERM.) The British volte-face had been a long time coming and the decision came, in a sense, from the fact that Britain had run out of reasons not to join, rather than from any sense of genuine enthusiasm. The superiority of an exchange rate target over a monetary target, particularly if the former was connected to the deutschmark, was becoming more widely accepted and many of the barriers to sterling's involvement (such as Britain's position as an oil exporter) simply seemed less important. However, British scepticism remained and there was some question as to whether the pound had entered the ERM at too high a rate.

The storm broke in September 1992. There was no single trigger but a combination of factors, notably economic recession in Europe, high German interest rates, falling American interest rates and a stagnant US economy, and political uncertainties stemming from problems over the ratification of the TEU. The ERM's Nordic satellites were the first targets: the Finns were forced to float their currency in early September and the Swedes only maintained their peg by raising overnight lending rates to draconian levels (and were ultimately forced to abandon their link in November). The Italians devalued by 7 per cent on 13 September but were then, along with the British, forced to leave the system altogether on 'Black Wednesday' (15 September); on the same day the Spanish devalued by 5 per cent. Moreover, the British departure was acrimonious: it was accompanied by accusations that the Germans had been more willing to support the franc than the pound and that remarks made by the Bundesbank President had been unhelpful. The Spanish, Portuguese and Irish introduced exchange controls (in violation of the single market rules) but they could not stave off the inevitable: the peseta (again) and the escudo devalued by 6 per cent in November and the punt by 10 per cent in January 1993. The malaise continued. In May the peseta (8 per cent) and the escudo (6.5 per cent) devalued again. Then in the middle of the year, as the French cut interest rates to try and alleviate their recession whilst the Germans showed little inclination to cut theirs, matters came to a head and the ERM virtually collapsed at the end of July. The possibility of the deutschmark leaving the ERM was discussed but the eventual decision was to continue but with the fluctuation bands widened from

2.25 to 15 per cent. Such wide bands might have been expected to preclude any speculative pressures and consequent devaluations but the respite was for only eighteen months and in early March 1995 the peseta and escudo were forced to devalue again by 7 and 3.5 per cent respectively.

The consequences of all this for EMU are clearly inauspicious. As one commentator put it, the provisions for EMU set out in the TEU 'received rough treatment at the hands of both markets and voters'.[35] Indeed, despite the continued bullishness of the Commission, the Finance Ministers of at least four EC member states (Britain, Germany, Ireland and Luxembourg) were openly sceptical about the prospect of a move to the final state of EMU in 1997 on the grounds that 'the economic fundamentals were not in place'.[36] Whether EMU will be any more feasible in 1999 remains to be seen. One possibility is that the convergence criteria might be relaxed to make participation easier. However, this is a dangerous course of action as accepting weak members amounts only to storing up future problems; in any case, such a change would be strongly opposed by the Germans. Meanwhile, the Commission is attempting to respond to the economic recession in Europe by a number of more positive measures, notably its White Paper on growth, competitiveness and employment[37] which sought to establish a medium-term economic strategy for the Community.

More enlargement: from ten to fifteen and beyond?

In parallel with the efforts to press forward with further integration the EC had continued to enlarge by admitting Spain and Portugal;[38] both had applied for membership as early as 1977 (in July and March, respectively). These countries were similar to Greece in that they were relatively poor Mediterranean states which had just emerged from periods of military dictatorship, but they were to prove much less problematical in the long run and more *communautaire* than the Greeks had been. However, the actual negotiations were more arduous than those with Greece (which had rather taken the view that it should join now and resolve its problems later). The motivation for accepting the Iberian applications was political – locking these nascent democracies into the Western European democratic system – but the difficulties were economic. Problems arose on both sides and almost exclusively with regard to Spain. In the Community delays were caused by the French insistence that the EC should resolve the problems of the first enlargement – that is the British budgetary dispute – before it embarked on another. These budgetary problems were significant as accepting two new members, which would clearly be net beneficiaries from the budget, at a time when the 'own resource' ceiling was being rapidly approached was incongruous (if not impossible). Thus the negotiations experienced considerable delay as the internal EC wrangle dragged on. There were several issues relating to Spain:

- the Common Fisheries Policy was threatened by the Spanish fishing fleet which was nearly equal in size to that of the entire existing Community;
- France and Italy were concerned about the impact of absorbing the Spanish agricultural sector on their producers;
- in the industrial field there were a number of worries, relating notably to the low wages of Iberian producers and their steel and textile industries, areas in which the EC was already suffering from overcapacity problems.

It was not until after the Fontainebleau summit in 1984 that progress could be made paving the way for the Iberian accession in 1986. Portugal, as a small and relatively poor country, posed little threat to the economies of existing EC members so the Portuguese were somewhat unlucky to find their application linked with that of Spain and therefore delayed.

The beginnings of the Iberian enlargement had preceded the relance of the EC and had been relatively straightforward. However, from the late 1980s the events triggered by the SEA and the collapse of the Soviet bloc were to lead to a deluge of membership applications, some of them from the most unlikely sources, which were to raise the issue of further enlargement to a critical level. The most important, single catalyst for this increased interest in the EC was the SMP which raised the profile of the Community and caused fears of a 'Fortress Europe'. The effect of this was to make many countries around the world re-examine their relationship with the EC and those that were eligible have virtually all applied to join or signalled an intention to do so. There are three groups:[39]

- the countries of EFTA, three of which actually joined the EU in 1995;
- the countries of Central and Eastern Europe which had formerly been Soviet satellites or republics;
- a diverse group of northern Mediterranean states.

The first to formally apply was Turkey (1987) followed by Austria (1989), Cyprus and Malta (1990), Sweden (1991), Finland, Switzerland and Norway (1992), and Poland and Hungary (1994). The Community was anxious to hold back this flood and to set itself firmly on the course of further integration before accepting new members. Consequently, it sought to delay any enlargement negotiations until it had completed the SMP, ratified the TEU and agreed the Delors II budget package. Indeed, in the short run (and probably, in some cases, in the long run), the Community preferred to offer an alternative to accession, the precise nature of which differed between the three groups.

The 'EFTAns'[40] were on the top of the EC's list as they were its largest trading partner, accounting (before 1995) for a quarter of its total external trade (as much as Japan and the USA combined). There were longstanding bilateral agreements between the EC and individual EFTA states but, from 1984, EFTA and the EC began to move towards a multilateral relationship which culminated in the European Economic Area which finally came into effect in 1993. The EFTAns were driven to this by their deep concern about the impact of the SMP on their economies, in particular the fear that they would be excluded from the EC market. The EEA allowed them to be part of the single market whilst remaining outside the EC. Initially this suited both sides: it allowed the EC to postpone further enlargement and the EFTAns to continue to indulge their preference for intergovernmental cooperation which had led them to join EFTA and not the EC in the first place.

However, it quickly became clear that the EEA was not wholly satisfactory as it forced the EFTA countries to obey rules made by the EC12 since, as non-members, they did not have a seat at the EC decision-making table; furthermore, it was the EC's Court of Justice that was the ultimate legal authority. Thus, in a sense, EEA membership implied a greater loss of sovereignty than EC membership. In the light of this, the continued economic imperative of the single market, and the relaxation of their security constraint due to the demise of the Soviet Union, three EFTA neutrals – Austria, Sweden and Finland – successfully pursued EU membership and joined the Union at the beginning of 1995. In a re-run of the events of 1971–2 (and for much the same reasons) Norway also negotiated terms of accession but then decided not to join after a negative referendum. Turning briefly to the remaining EFTAns: Iceland continues to stand aloof from the EU for the present, Liechtenstein is content with the EEA, and Switzerland, which is a unique case,[41] could not even bring itself to vote to join the EEA in its 1992 referendum and, therefore, its relationship with the EU continues to be governed by bilateral agreements.

The Central and Eastern Europeans pose a difficult problem. The EC is essentially caught between the political necessity of being very positive towards them and the economic reality that these countries are very far from being economically ready for accession. The dilemma has been resolved for the time being by negotiating (or in the case of the weaker countries offering the possibility of) 'Europe Agreements' which are a form of association involving a free trade area in industrial goods and rather more limited concessions in agriculture, political dialogue, economic, financial and cultural cooperation and an institutional framework; in addition, there is a reference in the preamble of these agreements to EU accession as an ultimate (but not automatic) goal, although this was conceded only very reluctantly by the Union. However, association is even further away from full EU membership than the EEA and is unlikely to satisfy the aspiring members in Central and Eastern Europe for long. The frontrunners are the Visegrad Four – particularly Poland and Hungary which have already applied, the others being the Czech and Slovak Republics – followed, at some distance, by Bulgaria and Romania. In the longer run the Baltic Republics will probably apply and, coming up rather more quickly perhaps, is Slovenia.

The final (Mediterranean) group is rather heterogeneous.[42] The EU's favoured relationship with these countries is probably a customs union and indeed, for the time being, this is all that is scheduled to happen with Turkey (at the end of 1995).

Turkey has aspired to EU membership for longer than any other current candidate and, indeed, some actual members. However, the prospect of Turkish accession raises questions on virtually every front – economic, political, social, demographic and cultural – and only in the security sphere, as a valued member of NATO, does Turkey appear to be an asset. The likelihood of Turkey joining in the immediate future is therefore very limited. However, the EU has been driven to go much further with Cyprus and Malta. Greek pressure has led to a commitment to open negotiations with Cyprus six months after the end of the 1996 IGC. The main problem is the political divide on the island, since economically the Greek Cypriots are comfortably on a par with the poorer EU member states. Conversely the drawback with Malta is economic rather than political. Accession requires reform in 'so many different areas (tax, finance, movement of capital, trade protection, competition law, etc.) and require[s] so many changes in traditional patterns of behaviour that what is effectively involved is a root-and-branch overhaul of the entire regulatory and operational framework of the Maltese economy.'[43] Malta is in the process of making these adjustments.

The 1995 enlargement to 15 and the almost certain further enlargement to the east and south to 20-plus raises critical issues for the European Union, both specific and general. In the first place there are a whole range of policies which could be radically affected, for example:

- Will the CFSP be undermined by the accession of three neutral EFTAns and the subsequent accessions of non-aligned Malta and Cyprus?
- How will existing EU members respond to the radical overhaul of the CAP that would be inevitable following the membership of Poland, Hungary and other former Soviet satellites (and Turkey) since agricultural support could not possibly continue at current levels?
- What will EMU look like given that few, if any, of the post-1995 new members are likely to fulfil the convergence criteria? Is a multispeed EMU therefore inevitable?
- What will be the impact on the EU budget of accepting so many relatively poor members?

There is also a wide range of institutional questions stemming from two essential issues:

- How does a structure designed for a Community of 6 cope with a European Union of 20 or more – does it mean, for example, more majority voting in the Council and a smaller Commission with some countries sharing a Commissioner?
- How are the differences in the size of member states reflected in the institutions? The main question relates to whether or not the disproportionately high representation of smaller states can be continued when they are in the majority. An important subsidiary issue concerns the role of micro-states like Malta and Cyprus – is it credible for them to take their turn as Council President?

Finally, there is the old 'widening' (enlarging) versus 'deepening' (further integration) debate in which the compatibility of accepting new members with more substantial integration is questioned. Certainly, the EC12 were well aware of this which is why they sought to complete the single market and agree the TEU and the 1993–9 financial profile before accepting any more members. The most basic fear is that with too many members the EU decision-making system may suffer from the institutional equivalent of 'gridlock'. More fundamentally, there are concerns, particularly within the original EC6, that some of the new members may not share the supranational aspirations of the EU's founding fathers but may have a preference for intergovernmental cooperation or be driven by economic ambitions.

Towards the 1996 Intergovernmental Conference

Thus, in the mid-1990s the European Union finds itself facing major challenges both internally and externally. A remarkable transformation was effected in the 1980s and major steps have been taken since 1985. However, much will depend on the outcome of the 1996 IGC to which, increasingly, all roads seem to lead. In fact, the TEU set the provisional agenda for the IGC which includes:[44]

- consideration of a report on the progress of the CFSP (including the WEU) with the possibility of amending the policy;
- reappraisal of the three pillar structure of the EU;

- consideration of widening the scope of the co-decision procedure;
- a review of the classification by hierarchy of Community legislative acts;
- examination of the possibility of adding to the TEU specific clauses in the fields of civil protection, energy and tourism.

To these three others have been effectively added: the size of the Commission, voting rights in the Council, and the balance between small and large states and the implications of this for the EU's institutions in general.[45] In fact the range of discussion could be much broader as the 'Group of Reflection' which is charged with preparing for the IGC is mandated to consider not only the above items but also 'any other measure deemed necessary to facilitate the work of the institutions and to guarantee their effective operation in the perspective of enlargement'.[46]

The 1996 IGC is therefore likely to be very wide ranging. There is a widespread presumption that the preferred agenda will tend towards the federalist vision at least for a 'hard core' of member states. Indeed, since the majority of those writing on the EU are 'Euro-enthusiasts', it often seems that this is the only admissible vision. But the intergovernmental alternative favoured by the majority of Britons and Scandinavians, a version of which was elaborated by Mrs Thatcher at Bruges in 1988,[47] is equally legitimate; the federalists do not have any automatic, moral right to the high ground. The EU is sometimes compared to a bicycle which has to be pedalled (and go forward) otherwise it will fall over. What the federalists forget is that most bicycles have stands and you can get off, stand the bicycle up and stay where you are (and that this may be a more pleasant place than where you would end up if you kept on pedalling). None of this is intended to prejudice the issue either way but rather to strike a note of balance since any account of the development of the EU will inevitably lean towards the federalist perspective; therefore it is important to point out there are legitimate grounds for debate. Intergovernmentalism is not just footdragging by the British and others. An intergovernmental Europe is not intrinsically inferior to a federal one, it is just different.

Finally, turning to the probable outcome of the IGC, there are two extreme schools of thought. On the one hand, there is what might be called the 'optimist federal view' that the IGC will move the EU significantly further down the road of integration with major institutional reforms, perhaps some progress on the CFSP and steps forward in various other areas. On the other hand, there is the more pragmatic, 'realist' view that experience since 1991 – the public reaction to Maastricht as evidenced by the ratification difficulties, the slow progress with the CFSP and Home Affairs and the virtual collapse of the ERM – has suggested that even the TEU is a bridge too far; consequently, the IGC will be about consolidation, tidying up the TEU, and may even include some backtracking away from more integration. There is also the question of how further enlargement will be handled at the IGC and whether commitments undertaken in this connection will impede further integration. Somewhere between there is a genuinely intermediate position in which some member states tend to one extreme and some to the other. This would create a multispeed or multitier Europe. As already indicated, the TEU itself includes elements of this and a recent German paper[48] from the parties in government addressed this issue very openly. Clearly all this raises fundamental questions about the shape European integration and the European Union should take and, in the present context, what kind of international organisation the EU is going to become.

Conclusion: the European Union as an international organisation

The character and purpose of a regional organisation can perhaps best be judged by examining two factors: its relationship with the outside world and its own internal structure. Unfortunately, in both regards, the European Union lacks clarity. With regard to the first of these, it is clear that the EU does have an external policy, notably:

- the EU has a trade (or trade and aid) agreement with virtually all parts of the world including association agreements, the Lomé Convention and, of course, the EEA;
- the EU has negotiated as a group in the GATT talks, most recently the Uruguay Round and in the four-yearly UNCTAD meetings;
- the EU member states have worked as a unit in the CSCE (even though separate EU representation was not allowed)

and, to some extent, at the UN (although with much less co-
herence);

- the EU has had a seat at Western economic summits since
  1975;
- the EPC procedure, subsequently replaced by the CFSP, has
  led to a range of EU joint statements and actions (although
  there have been failures).

However, whilst the economic element is fairly well defined, this
is not true of the political identity projected by the EU (although it
has to be said that one of the more curious facts about the EU is that
outsiders always perceive it as being much more integrated and
coherent than it actually is). Moreover, even the economic aspect is
muddied by the fact that member states continue to act separately
in their own right (alongside EU actions).

The internal structure of the EU is, in some ways, even more difficult to define because it is obviously a highly contentious issue.
The uneasy compromise between the 'federalists' and the 'intergov-
ernmentalists' may be strained to breaking point at the 1996 IGC
and a 'hard core' may seek to integrate further without their more
reluctant partners. Several possible scenarios can be identified:

- a 'multispeed' Europe is where all member states pursue the
  same objectives but some achieve them later than others because of economic weakness or political disposition;
- a 'multitier' or 'multilayer' Europe or 'Europe of concentric
  circles' is where there is a 'hard core' of member states on a
  kind of fast track surrounded by a 'soft core' of members who
  have only agreed to pursue a (common) subset of the objectives of the 'hard core'; beyond them there could also be a suc-
  cession of 'softer cores' with progressively, more limited
  agendas;
- a 'Europe à la carte' or 'Europe of opt outs' is where every
  member has its own agenda and participates only in those
  policies in which it wants to.

These various expressions are frequently discussed very loosely but
clearly there are important differences amongst them. The alternative to all three is for the EU to continue to integrate 'en bloc' – a
'single speed' Europe – but as ideologies clash in 1996 this may

prove impossible and the possibility of a 'multispeed' or 'multitier' compromise is becoming increasingly likely. All this clearly has an impact on the external face of the EU and adds to the confusion.

Thus, as international organisations go, the European Union remains something of an enigma. It is a curious mix of the supranational and the intergovernmental which incorporates both elements with a degree of the former (the 'European Community') and others which are clearly run along the lines of the latter (the CFSP and Home Affairs). This uniqueness is reflected in the EU's budget which is radically different from those of other international organisations in that the overwhelming majority of it – 95 per cent – is spent, not on administration, but on actual policies. Furthermore the EU is not a 'finished' organisation. It was created in an evolutionary form and continues to evolve. However, there is significant disagreement amongst its members as to the direction that this evolution should take and over what the final form of the organisation should be. This is much more marked than in other organisations. Finally there is the question as to whether the EU is a role model for regional integration elsewhere. There have indeed been many imitators but none have been very successful. Arguably the EU is a product of a unique time and unique circumstances and is and will continue to remain outside the behaviourial norms of other international organisations. Perhaps it is not an organisation at all but really is a superstate in the making. The 1996 intergovernmental conference will provide some pointers but the debate will continue.

9 Regional Organisation Outside Europe

There is now a vast number of regional and subregional organisations with a range of functions embracing military, economic, political and cultural cooperation. Rather than attempting to discuss all or even many of these – a task which in one chapter would produce little more than a list of names – I will confine myself here to considering briefly the history and functions of three of the more important regional organisations together with some of their offshoots.

The Organisation of American States (OAS)

The central fact to note about the OAS is the enormous disparity in wealth and power between one of its members, the United States, and the others over most of the postwar period. It was only in 1990 that this bipolarity was diffused by the acceptance of Canada into membership.[1] Indeed it is no exaggeration to say that the history of the OAS and more generally of regional integration in Latin America is largely identical with the history of US policies there and the Latin American response. But alongside this central theme (and to some extent an aspect of it) has emerged another: the search for a distinct Latin American identity. The OAS and other regional organisations have provided an important channel through which both themes have been expressed.

Tensions between US objectives in Latin America and Latin American aspirations for their own region may be seen as part of a more fundamental conflict between two sets of ideas about the American hemisphere, ideas which one author terms 'unilateralism' and 'multilateralism'.[2] The most famous early expression of the 'unilateralist' idea was the Monroe Doctrine of 1823, in which

President Monroe declared a US special interest in the hemisphere as a whole and a determination to exclude European influence from it. In 1905 President Theodore Roosevelt added a 'corollary' to the Monroe Doctrine by which the USA asserted a right to intervene in Latin American affairs to maintain order there. At about the same time as Monroe's statement, Simon Bolivar was proposing one version of the multilateralist idea: a union of the former Spanish colonies of South America.[3] The other version of multilateralism was the concept of Pan-American union (that is including the United States), which first appeared in the 1880s and which was the origin of the present-day OAS.

Pan-Americanism was first promoted by the United States at the first International Conference of American States in 1889, whose aims were to discuss and recommend:

> some plan of arbitration for the settlement of disagreements and disputes that may hereafter arise between them, and for considering questions relating to the improvement of business intercourse and means of direct communication . . . and to encourage such reciprocal relations as will be beneficial to all and secure more extensive markets for the products of each of said countries.[4]

As this makes plain, the primary objective of the Conference – and the chief US interest in calling it – was the development of economic relations amongst the countries involved. This was also the aim of the first regional organisation to be established, the International Union of American States (1890), whose purpose was to collect and disseminate commercial information.[5]

Despite some marginal changes over the next 40 years, including the first steps towards a system for the peaceful settlement of disputes through arbitration and other means, the organisation remained, in effect, what its name suggests: a typical nineteenth-century international union with strictly limited functions. Its four- or five-yearly conferences did, however, provide a forum for the expression of Latin American opposition to the US assumption of a general right of intervention in Latin American affairs: a right implicit in the Monroe Doctrine but which was becoming more of a live issue with the growth of US power. So great was the pressure from its neighbours that at two Pan-American conferences in 1933 and 1936, the United States formally accepted the principle of non-intervention between states.[6] A period of substantial cooperation followed, which reached a peak during the Second World War, and the desire to continue this after the war gave a major impetus to the formation of the OAS.[7] The Latin American countries were also anxious to place their special relationship with the United States on a distinctive institutional basis in order to prevent that relationship from being subordinated to America's global interests in the newly formed UN. It was to a great extent the efforts of the Latin American states at the San Francisco Conference which resulted in Articles 51, 52 and 53 of the UN Charter, encouraging regional organisations to have a substantial role in the settlement of local disputes.

The OAS rests on three treaties. The Inter-American Treaty of Reciprocal Assistance (the Rio Treaty), signed on 2 September 1947, is both an alliance and a collective security pact: it provides for cooperation against aggression from outside as well as by any of its signatories. It also reflects a growing concern with what were seen as Communist techniques of subversion by referring to 'aggression which is not an armed attack'.[8] The OAS Charter, agreed at a conference in Bogota, Colombia, between 30 March and 2 May 1948, set out the Constitution of the new organisation. The American Treaty on Pacific Settlement (Pact of Bogota), agreed at the same time, provided for an extensive system for the pacific settlement of disputes, but this has had little subsequent impact.

The OAS Charter reflects the varied concerns of its members. For example, the principle of non-intervention is firmly enshrined in Articles 15 to 20.[9] These prohibit not only military intervention but 'any other form of interference or attempted threat against the personality of the State or against its political, economic and cultural elements'. This is a clear, albeit indirect, statement of the widespread Latin American fear of becoming dependencies of the United States in ways other than the normal political ones. Equally, however, US concerns are reflected in various affirmations of the principles of representative democracy and individual liberty. In other respects the Charter is a sweeping proclamation of a great range of supposedly shared values and beliefs which are virtually meaningless as guides to action – the statements, for instance, that 'the education of peoples should be directed towards justice, freedom and peace', or that 'the spiritual unity of the continent is based on respect for the cultural values of the American countries and requires their close co-operation for the high purpose of civilisation'.

The OAS has had a troubled history from the outset. On the one hand many Latin American states believed Washington to be using the Organisation to pursue its Cold War conflict with the Soviet Union and to legitimise US interventions against left-wing regimes in the region. Yet, from the other perspective, despite the affirmation of democracy which is at the heart of the OAS Charter, it is only in the present decade that freely elected governments predominate in the region. A second source of dissension in the middle years of the postwar era was the divergent US and Latin American views about the OAS role in relation to economic development and the tendency for Latin American countries to align themselves with the third world in questions of international economic relations. During these years the deficiencies of the OAS Charter became increasingly apparent, a matter only partly resolved by the revisions of the Charter in 1967, which came into force in 1970. However during the first 20 years of its existence the OAS demonstrated a modest success in peacekeeping and some 40 disputes were resolved by its machinery.[10]

The first major intervention came in 1954, when the leftist government of Guatemala, which had expropriated land owned by an American company, was overthrown by an invading force of exiles who apparently enjoyed the support of the United States as well as Guatemala's neighbours, Honduras and Nicaragua. Washington had earlier called for united Latin American action against what it termed a 'bridgehead of international communism'.[11] The United States was able to prevent the UN from taking up the issue by arguing that, as an essentially regional matter, it should be left to the OAS to deal with, a claim resented by several Latin American states because it seemed to deny them some of the benefits of UN membership.[12] The Guatemalan case foreshadowed what was to be a lengthy OAS involvement with the affairs of Castro's Cuba. The United States had been unable to obtain support from the other American countries for a joint intervention against the Cuban government, but in January 1962 it secured OAS agreement to economic sanctions against Cuba for the latter's activities in support of guerrillas in Venezuela. The OAS also declared that 'adherence by any member of the OAS to Marxist-Leninism is incompatible with the Inter-American system' and that, 'this incompatibility excludes the present government of Cuba from participation in the Inter-American system'.[13] Further diplomatic and economic sanctions were voted against Cuba in 1964 and 1967, although several OAS members did not vote for sanctions and Mexico refused to impose them. Following the example of Dr Allende's Marxist government in Chile in 1970, a number of Latin American states re-established relations with Cuba and in 1975 the sanctions were formally ended.[14]

Washington's determination to prevent another Cuban-style government from emerging in Latin America was primarily responsible for its intervention in the Dominican Republic in 1965, for which it sought OAS endorsement. The OAS had earlier become involved in Dominican affairs during the much-hated dictatorship of Trujillo in 1960, when after an OAS investigation into Venezuelan charges of Dominican interference in Venezuelan politics, it was decided to impose economic and diplomatic sanctions against the Dominican Republic. Partly as a consequence of OAS sanctions, Trujillo was overthrown and a period of instability ensued. The US intervention came in April 1965 when a revolutionary group seemed likely to gain control of the government. The OAS as such was not consulted, and its first efforts were directed towards bringing about a ceasefire, with many OAS members highly critical of what they saw as an outright US intervention in the Dominican Republic's domestic affairs. However, a majority agreed to Washington's request that an inter-American peace force be set up to take over the US role in the Dominican Republic. From the US perspective, this would lend a degree of legitimacy, if not respectability, to its operation, and although some Latin American states refused to approve the peace force for this reason, others clearly hoped that it might at least set some constraints on the United States. But there was little support for the US proposal that a permanent peace force be established with the capacity for dealing with similar eventualities in the future.[15]

In disputes where the Cold War did not play a crucial part, the OAS proved to be a useful instrument for effecting a peaceful settlement. It has employed the full range of techniques available to international organisations for this purpose, including fact-finding missions, behind-the-scenes diplomacy by the OAS Secretary-General, mediation, diplomatic pressure and, in the 1960 Dominican case, economic sanctions. Disputes where the OAS has helped to reduce tension include conflicts between Costa Rica and Nicaragua (1948–9), the Dominican Republic and Haiti (1949–50), Cuba and Guatamala (1950), Costa Rica and Nicaragua (1955–6), Honduras and Nicaragua (1957) Panama and Cuba (1959), the Dominican Republic and Haiti (1963–5), El Salvador and Honduras (1969), Costa Rica and Nicaragua (1977), Peru and Ecuador (1981).[16] Several of the earlier disputes were resolved partly through the efforts of the Inter-American Peace Committee, which had been created by the OAS for this purpose, but in 1956 the powers of this body were severely curtailed when it was decided that it could not send an investigative mission to the location of a dispute unless both sides invited it to do so. Without decrying what was undoubtedly a useful role, it may also be observed that, as with other successful exercises in peacekeeping, success was greatest where the OAS was offering, in essence, a way out with the minimum loss of face for two sides which did not really wish to raise the level of hostility between them. In the 1980s the Organisation became increasingly paralysed by the growing divergence between the United States and the Latin American majority. The Falklands war in 1982 was played out on a larger stage than that of a regional organisation but its ramifications were felt within the OAS. There is also a view that in the latter half of the 1980s the Falklands issue was used to deflect attention from the interventionary role being played by the US in Nicaragua and later Granada and Panama.[17]

More recently, OAS conflict resolution efforts have been directed towards assisting the settlement of internal conflicts and crises. This is itself a reflection of the resurgence of the Organisation in the present decade and its emergence from a period of stagnation and marginalisation during the height of the Cold War. The end of the Cold War has provoked a re-evaluation by the United States of its own future role and interests in the region. In June 1990 George Bush launched the Enterprise for the Americas Initiative (EAI) which proposed writing off part of the debt owed to US Agencies, steps to increase foreign investment and the eventual creation of a free trade area covering the whole of the hemisphere.[18] The proposal was received well by the Latin American countries where it was interpreted as heralding a greater equality in approach to solving the region's problems. At the same time there is an increased confidence generated by the Organisation's successful monitoring role, for example in the 1990 Nicaraguan general election and the Contra rebel resettlement, and the Surinam peace agreement of August 1992. However, a partial collapse of the Mexican economy in 1995 demonstrated that earlier hopes that the longstanding Latin American debt problem was effectively resolved were unfounded.

The OAS member states took a significant step forward from the rather aimless *laissez-faire* approach of the past decades when at the 21st General Assembly in June 1991 they strongly reaffirmed their commitment to democracy. The Santiago Commitment to Democracy and the Renewal of the Inter-American System pledged defence and promotion of representative democracy and human rights in the region, and stated a firm resolve to stimulate the process of renewal of the OAS to make it more effective and useful. This was seen by many to be a milestone in the Organisation's history comparable to the 1948 conference which created the original OAS Charter.[19] It has been followed in subsequent years by equally strong commitments. The Protocol of Washington which emerged from the 16th special session of the General Assembly in December 1992 amended the OAS Charter, empowering the General Assembly (by a two-thirds vote) to exclude any member state whose democratically constituted government is overthrown by force. In June the following year, the 23rd session of the General Assembly in the Managuan Declaration confirmed the Organisation's awareness that 'progress made in defence of democratic institutions must be completed by mechanisms which foster and reinforce democratic government in an integral way, thereby improving its ability to face the challenges of economic, social, and cultural development in all the member states.'[20]

The recognition that political, economic, environmental, educational, scientific and security considerations are inextricably linked in the quest for development is a recurring theme of the OAS. However, whilst showing increasing concern to publicise the problems of extreme poverty in the region and recognising that economic development is one of the more significant keys to unlocking some of the other goals, this is not an area where the OAS is particularly well placed to do more than provide a forum for debate. Indeed, there has been a longstanding Latin American discontent with the OAS over its relative ineffectiveness in helping to promote economic development, with some fearing in past years that it was instead an instrument of US economic domination. This was especially so in the immediate postwar years, when the Latin American states failed to achieve their main aim of persuading the United States to introduce a Marshall Plan for the region. It was not until clear signs of Latin American restlessness appeared in the late 1950s that the United States moved to expand the economic role of the OAS by creating an Inter-American Development Bank. This first step was followed by the launching of President Kennedy's Alliance for Progress in 1961. The Alliance for Progress was an ambitious and wide-ranging two-year programme, whose objectives included not only accelerated economic growth in Latin America but internal political, social and economic reforms. Perhaps inevitably such ambitious aims proved impossible to attain, although there is general agreement that the Alliance and the OAS in general performed a useful service in providing some economic aid and technical assistance and also in coordinating economic planning in Latin America. However, the opposing viewpoint is that the Alliance for Progress was merely another device to enable the United States to pursue policies of economic neo-colonialism in Latin America. It was certainly the case that Washington linked its aid programmes under the Alliance for Progress to its general anti-Communist policies in the region. In the United States itself another ground for opposition to allocating a larger economic role to the OAS was that this would merely entail a wasteful duplication of work already being carried out by UN agencies.

Although the most optimistic aims of the early 1960s failed to materialise in the following three decades, there were some steady, if unspectacular, achievements in certain areas. One was in the field of technology transfer: an important aspect of the wider demands from the Third World for a New International Economic Order. The OAS decided in 1967 to embark upon a major programme to promote the transfer of technology to Latin America. An evaluation of this programme ten years later found that, despite various shortcomings, genuine progress had been made in this field and a foundation had been laid down on which it was possible to build further.[21] To the present day the continuance of this technical assistance activity receives support from OAS member countries: $24 million in 1992. Unlike other agencies such as the World Bank which has its own projects and priorities, the OAS is structured to meet direct requests from its members. The smallest countries in particular which have little or no access to alternative sources of technical advice and training are anxious for this situation to continue.[22] Other commentators have suggested that an organisation so starved of funds might sensibly leave such projects to the larger institutions.[23]

The sense of dissatisfaction with the more general economic dimension of the OAS was one of the factors which underlay the 1967 revisions of the OAS Charter. These raised the status of the OAS Economic and Social Council and incorporated as an ultimate objective the economic integration of Latin America. They also replaced one of the OAS bodies, the virtually moribund Inter-American Conference, with a General Assembly, which was to meet annually and whose powers were to be enhanced.

By the time the amendments came into force in 1970, they had already been overtaken by the rapidly changing climate of international opinion. In particular the Latin American countries increasingly saw themselves as part of a third world that was engaged in a fundamental confrontation over international economic matters with the industrialised countries, at whose head stood the United States. During the 1970s the Latin American states proposed sweeping changes in the OAS Charter, by which it would enunciate the principle of 'collective economic security' with sanctions against 'economic aggression'.[24] Understandably, perhaps, Washington resisted these demands.

The economic agenda for the hemisphere in the 1990s is very clearly dominated by trade agreements both internal – Bush's vision of a single free trade area 'from Alaska to Patagonia' – and also the trade bloc that the region is able to present to the rest of the world. When Mexico agreed the draft North America Free Trade Area (NAFTA) with the US and Canada in August 1992 it acted as a spur to other countries in Central and Latin America to make progress on their own plans towards greater integration. This is not at variance with the previous focus. The emphasis of all postwar schemes for regional integration has been primarily economic rather than political and as such as been represented in a variety of subregional groupings rather than through the OAS proper.

The Organisation of Central American States (ODECA) was established by the Charter of San Salvador in October 1951 (revised in December 1962) between Costa Rica, El Salvador, Guatemala, Honduras and Nicaragua. Its purpose was stated to be the formation of an 'economic-political' community.[25] ODECA was followed in December 1960 by the creation of a Central American Common Market (CACM), which aimed to establish a customs union in the short term, and in the long term to unify the economies of its members and jointly promote the development of Central America.

The Central American experiment has enjoyed only a limited success. It led to a massive growth in intra-regional trade in the earlier years although this fell off later.[26] There was also a significant increase in industrial production and investment, although the vital agricultural sector was much less affected by the union.[27] Also, the two poorest countries, Honduras and Nicaragua, gained less than the others from the grouping; an outcome which caused much dissension.[28] An unexpected paradox was encountered during the 1960s when it became apparent that a union set up in part to liberate its members from foreign economic domination had actually succeeded in attracting greater foreign investment. Increasing revolutionary violence in the 1980s undermined the possibilities of developing closer economic links over this period. However, in 1990 ODECA members (with Panama, later to become a member, as an observer) signed an Economic Action Plan for Central America which agreed that discussions should proceed on the revival of CACM. Six months later these heads of state, together with Mexico and the Foreign Ministers of Venezuela and Colombia, agreed to accelerate negotiations for a free trade agreement, to be implemented by 1996 at the latest.

The Latin American Free Trade Association (LAFTA) established in February 1960 by Argentina, Brazil, Chile, Mexico, Peru and Uruguay – with Bolivia, Colombia, Ecuador, Paraguay and Venezuela joining later – experienced similar difficulties to CACM. Its goal was the achievement of a free trade area through the progressive reduction of tariffs and other restrictions on trade. Intra-regional foreign trade grew after its establishment but only to around 10 per cent of the region's total trade. As with CACM, unexpected beneficiaries were foreign investors and the much feared multinational corporations, who were better placed than indigenous industries to exploit the opportunities provided by a larger market.[29] It also had in common with CACM the apparently inequitable distribution of benefits amongst richer and poorer members. In 1990, LAFTA, reconstituted as the Latin American Integration Association (ALADI) sought to address this issue. The retitled organisation comprises the

11 original LAFTA members grouped into three categories: most developed, intermediate and least developed. Tariff treatment varies by category with the least developed countries getting the best terms.[30] However, a certain suspicion has attached to Mexico's apparent reluctance to agree tariff reductions, with some members believing that trade with the developed world, especially the US, preoccupies Mexico to the exclusion of regional needs.[31]

The Andean Group was established in May 1969 by the Cartagena Agreement, as a direct response to LAFTA's inadequacies, by a subgroup comprising Bolivia, Chile, Colombia and Peru, with Venezuela joining in 1973 and assuming something of a leadership role.[32] Its underlying philosophy represents a break with earlier Latin American projects and with the liberal economic assumptions of the Economic Community.[33] Its stated aims include a reduction of economic inequalities amongst its members, with preferential treatment for Bolivia and Ecuador actually specified in the Agreement. One author describes its basic ideology as one of 'developmental nationalism', with individual countries allocated a virtual regional monopoly in the production of certain industrial goods, rather than the pursuit of industrial development through the creation of regionwide enterprises.[34] Moreover the programme is marked by a much stronger element of central planning than previous regionalist endeavours.[35] The Group has also attempted to develop an imaginative response to the problems posed by foreign investment, by which the necessary foreign capital would not be frightened away but its worst features, such as foreign domination of the national economy, might be prevented. This, however, was one of the factors that led to a crisis in the mid-1970s, leading to the withdrawal of Chile, partly on the grounds that the investment code was too restrictive.[36] Before the crisis the Group had achieved substantial increases in trade, although its industrial development programme was already lagging behind the earlier optimistic projections. The Group survived the loss of one of its members and has gone on to make some progress towards trade liberalisation within the remainder, although in 1992 a suggestion of a common foreign tariff which would allow members countries to compete under the same conditions met considerable opposition from Ecuador.[37]

A third group of countries which, while coming under the umbrella of the OAS, needed to form their own subgroup for mutual support and development, were the Caribbean countries. The early years of the postwar period were dominated by their need to achieve independence and self-government. However, their continuing economic and political viability was seen to rest on an ability to integrate sufficiently to offset the disadvantage of their individual small size. The Federation of the West Indies created in 1958 lasted only three years but the need for economic and financial cooperation became if anything more acute. The Caribbean Free Trade Area was created in 1968, encompassing the ten members of the earlier Federation and Guyana. Belize joined in 1971.[38] At the same time, perhaps mindful that the collapse of the earlier Federation was in part due to conflict of interests between the larger and smaller countries of the group, the seven smaller members of CARIFTA founded the Eastern Caribbean Common Market (ECCM).[39] CARIFTA itself was reformed as CARICOM under the Treaty of Chaguaramas in 1975 but like its predecessors failed to achieve the desired economic progress for its members and in the early eighties the advice of a 'Group of Experts' was sought[40] which generated a blueprint for action for the decade, but to little effect. The modest success story of this period was in the Eastern Caribbean with ECCM (later OECS) achieving growth and expansion of trade amongst its members. However this was not matched by harmonisation in, for example, fiscal structures, rather the reverse, and may therefore be self-limiting.

The Organisation of African Unity

As with most international organisations, the OAU was both the culmination of developments over many years and the product of a series of political bargains struck at its inception. Pan-Africanism, the idea of a United States of Africa as an ultimate aspiration, goes back to the beginning of this century[41] and became a dominating theme for several African leaders, notably Kwame Nkrumah of Ghana, which became in 1957 the first African state to gain its independence in the postwar period. However, pre-independence support for the ideal of pan-Africanism soon evaporated amongst leaders of newly sovereign states whose first concern was with the preservation of that sovereignty. Moreover, it was increasingly apparent that what had seemed strong bonds among Africans fighting the common enemy of colonialism were less effective in forging unity after independence. Divisions emerged between Anglophone and Francophone states, between radicals and moderates, and between neighbours now able to dispute what treaties drawn up amongst Europeans had allocated them as borders. Finally, the tensions caused by the outbreak of the Congo crisis in 1960 seemed for a time to push African states into various subregional groupings rather than a single all-embracing entity. During 1961 and 1962, three such groupings were created, known as the Casablanca, Brazzaville and Monrovia groups.[42] Such was the reality confronting the pan-African ideal when a summit conference of all 31 independent African states was held at Addis Ababa in May 1963 to prepare a Charter for an Africa-wide international organisation.

Nkrumah's dreams of a superstate with its own army, parliament and government had been outlined at an earlier Foreign Ministers' conference,[43] but a more pragmatic conception of a loose association of sovereign authorities won the day with only a token bow to pan-Africanism. Ethiopia was prominent in advocating this more modest scheme, but it was widely supported at the conference. The radicals who pressed the case for African Unity were partly appeased by a clear affirmation in the OAU Charter of support for the liberation of Southern Africa: another of their cherished goals.[44]

The OAU differs from other regional organisations in that its principal aims are neither collective security nor the pursuit of economic integration. However, the OAU was given from the outset another of the classic functions of international organisations: the peaceful settlement of disputes. Its role in this regard was referred to briefly in Article 19 of the Charter and set out in more detail in a Protocol of 21 July 1964 (amended in September 1970). This established a Commission of Mediation, Conciliation and Arbitration, although as it turned out most of the OAU's peaceful settlement work was done through informal or ad hoc means. But, not withstanding its possession of this function, the OAU was essentially seen as the embodiment of certain principles and, in a vague way, as the expression of an African identity, rather than as the means of achieving certain specific goals. Its principles are set out in Article 3 of the Charter:

- The sovereign equality of all member States.
- Non-interference in the internal affairs of States.

- Respect for the sovereignty and territorial integrity of each State and for its inalienable right to independent existence.
- Peaceful settlement of disputes by negotiation, mediation, conciliation or arbitration.
- Unreserved condemnation, in all its forms, of political assassination as well as of subversive activities on the part of neighbouring States or any other States.
- Absolute dedication to the total emancipation of the African territories which are still dependent.
- Affirmation of a policy of non-alignment with regard to all blocs.[45]

Within a few years an inherent clash was revealed between the principles of territorial integrity and the right of independence, with the latter cited by breakaway movements within African states. The most serious illustration of this came with the 1967–70 Nigerian Civil War, when the breakaway state of Biafra was actually recognised by several African states. Since all African states were located within artificial borders determined to suit the interests of the colonial powers rather than any ethnic or tribal division, this was an issue with potentially disastrous implications throughout Africa. Not unnaturally the OAU adhered throughout the Civil War to a doctrine it had earlier agreed at a Cairo summit conference in July 1964: that 'the borders of African states on the day of their independence constitute a tangible reality'.[46]

The principal institutions of the OAU are an Assembly of Heads of State and Government, meeting at least annually, a Council of Ministers and a General Secretariat. Although there were moves by a few representatives at the Addis Ababa conference to give the Secretariat more than purely administrative functions, these were strongly resisted by the majority.[47] Various specialised commissions were also established which, after a reorganisation in 1967, included an Economic and Social Commission, an Educational, Cultural, Scientific and Health Commission, and a Defence Commission. In 1968 a Bureau for the Placement and Education of African Refugees was added to these. The commissions were to have little impact, although to some extent they, like the OAU in general, acted as fora where ideas and policies could be given a preliminary ventilation prior to their re-emergence at the UN.

Measured by the yardstick of concrete achievement, the OAU would probably be judged a failure. Yet it has survived and in some respects grown, something which can only be explained by examining the role that the OAU has played both in diplomacy amongst African states and in Africa's relations with the rest of the world. Two main facets of its work will be used here to illustrate these themes: its involvement in the peaceful settlement of disputes and its role in the liberation of southern Africa.

The OAU was almost immediately faced with a serious conflict between two of its members: Algeria and Morocco.[48] This involved a typical border problem bequeathed from the colonial past, complicated by the economic importance of the disputed region and ideological tensions between the leftist government of Algeria and the conservative Moroccans. An important precedent was set when a dispute between the two sides over whether the issue should go before the UN or OAU was resolved in favour of the OAU. It should be noted, however, that this was decided partly as a result of pressure from France and the United States, who wished the matter to be settled within an African context, rather than at the UN where it would inevitably become entangled in Cold War politics. The OAU set up a special committee of mediation in November 1963, and in 1964 the two sides announced a ceasefire, with a settlement eventually being arrived at in 1968. This peaceful outcome was hailed by some as a great achievement on the part of the OAU, although it owed at least as much to the determination of the major powers not to become involved and of the two disputants not to let the matter get out of hand. None the less, the OAU had played a useful, if undramatic, role as an intermediary and by its consistent reiteration that borders inherited from the colonial period were inviolable.

Other conflicts were to prove more intractable. For instance, in 1964 serious fighting broke out between Ethiopia and Somalia over Somalia's irredentist claims in Ethiopia. Although there have from time to time been periods of truce in this conflict, occasionally arranged through OAU auspices, this conflict persisted and intensified. The dispute was to confirm what the Congo crisis had already made clear: that the OAU was powerless to prevent great power involvement in a conflict if the powers were determined to intervene. An equally bitter conflict developed between Rwanda and Burundi, where refugees from both sides were accused of subversive activities across the borders, leading to frequent military clashes between the two countries. This, too, was a classic postcolonial situation, resulting from borders which cut across tribal areas, and here again the OAU could do little other than organise temporary cease-fires.[49] The OAU's relative impotence to influence outside intervention, either to prevent its arrival or its departure, was further underlined by the most recent ethnic conflicts in Rwanda. The United Nations sent a mission to Rwanda (UNAMIR) following the death of President Habyarimana on 6 April 1994 and the consequential escalation of fighting between the majority Hutus and minority Tutsis. However, after unsuccessful attempts to mediate a ceasefire, the force was reduced to observer-level numbers by late April. This move was condemned by the OAU as indicating double standards applied by the UN to Africa and Europe, given the ongoing and significant UN presence in Bosnia.[50] Earlier, a similar lack of muscle was exposed in the long-running feud between Uganda and Tanzania following Idi Amin's coup in Uganda. This was not finally resolved until Tanzania was provoked into invading Uganda and overthrowing Amin, thereby violating several cherished OAU principles.

A few disputes were resolved through OAU mediation. In 1972 a quarrel between Gabon and Equatorial Guinea over the ownership of certain islands was settled after both sides accepted the appointment of an OAU commission to define the maritime border.[51] The OAU was similarly useful in 1964 in assisting President Nyerere of Tanzania to end his embarrassing dependence on troops from the former colonial power, Britain, which had been called in to quash an army revolt. However, this was an unusual example of a case where the OAU was able to aid in the resolution of an internal conflict. In general the OAU has not been encouraged to intervene in the internal affairs of its members and since these, rather than interstate disputes, have produced the most serious situations of the OAU's first 15 years, the OAU has inevitably been precluded from involvement in many of the major crises. Thus hundreds of thousands of lives were lost in Uganda, Sudan and Burundi with the OAU barely able even to comment. But in some respects the OAU was presented with an even more difficult problem in the Nigerian Civil War because here the OAU itself became a factor, albeit a minor one, in the conflict.[52] Initially the federal government of Nigeria was adamant in refusing to permit the OAU even to discuss the war because it felt that this might go some way towards legitimising Biafra as an independent entity, while the Biafran leadership was equally intent upon encouraging OAU involvement. But here too, many thousands were being killed and the crisis was receiving worldwide press attention, so the OAU would have laid itself open to considerable ridicule if it had simply ignored the Nigerian situation. In the event, it established a Consultative Committee on Nigeria, but this, in line with general OAU policy, declared after its first visit to Nigeria that 'any solution of the Nigeria crisis must be in the context of preserving the unity and territorial integrity of Nigeria'.[53] Hence, because of its adherence to the territorial integrity principle, the OAU was put in the position of having to support one side in the Civil War, which inevitably damaged its chances of mediating. By 1969, the Biafran leader, Colonel Ojukwu, refused to accept any OAU role, while the federal government, in contrast, insisted that it would only accept mediation from the OAU.[54]

The other major issue which has concerned the OAU from its inception has been the liberation of the remaining African countries governed by white minority regimes, mainly in southern Africa. This has been the primary concern of the OAU Liberation Committee which was set up at the same time as the OAU itself in 1963. The tasks of the Committee, as outlined in 1963, were to bring pressures on the colonial powers, to provide moral and material support for the liberation movements, and to act diplomatically both to secure international legitimisation of armed struggle in the UN and elsewhere and to isolate the minority regimes.[55] It was also to work to unify the separate liberation movements in each country.

With the 1994 free elections in South Africa seeing the final demise of the original white minority governments, the liberation movement as such has clearly succeeded and the OAU has played a significant if limited role which it will continue by participating in the monitoring of future elections in South Africa. To a considerable extent it has shaped the response of those external powers who supported the liberation struggles or who wished to give humanitarian aid by indicating to them which struggles and movements it regarded as legitimate.[56] It has helped to coordinate the activities of those states which allowed their territories to be used as bases by the guerrilla movements, although it was unable to agree upon measures to aid those states when they came under military attack from the white regimes. It also succeeded in making the cause of the liberation of Southern Africa an international issue by repeated pressure at the UN. Finally, a committee of military experts established in September 1967 proved to be a valuable source of technical advice on fighting a guerrilla war.[57] However, in one important respect the OAU had little success. Despite bringing very strong pressures to bear it was unable to unify the different liberation groups for any length of time. Its attempts in the face of this failure to single out individual groups for its recognition as the legitimate revolutionary forces often brought more confusion than clarity.[58]

A mark of its failure in this respect is the bitter divisions and in some cases continued fighting that still persist. It should also be noted that many African states have been less than willing to back their verbal militancy in OAU debates with material assistance: the Liberation Committee was consistently short of funds. There was also a noticeable lack of unity whenever the OAU called upon its members to take some concrete action. For instance, after an OAU Council of Ministers meeting in 1965 (following Ian Smith's Unilateral Declaration of Independence in Rhodesia) called upon members to break off diplomatic relations with Britain should the latter not use force to end the Smith regime, only ten African states did so. Moreover, different African states have supported different wings of the liberation movement, which was hardly likely to assist the OAU in its avowed aim of seeking to unite the different groups.[59]

In many respects, the OAU's most important function, both with regard to the liberation movements and in other matters, has been to provide one stable reference point for foreign countries in their attempts to formulate policies towards an Africa where governments could be replaced overnight by military or other regimes with opposite political persuasions. It would not have been difficult for an external power seeking influence to sponsor breakaway movements following the Biafran example. That this has not happened to any great extent is at least in part because the OAU has been able to present a united front in favour of the territorial status quo. This has also meant that several African states have refrained from pressing what in some respects might have seemed reasonable claims for territorial revisions along tribal lines. In a similar vein, the OAU played a significant part in important negotiations that led to a new economic relationship with the European Community.[60]

For these reasons an assessment of the OAU and the reasons for its continuing existence should not be confined to a search for specific concrete achievements in any field. In many areas, notably the economic, social, scientific and cultural spheres, the OAU has little or nothing to show for 30 years of existence.[61] Its importance lies in less tangible factors, as is suggested by one writer: 'The OAU has functioned as a neutral meeting site, an agent for interstate communications, a forum for expressing widely held opinions and as an agent able to disperse legitimisation for policy decision.'[62] Africa's problems of desperate poverty, ethnic and tribal conflict, corruption, unstable and dictatorial leadership, and continuing interference by major powers will not be resolved by the OAU. But without some such institution, Africa will be in danger of losing even the flimsy foundation of unity that exists over certain basic principles and with regard to such important contemporary issues as the development of a new international economic order.

If it is unreasonably optimistic to expect the OAU to take the leading role in meeting the many challenges that Africa will face in the 1990s, it is nevertheless the case that, in common with regional organisations in other parts of the world, it will need to have regard to the shifts in emphasis which have resulted from the end of the Cold War and adjust accordingly. In particular the growing concentration of other areas of the world into trade blocs needs to be urgently addressed by Africa. Set against the European, North American and Asia and Pacific Basin groupings, Africa is a late starter and there is concern in some quarters that it may be left behind. The 1980s is seen as being a lost decade in economic terms with falling per capita incomes, per capita food production lower in 1989 than in 1980 and a smaller share for the region in the world market for exports.[63] By this year also, intra-African cooperation and intra-African trade were perceived to be less than they had been two decades earlier.[64]

As with the OAS in Latin America, the OAU has, in the past, looked to subregional organisations to promote economic cooperation to serve common interests. Several subregional organisations have been created in Africa, but these have generally had a troubled history with some outright failures and no clear-cut successes. The East African Community, established as a common market in 1967, collapsed after a promising start under the weight of discord amongst its members following Idi Amin's accession to power. Similar problems have beset the Central African Customs and Economic Union (established in 1964) and the Common African, Malagasy and Mauritian Organisation (1966). There are also many smaller groups of states, usually with more limited objectives, and these have had varying results. The most ambitious addition to the list of subregional organisations was the Economic Community of West African States (ECOWAS) established by the Treaty of Lagos in May 1975. The Community was the culmination of nearly 15 years of discussion and partial and preliminary steps towards integration, promoted in the main by its largest member, Nigeria.[65]

ECOWAS broke through one longstanding barrier to African unity, the division between Anglophone and Francophone states, in bringing together 15 countries from both wings (as well as one former Portuguese colony, Guinea-Bissau). It has the standard bodies, including an 'Authority' of heads of state and government, a Council of Ministers, a Secretariat and a tribunal to settle disputes. Its objectives as set out in Article 2 of the Treaty are:

> to promote co-operation and development in all fields of economic activity, particularly in the fields of industry, transport, telecommunications energy, agriculture, natural resources, commerce, monetary and financial questions and in social and cultural matters for the purpose of raising the standard of living of its peoples, of increasing and maintaining economic stability, of fostering closer relations among its members and of contributing to the progress and development of the African continent.[66]

As with the European Community, progress towards integration and harmonisation of the national economies was to take place by carefully thought out stages, with the ultimate aim of 'the creation of a homogeneous society, leading to the unity of the countries of West Africa by the elimination of all types of obstacles to the free movement of goods, capital and persons'.[67]

Although driven ostensibly by the desire for economic cooperation it was quickly recognised by ECOWAS that these aims could not be furthered without an accompanying political agenda. In 1978 a Non-aggression Protocol was agreed which forbade the use of force as a means of settling disputes between member states, recognising that stability and the reduction of fear of attack were important preconditions to economic achievements.[68] However, it was not until the Protocol on Mutual Defence Assistance, signed in May 1981 but not effective until October 1987, that the issue of external aggression was addressed.[69] Two years later, in December 1989, the Defence Pact was put to the test by the Liberian Civil war which threatened to escalate beyond Liberian boundaries. ECOWAS authorised the creation of a peacekeeping force, the Economic Community Monitoring Group (ECOMOG) with a mandate to suppress tribal fighting, restore peace and to organise both a transitional government and elections for the appointment of a legitimate government. There was a danger that this would in turn sour the fragile anglophone/francophone accord since of the francophone countries only Guinea contributed troops. Despite some short-term success on the part of ECOWAS it was not until the middle of 1993 and the involvement of the UN that the warring sides agreed to try to negotiate a peaceful settlement. Some authors see the greater success to ECOWAS as lying in the process of shared 'felt needs' and the enhancement of members' sense of collective responsibility.[70] However, a continuing decline during the 1990s in the political stability and economic prosperity of ECOWAS's leading member, Nigeria, does not bode well for the region.

ECOWAS was followed by the Preferential Trade Area for Eastern and Southern Africa (PTA) in 1981 and then by the Economic Commission for Central African States (ECCA) but to little effect. Then, at its 27th Assembly in Abujan, Nigeria, I June 1991 the OAU formally signed the treaty to set up the African Economic Community (AEC) a structure which had been formulated as early as the Declaration of Algiers in 1968. The Treaty provides for the establishment of a continental framework for the development of resources; for economic and trade cooperation between member states and for adoption of common trade policy towards non-members. It envisages a 34-year, six-stage timetable for adoption which would come into force 30 days after ratification by two-thirds of the OAU membership. The revival of such an ambitious proposal at the start of the 1990s undoubtedly marks the concern both individually and collectively that African states have concerning the economic prospects for the continent. However, whether collective action will be preferred to individual has yet to be revealed. Certainly, a year after the approval in principle of the AEC and its aims, less than one quarter of the OAU membership had signed up to the plan.

ASEAN

Asian regionalism in the immediate post-Second World War period and through the 1950s was limited and, to some extent, externally prompted. There was some economic cooperation under the auspices of the UN's Economic Commission for Asia and the Far East (ECAFE) and, for Pakistan, Thailand and the Philippines, a strategic alliance with the United States and other Western powers in the form of the South East Asia Treaty Organisation (SEATO) in 1954. The first moves towards an exclusively south east Asian grouping did not take place until July 1961 when the Association of Southeast Asia (ASA) was formed by the Philippines, Thailand and Malaysia. This had the objective of promoting economic and cultural cooperation through schemes for student exchange, joint shipping and airlines and the like, but a major rift between Malaysia and the Philippines and various practical difficulties prevented any real progress from being made.[71]

However, this proved to be only a temporary setback; in the wake of the success of the EEC, regional integration became very fashionable in the 1960s and ASEAN (Association of South East Asian Nations) was created by the Bangkok Declaration in 1967. Indonesia, Malaysia, the Philippines, Singapore and Thailand were the founding members; Brunei became the sixth member in 1984. There were also four factors specific to South East Asia which prompted a revival of regionalism there at this particular time:

- the fall from power of President Sukarno of Indonesia, who had pursued a policy of 'confrontation' against Malaysia, and his replacement by the more pragmatic President Suharto, who quickly expressed an interest in reconciliation with Malaysia;
- the threat to the region created by the Vietnam War and the fear that a Communist victory over South Vietnam would be followed by more North Vietnamese military incursions creating a 'domino' effect in the region, probably beginning with Thailand;
- the concerns about the regional instability caused by the Chinese Cultural Revolution and, specifically, calls to other Asian Communist parties to embark upon 'peoples' wars';
- a feeling that there was a need for closer economic association, especially in the face of the rise of Japanese economic power.

It is clear from the above that ASEAN was very much a response to external threats and that its economic rationale was only articulated in the vaguest of terms. This explains much of the subsequent development of ASEAN (or lack of it).

In fact, ASEAN is sometimes presented as the next best example of regional cooperation after the EU, although this is a rather exaggerated plaudit. Nevertheless, in the light of the rather dismal history of regional integration outside Western Europe in the last 40 years, the very survival of the organisation for nearly 30 years is clearly of some merit. This probably reflects two factors: firstly, that ASEAN's main activity has been reacting to external political and security threats and, as these threats have been present for most of the period since 1967 then there has been a reason for continuing with ASEAN; secondly, since ASEAN has been essentially moribund on the economic and most other fronts, no internal group or member state has felt threatened and, therefore, there has been no scope for conflict. These are perhaps rather negative reasons for continuing but it does mean that ASEAN has a clear identity, and to some extent also a clear purpose, unlike the more recent, larger Asia–Pacific groupings like the EAEC and APEC.

Nevertheless, the first eight years of its existence were little more than 'symbolic'.[72] This largely reflected its negative foundations. Unlike the European Union which in its early years had a shared vision of a politically and economically integrated region, ASEAN was essentially an attempt to ward off external threats by showing solidarity and, in particular, 'to demonstrate determination to ward off Communist infiltration'.[73] Indeed it was this common thread of anti-Communism which led to the first major development of ASEAN when the collapse of the (non-Communist) governments in Cambodia and South Vietnam led to fears of Communist-led revolutionary activities within ASEAN and to the Bali summit in early 1976 at which it was decided to press ahead with ASEAN cooperation on virtually all fronts. Two major documents were signed:

- The Treaty of Amity and Cooperation. This had four main elements: the principles of mutual respect for the independence and sovereignty of all nations; non-interference in each others' internal affairs; settlement of disputes by peaceful means; and effective cooperation amongst ASEAN members.
- The Declaration of Concord which covered economic, social and cultural relations, including cooperation in economic

development and the establishment of a 'Zone of Peace, Freedom and Stability' (ZOPFAN).

However, the main focus of attention was on economic cooperation, particularly intraASEAN trade liberalisation and the development of large-scale ASEAN industrial projects.

Unfortunately it proved extremely difficult to convert intentions into actions in almost every respect for a number of reasons, which have been to some extent responsible for the limited success achieved by the many attempts to establish regional groupings outside Europe.[74] These include:

- differences in political systems and ideology (which are extreme in ASEAN – for example between Indonesia, Singapore and Brunei);
- lack of political harmony – there is a long history of disputes and distrust between numerous combinations of the ASEAN membership;
- differences in levels of economic development and national wealth – these are quite large in ASEAN and can make economic cooperation, in particular, very difficult;
- variations in size – both in terms of population and area and also economic size (gross national product);
- disparities in attitudes to trade (ranging from the openness of Singapore and Brunei to the protectionism of Indonesia);
- the similarity (and hence lack of complementarity) of production and export patterns.

It is therefore not surprising that only minimal tariff reductions could be agreed and that intra-ASEAN trade has generally remained below 20 per cent of total ASEAN trade. Furthermore, only two of the projected five (one in each of the then five ASEAN members) large-scale industrial projects have materialised (in Indonesia and Malaysia).

In fact, the most successful area of ASEAN economic cooperation would seem to be external relations. In particular, ASEAN has established seven 'dialogue partners' – the EU, USA, Japan, South Korea, Canada, Australia and New Zealand – with which it has regular meetings. These relationships grew out of ASEAN's discussions on trade issues with the EU and Japan in its early years and such issues remain important although the negotiations are now much more wide ranging. Similarly, in the political domain – where ASEAN is generally considered to have been most successful[75] – the success has been on the external front. In particular, in the late 1970s, the development of a coordinated and credible response to the increase in the number of Indochinese refugees (particularly, the Vietnamese 'boat-people') and, especially, to the Vietnamese invasion of Cambodia, considerably enhanced ASEAN's international reputation.[76]

Thus it seems that ASEAN's progress has been relatively modest and observations to the effect that it is 'evolutionary rather than revolutionary'[77] and ought to be considered as a 'state of mind'[78] tend to support this conclusion. More fundamentally, it is clear that much of the economic success of the ASEAN member states has been due to the successful efforts of the individual countries rather than ASEAN membership; indeed, it may well be that the continued existence of ASEAN has been facilitated by the high economic growth of its members. Quite apart from the general problems (described above) that have undermined all efforts to establish regional cooperation outside the European Union,[79] ASEAN has to address a number of specific issues, most particularly:

- The question of the leadership role within ASEAN. Indonesia has always felt that it ought to be considered pre-eminent or at least to have a right to be consulted in advance of major initiatives and was irritated when Malaysia failed to do so about the EAEC proposal. Subsequently, there appears to be some rivalry over ASEAN leadership between the two.
- This is part of the more general friction within the Indonesia–Malaysia–Singapore triangle. For example, in recent years Malaysia and Singapore have clashed over tourism and the Malaysian arrest of two alleged Singaporean spies,[80] Malaysia and Indonesia over the Malaysian EAEC proposal[81] (and the leadership issue) and Indonesia and Singapore over the latter's advocacy of closer ASEAN ties with China.[82] Indeed, it has been argued that the 'greatest obstacle . . [to] . . ASEAN economic integration is nationalist sentiments'.[83]
- One potential source of friction might be alleviated by more integration – the flow and distribution of investment into ASEAN. It may well be that the principal advantage of an

ASEAN free trade area would not be the internal trade (creation) generated, given the similarity of the ASEAN economies, but rather the encouragement it would give to third
countries to invest even more within ASEAN countries and
make use of the free access to the whole ASEAN market.
Greater investment flows into ASEAN would obviously reduce
the friction within ASEAN over the distribution of foreign investment.

- The question of ASEAN enlargement to include Vietnam,
  Laos, Cambodia and Myanmar (Burma) has begun to arise. All
  four countries appear to favour eventual ASEAN membership
  which has been actively courted by Vietnam[84] to the point of
  acceding to the Treaty of Amity and Cooperation, along with
  Laos, in 1992. However, there are political problems in the
  shape of mistrust and various territorial disputes between the
  current and aspiring ASEAN membership.[85] There are also
  economic difficulties created by the comparatively lower levels
  of economic development and national income levels in the
  potential applicant states. The current ASEAN membership
  are wary of the internal economic dualism that enlargement
  will create and of the implied responsibilities that will have to
  be taken on by the more economically developed (existing)
  members. In addition to these specific concerns, enlargement
  of ASEAN could inhibit further integration in ways that are all
  too familiar to the European Union.
- ASEAN has to face (and relate to further ASEAN integration)
  the successful completion of the Uruguay Round negotiations,
  on the one hand, and moves towards enhanced Asia–Pacific
  cooperation, through the EAEC and APEC, on the other. In a
  sense, the two may be mutually incompatible in that APEC was
  perceived, to some extent, as a fall back position in case there
  was no successful outcome to the Uruguay Round. However,
  perhaps the more important dilemma for ASEAN is how to
  participate in these developments without undermining its
  cohesion and independence.

The first dilemma expressed in the final point may hold the key
which explains why economic integration has been so limited in
ASEAN. The rapid growth of the ASEAN economies has been based
on export performance, particularly to OECD countries, and not

on ASEAN integration. Consequently, ASEAN has had a vested interest in the success of the GATT and the maintenance of an open world trading system which has made it reluctant to engage in any activity that might undermine such a system (such as regional economic integration). With the completion of the Uruguay Round it is not clear that much has changed.

However, for the sake of appearances and for political reasons, ASEAN still feels the need to pursue economic integration. At the fourth ASEAN summit at Kuala Lumpur in January 1992, there were two significant economic agreements, although both were much watered down versions of the original proposals. The first of these was the 'Framework Agreement on Enhancing ASEAN Economic Cooperation'. This has its origins in a Philippine proposal for a wide ranging but ill defined ASEAN economic treaty. It binds ASEAN members to strengthen economic cooperation and covers various sectors, specifically trade, industry, transport, communications, finance and banking. It also provides for subregional growth areas both within ASEAN and between non-ASEAN states. This would allow the development, for example, of Singapore's growth triangle linking Singapore, Johor (Malaysia) and Riau province (Indonesia). The agreement is potentially very useful as it sidesteps the stumbling block of having to have full agreement within ASEAN before any cooperation can proceed; the Agreement allows two or more ASEAN members to initiate economic cooperation amongst themselves and not to have to wait until all ASEAN members are ready.

The second measure agreed in Kuala Lumpur was the creation of an ASEAN free trade area (AFTA) over a 15 year period beginning on 1 January 1993 and ending in 2008. Basically tariffs on all goods with a 40 per cent or more ASEAN content are to fall to 0–5 per cent; within this there is a 'fast track' programme which covers 15 special categories which are suppose to reach this target after only ten years (in 2003). On the face of it, this is an exciting development: it aims to create an integrated market of 330 million people with a combined GNP of US $300 billion and a growth rate of 7 per cent per annum. Unfortunately, there are difficulties (and consequent scepticism):

- AFTA is based on a Thai proposal which provided for only a ten-year transition period; thus, there has been some slippage before the scheme even started.

- There is a very mixed attitude within ASEAN to AFTA. The Thais are very positive (not surprisingly as the original sponsors), as is Singapore, which already has an open market and therefore has everything to gain. On the other hand, Indonesia, with its protected and precariously balanced, export-led economy, is dragging its feet. In addition, Malaysia, despite strongly backing AFTA, had failed to publish full details of its new tariff regime four months into 1993.
- There is an opt out clause which allows individual members to decide not to lower tariffs in areas they feel would harm their industry. Thus, for example, the Philippines was very quick to opt out of tariff cuts on cement.
- The agreement is only partial in that unprocessed agricultural goods and services are excluded, at least for the time being.
- Different ASEAN members are to cut tariffs at different speeds, thereby creating a very complex formula. Malaysia and Singapore were to begin immediately (and are also at the forefront of the 'fast track' programme) whereas Thailand and Indonesia are not scheduled to begin their tariff cuts until 1998.
- Non-tariff barriers are not covered by AFTA, not even quantitative restrictions.
- Business interests in ASEAN have been confused, concerned and special about AFTA.

None of this augurs well for the future of AFTA. Indeed, AFTA got off to such a bad start that the ASEAN leaders felt that it was necessary to relaunch it in October 1993. The scheme remains substantially the same except the start date was rolled back until the beginning of 1994 (although the end date remains 2008) and unprocessed agricultural goods are now included (as well as processed agricultural goods and manufactures). The optimistic justification for the relaunch was that the original scheme had been launched too hastily with insufficient attention to detail. However, a further, and more ominous reason was that only Malaysia (eventually) and Singapore had actually stuck to the agreed schedule of tariff cuts.

However, the doubts continue. AFTA still maintains a wide range of exemptions, a staggered timetable and baffling distinctions between included and excluded items. Consequently, there is considerable opportunity for business interests and pressure groups to lobby successfully to keep their protection by delaying or causing the abandonment of scheduled tariff cuts. Excessive activity of this kind could completely undermine AFTA. Furthermore, and to some extent following on from this, there remains the fundamental fact that ASEAN members are essentially competitive. Free trade areas do not work well without industrial complementarity. In the light of all this, it is difficult not to conclude that AFTA lacks credibility.

The other, and arguably more appropriate, field in which ASEAN is trying to make progress is regional security. Like economics, this is a difficult area even though it is common (external) security concerns that have held ASEAN together. In particular, there are numerous aspects of security which remain contentious and impede cooperation, notably:

- There is disagreement over what 'security' means in practice: Singapore and the Philippines would like to add a military dimension but this is opposed by Indonesia which prefers to define security in broader economic and political terms.
- Singapore would like ASEAN to engage in a regional security dialogue with its Asia–Pacific neighbours but others are less enthusiastic, particularly Indonesia which considers that it may invite external interference.
- Thailand and and Singapore would like a closer relationship with mainland China. (Of course, Singapore already has a close and profitable economic relationship with the Chinese.) However, Malaysia, Indonesia and the Philippines are somewhat ambivalent about and wary of such a development.
- External security relations are complicated by territorial disputes involving (in various combinations) members of ASEAN, a prospective member (Vietnam) and China.[86]
- Partly because of this there remains some mutual mistrust within ASEAN over national security objectives.
- More generally, there appears to be a general preference amongst the ASEAN membership for conducting defence relations on a bilateral rather than multilateral basis.

The first ASEAN regional forum to discuss security matters finally took place in July 1994, after the annual ASEAN ministerial meeting.[87] However, this is only a beginning and it will take time for the ASEAN membership to resolve its differences over security issues.

In some ways ASEAN remains an enigma. It is widely regarded as the second most successful attempt to achieve regional integration (after the European Union). However, if the measure of achievement is the successful implementation of agreed policies, then the story of ASEAN is largely a catalogue of failure; its success mainly stems from actually continuing to exist as similar initiatives elsewhere have floundered. Moreover, it is not entirely clear that economic integration within ASEAN is actually desirable as its members owe much of their economic success to an open world trading system in which regional trade blocs are the exception rather than the rule.

More generally, the ASEAN case raises the fundamental questions about how regional integration should proceed. There seems to be an implicit assumption that because it has been successful the European Union model is the one that has to be followed – that is, economic integration should be the driving force. Efforts elsewhere in Africa and Latin America have followed this road and have all failed. Arguably the reason why ASEAN has hung together has been that, despite its best efforts, it has failed to imitate the EU. In fact, it has actually followed its own unique path of limited political integration based on responding to common external threats. There is potentially a lesson both specifically for ASEAN and more generally from this experience. The lesson for ASEAN is that it may be better advised to pursue regional security concerns and related matters and to abandon its efforts to pursue economic integration except on a very modest scale. More fundamentally, perhaps organisations pursuing regional integration should follow their own unique agenda. There is no reason why economic integration should come first or indeed why regional integration cannot proceed to a mutually acceptable end point involving a degree of political cooperation but only limited economic integration.

Conclusion

The assumption is commonly found in political science literature on regionalism that regional organisations should be measured against a single yardstick: the extent to which they contribute to the political and economic integration of their members. The ultimate goal is federation under one government. The distance travelled by a regional organisation towards that goal determines its success or lack of it. The practical experience of the three main institutions examined here shows that this may be a misguided approach, for none is in any sense close to substantial integration yet all have served a purpose in quite distinct ways that have little to do with any longer-term process of integration.

The OAS has provided an arena for the working out of the relationship between the United States and Latin America, in the course of which it has also played other roles in disseminating information, promoting economic development, settling disputes, devising common policies and negotiating positions for some of the important international conferences. The OAU has had only a marginal significance in the resolution of disputes and even less in economic affairs. Far from its members growing in unity as has been the case with ASEAN and to a lesser extent the Latin American members of the OAS, some of their conflicts have become increasingly bitter. But it has survived because it has performed other important functions. It has laid down norms and guidelines that have had a remarkable durability and measure of acceptance, notably over the maintenance of the territorial status quo. It has provided a means of arriving at an African consensus over issues such as colonialism and racism and has helped to internationalise these questions. It has gradually gained acceptance as a source of international legitimisation, and has acted almost as a compass for foreign powers trying to steer a safe course through the turbulent waters of African politics.

ASEAN, too, started life in unpromising circumstances, with serious disputes amongst its members and few common interests beyond a general unease about the future of their region. It lacked a plan for gradual political and economic integration and for some years appeared to be an inactive irrelevance. But merely by bringing its members into regular contact with each other it helped to defuse their own conflicts and obliged them to seek consensus viewpoints on various matters. It encouraged a habit of consultation which grew inevitably into collaboration over matters of substance. Even more than the OAU it provided a focal point for outside powers as well as industrial corporations, while it also added to its members' capacity to deal on equal terms with the latter.

10 International Regimes

The process of international organisation is concerned with the development by states of ways of regulating their conflicts, jointly managing for their collective benefit various specific areas of activity and, most ambitiously, planning for peaceful change towards agreed goals. Sometimes this has involved the creation of large multipurpose institutions such as the League, UN or EU. However, the essential core of international organisation is not the various administrative buildings in New York, Brussels, Geneva and elsewhere which represent the relevant institution in the public mind, but the rules, regulations and agreed procedures for which the institutions have assumed responsibility. In this sense the main thrust of international organisation is the development of 'international regimes': sets of rules which aim to regulate some specific activity of international interest. Thus defined, regimes encompass not only formal institutions but many informal, decentralised arrangements among states, and sometimes among non-state actors, such as the Swiss-based International Committee of the Red Cross which has an important role in relation to the Geneva Conventions on war.

International regimes have attracted a great deal of academic attention since they first emerged as a distinct analytical category in the 1970s.[1] Much of this has been concerned with fundamental theoretical issues, such as the conditions in which international cooperation is possible, the problems of 'free riding' and cheating that are intrinsic to collective action, and the role of hegemonic power in upholding particular regimes. This theoretical literature is valuable, not least because it focuses upon the policies and behaviour of states, as is also evident in the following widely accepted definition of regimes as: 'sets of implicit or explicit principles, norms, rules and decision-making procedures around which actors' expectations converge in a given area of international relations'.[2]

A complete list of regimes would embrace almost every area of international life which is marked by some degree of orderliness and cooperation among states. Technical fields such as civil aviation, meteorology, telecommunications, the environment, a large part of international economic or monetary relations and certain aspects of arms control are among the subjects of contemporary regimes. The different organisational forms taken by the regimes range from substantial formal institutions such as the World Health Organisation (WHO), which is actually the parent body of several smaller regimes, to a treaty approved by the UN General Assembly in December 1979 declaring that the moon and its natural resources are the common heritage of mankind, and hence not subject to national appropriation.[3] Here we shall consider four regimes, all of which affect vitally important aspects of international affairs, and which illustrate the problems, as well as the possibilities, of international regimes.

International economic order

The Great Depression of the 1930s, which was exacerbated by competitive and self-defeating devaluations and protectionist policies and which helped to create the conditions that gave rise to fascism, had demonstrated clearly the need for an international economic regime that would both provide some degree of stability, especially with regard to exchange rates, and also promote trade. Keynesian economic theories in addition encouraged governments to believe in the contribution of more interventionist economic policies to full employment. It was a natural next step from this perspective to a belief in the possibilities of economic management at the global as well as the national level, especially as Keynes himself was an important figure at the 1944 Bretton Woods conference, which laid down the foundations of the postwar economic order for the next 25 years.

The conference established an international monetary system and also discussed plans for an International Trade Organisation (ITO). This latter did not materialise until 1995 but in 1947 the General Agreement on Tariffs and Trade (GATT) was established with the aim of fulfilling some of the functions of the ITO.

Bretton Woods created two new international organisations. The less important of the two was the International Bank for Reconstruction and Development (IBRD) or World Bank. This had the initial aim of helping to finance the rebuilding of those parts of Europe and Asia that had been devastated by war. Later it focused primarily on the provision of aid and advice to developing countries. The more important organisation was the International Monetary Fund (IMF) which was to undertake a key role in the international monetary regime devised by Bretton Woods.

The overall aim of this regime was to create a stable and predictable international monetary system that would avoid the competitive devaluations that had characterised the prewar era. It was to have three main features. First, it was to promote stability primarily through a regime of fixed exchange rates, in which states agreed to intervene to buy or sell each others' currencies with the aim of preventing sharp exchange rate fluctuations. Second, the members of the IMF all paid a subscription which was then used to provide short-term credits to countries experiencing balance of payments difficulties. This credit was not to be given automatically but was to be linked to the imposition of a set of policy changes that were intended to encourage financial discipline in the recipient state. Third, and most importantly, the regime rested upon the assumption by the United States of international economic leadership. There were several elements to this American hegemony. Most critically, the United States committed itself to exchange gold for dollars at any time at a fixed value of $35 per ounce. In practice this meant that countries tended to hold reserves in interest-bearing dollars rather than gold. The dollar became the international currency. The United States also undertook the responsibility of maintaining international liquidity, first by granting $17 billion in Marshall Aid loans to Western Europe after the war and second by its preparedness to run balance of payments deficits.[4]

The system worked well enough while the United States enjoyed unchallenged economic dominance. However, serious problems began to emerge in the 1960s. In part these stemmed from the fact that enormous financial power was beginning to build up outside the control of governments as international banks and multinational corporations accumulated huge financial assets, thus creating a global market in money outside the Bretton Woods regime. As there is inevitably a time lag in any system of fixed exchange rates between the first signs that a particular currency may be overvalued and a government's decision to devalue, this opened up the prospects of large and relatively risk free profits from speculating against weak currencies. Another set of problems was associated with the increasing inability of the United States to continue to play the role it had assumed after the war. Japanese and European economic power had grown beyond its initial dependence on the United States and those states were becoming resentful of what they perceived as an American ability to abuse its favoured position by increasing expenditure on domestic policies and the Vietnam War without bearing the normal cost of politically unpopular tax increases. By 1968 the regime was coming under ever greater strain, with which it was essentially unable to cope.

One of the problems with an international economic regime that depends critically on the hegemony of a single state is that the hegemon may feel constrained to take actions for essentially domestic reasons that have serious consequences for the entire global economy. This was the case in 1971 when President Nixon severed the link between gold and the dollar and took other steps designed to improve the US economic situation. This 'Nixon shock' marked the effective end of the Bretton Woods regime. In its place a system of floating exchange rates emerged in which rates were determined by market forces. This could not be described as a 'regime', since it lacked the essential elements of management and regulations, and in the view of some economists was all the better for it. Some degree of macroeconomic coordination was, however, attempted both through the IMF and through the 'Group of Seven' – the seven most important economies whose leaders held regular summit meetings from 1975. But the emergence in the United States, Britain and elsewhere of governments strongly influenced by 'new right' economic thinking created a climate that was hostile to any significant degree of intervention in the international economy, leaving the field clear for market forces and an ever increasing role for private capital.[5]

The international monetary system was thrown into further disarray by the Organisation of Petroleum Exporting Countries' (OPEC) decision in 1973 to quadruple the price of oil, with further large increases following in the wake of the overthrow of the Shah of Iran in 1979. This helped to fuel inflationary pressures that had already built up during the 1960s and created particularly severe problems for developing countries, which lacked the hard currency necessary to purchase oil at the new prices. Seeing an apparent opportunity of longer term profits, Western banks stepped in with offers of large loans. While these helped the developing countries through their short-term crisis, in most cases this was at a cost of huge indebtedness as the global recession made it virtually impossible for these countries to earn sufficient through exports to pay off their debts. For many in the third world, this was further proof of a thesis they had been advancing since the early 1960s: that the world economy was structurally imbalanced against the interests of developing countries. In their view what was required was nothing less than a new international economic order characterised by positive discrimination in favour of the third world.[6] This was also a constant refrain in the developing countries' contribution to the ongoing negotiations on trade within the framework of the GATT.

The underlying principles of the GATT reflected the same postwar concerns as the international monetary regime. During the early 1930s international trade had declined rapidly as a direct consequence of a series of competitive and self-defeating protectionist measures in a number of countries, led by the United States. After the war the predominant Anglo-American belief was that a liberal trade regime, underpinned by the United States, would promote a steady growth in trade that would benefit all through a general increase in prosperity and reduce the attraction of more extreme politico-economic doctrines. However the US Congress rejected the more ambitious Bretton Woods proposals on trade, leaving only the much weaker regime of the GATT. This was, in essence, a set of principles that provided an agreed framework within which more detailed negotiations could take place. The central principles were non-discrimination in trade, so that a preferential agreement between two members of the GATT would extend to all members, and reciprocity, so that a concession by one GATT member would be met by an equal concession from the others.[7]

The regime worked adequately in the area for which it was originally designed: the reduction of tariff barriers against manufacturing exports. A number of 'rounds' of negotiations sponsored by the US progressively reduced such tariffs to relatively insignificant levels. But by the 1970s serious problems had begun to appear in the GATT regime, largely because of loopholes in the regime itself and because of far reaching changes in the global economy.

The major problem was that a wide range of protectionist devices, known as 'non-tariff barriers', were available to countries wishing to protect certain industries from the impact of international competition. While the liberal economic theories that underpinned the GATT predicted that in the long run competition would benefit everybody, this was small consolation to groups such as American steelworkers or French farmers for whom competition meant unemployment. Politicians faced with a choice between the hostility of large numbers of their voting publics and the displeasure of their GATT partners were inevitably liable to favour the former and seek for ways round the GATT principles. Similarly, Japan and its subsequent East Asian imitators believed that their new industries needed a period to grow without too much external pressure. In the case of the Americans and Europeans, 'Voluntary Export Restrictions' (VERS) and 'Orderly Marketing Agreements' (OMAs) were negotiated with Japan in order to limit certain Japanese exports, arrangements that were certainly against the spirit if not the strict letter of the GATT. Japan (and many other countries) likewise introduced numerous non-tariff barriers to imports, such as systematic border delays, preferential government procurement strategies, and the use of a wide range of rules and regulations in areas like health and national standards that were designed to make it difficult, if not impossible, for imports to compete effectively with domestic alternatives.[8]

Another set of problems concerned trade in items that had not been included in the original GATT. For example, trade in commercial services such as insurance, data processing, and telecommunications was not subject to the GATT regime but only to various specific and limited regimes that had emerged in a random fashion over the years. The significance of this omission from the GATT regime may be deduced from the fact that trade in services grew by about 15 per cent per annum during 1982–92, as against an annual growth of less than 10 per cent in merchandise exports. Total world trade in services has now reached around a trillion dollars.

A further constant source of irritation in trade negotiations was governmental protection of the agricultural sector. Because agriculture is particularly subject to sharp fluctuations of production and income and because all countries regard it as a vital interest that they should be able to feed their people, agriculture has always received some degree of protection. This is particularly the case of the European Union, one of whose cornerstones is a Common Agricultural Policy designed to exclude foreign competitors. Since the European Union as a whole, together with many of its former colonies, operated as a more general protectionist arrangement, European as well as Japanese trade practices encountered increasingly vehement American criticism through the 1970s and 1980s.

All of these issues were the subject of the most comprehensive series of trade negotiations to date: the Uruguay Round, which ran from 1987 to 1993. After much heated debate, especially between the American and European sides, the negotiations produced agreement on a wide range of issues – so wide, in fact that the text of the main agreement was more than 400 pages long, with over 20 000 pages of supplementary agreements and specific commitments by countries. Chief highlights are the incorporation into the GATT of trade in services and trade-related aspects of investment and intellectual property, relatively modest commitments to liberalise trade in agriculture by reducing export subsidies and other measures, the phasing out of many existing quotas on textiles, subjecting government procurement activities to further regulation and liberalisation, improving dispute settlement procedures and establishing a World Trade Organisation (WTO) to take the place of the GATT.[9] The outcome of the Uruguay Round was less a set of immediate changes than a clear basis for progress towards substantial liberalisation, with the WTO having the task of coordinating developments. If all of the measures agreed in the Uruguay Round are properly implemented, some predict an increase in world GDP of more than $200 billion over the next ten years but this prediction is based on the unlikely assumption of all states living up to their promises.

The law of the sea and the seabed mining issue

Traditionally the law of the sea has been concerned with defining the rights of navigation through various kinds of waters: the high seas, the 'territorial sea' of coastal states, narrow straits between two or more sovereign states, and other international waterways. With increasing reliance being placed on the sea as a source of food, oil and, in the near future, minerals such as manganese, copper, nickel and cobalt, and with strategic and ecological problems also involved, potential areas of contention have accumulated in recent decades.

In line with a growing tendency for the international community to seek to codify and give its explicit consent to rules that had previously been left to the more informal and indirect processes through which customary international law was formulated, the first UN Conference on the Law of the Sea (UNCLOS I) was held in Geneva in 1958. It succeeded in drafting four conventions on the territorial sea, fishing and the conservation of the living resources of the high seas, the high seas themselves, and the rights of states to the exploitable resources of their continental shelves. The main purpose of the Conference was to clarify the limits to the power of coastal states outside their territorial waters, to which end it determined that states on the high seas had freedom of navigation and of fishing, the freedom to lay submarine cables and pipelines and the freedom to fly over the high seas.[10]

Although UNCLOS I was successful in its attempt to codify many aspects of marine law for the first time, some crucial difficulties were still unresolved. In particular, the exact extent of a state's legitimate territorial waters – a matter of growing controversy since 1945 – had yet to be determined. A second UNCLOS in 1960 just failed to reach agreement on this question, but already many new problems were emerging and it soon became clear that a completely fresh approach to the law of the sea was needed. This was the task of UNCLOS III, which, lasting from 1973–82, became the world's longest and, with 158 participants, largest international conference.

One reason for the long drawn out nature of UNCLOS III was its ambitious agenda, with just about every conceivable marine issue on it. In practice, the outcome of UNCLOS III was several different regimes, but the national delegations at the Conference insisted on treating all of the issues before them as a single package for negotiating purposes. This enabled them to maximise their voting power on issues that concerned them by trading off votes on less crucial issues for their national interests against concessions in more important areas. The overall outcome of this complex bargaining was a decision-making process that required consensus formation at each stage to pre-empt the possibility of any group of states blocking progress.[11]

By 1980 many of the questions before UNCLOS III appeared to have been settled, notably as a result of a successful session in that year, which was described by the leading American delegate, Elliott Richardson, as 'the most significant single event in the history of peaceful cooperation and development of the rule of law since the founding of the United Nations itself'.[12] This judgement proved premature because of the subsequent change of President in the United States, but broad agreement had been reached on a range of issues. These included a 12-mile territorial sea, with accepted rights of transit through 100 international straits which, being less than 24 miles wide, would normally come under coastal state jurisdiction. Agreement had also been reached on environmental protection, marine research and the system to be employed in settling disputes.

One of several novel concepts to be given legitimacy by UNCLOS III was the principle that states should enjoy an exclusive economic zone (EEZ) of 200 miles from their coastlines, giving them the sole right to the food and mineral resources of the sea and seabed in this area. All other states would have freedom of navigation and overflight in the zone as well as the freedom to lay submarine cables and pipelines. Coastal states would also have the obligation to pursue sound conservation measures in their EEZs.

The Reagan administration was prepared to accept much of this, but it had serious reservations about its predecessor's agreement to the UNCLOS III provisions on deep seabed mining (that is, beyond the EEZ limits). This had always been the most contentious and complex issue before the Conference. At stake was a potentially rich harvest of manganese nodules, polymetallic substances for which the technology now exists to engage in economic mining operations. The starting point for discussions on this matter was a General Assembly resolution in December 1970 declaring these resources to be 'the common heritage of mankind', but debate soon resolved itself into a conflict between three distinct interest groups. The developing countries at first insisted that mining should be carried out by an international authority in the interests of all. This they saw as an important and concrete application of their more general argument in favour of a new international economic order. The opening bargaining position of the richer industrialised nations was that any international authority should have only minimal powers, with the seabed open for any state to exploit: an outcome which would have suited them very well as they alone possessed the necessary technology. A third group of 'landlocked and geographically disadvantaged' states, who potentially stood to be the biggest losers, attempted to ensure that their interests were safeguarded in the new regime. An additional, much smaller interest group was the existing producers of the minerals involved, whose concern has been to place a production ceiling on seabed mining with the aim of preventing prices from falling because of overproduction.[13]

The proposed new regime had a number of entirely novel and potentially highly important features. The central element in the regime is to be an International Seabed Authority (ISA), able to conduct its own mining operations through an institution to be called the Enterprise, which will have overall control of all seabed mining. An ingenious rule designed to ensure that the big mining companies, with their vast resources and monopoly of technology, would be incapable of denying the ISA its fair share of future mining operations, sets out the principle that any company wanting to mine the deep seabed will first be obliged to ask for a licence to mine an area large enough to be split into two commercial operations. The Enterprise will then grant a licence for half of the area, reserving the other half for its own future use. It will also receive a tax from mining carried out by private or state companies, who are obliged by a complex set of provisions to make their technology available both to the Enterprise and to developing countries.[14]

Another novel aspect of the ISA is its decision-making processes, which were at first a source of profound disagreement. There are to be two decision-making bodies, a Council and an Assembly, with a complex system for arriving at decisions designed to encourage consensus formation so that all interests may be safeguarded. There will also be an Economic Planning Commission and a Legal and Technical Commission to provide expert advice. Decisions will be divided into three categories of importance, requiring three different degrees of consensus. There was also what later proved to be a controversial provision for a review conference 15 years after the beginning of mining operations to re-evaluate the seabed mining regime. If this could not reach agreement by consensus, it could revise the Convention by a two-thirds majority.[15]

In January 1982 President Reagan expressed a number of fundamental American reservations about the draft convention. This intervention, coming at a point when most participants in UNCLOS III were congratulating themselves on the successful completion of the Conference, reflected both a reassertion of American national interests and new ideological misgivings that stemmed from Reagan's free market philosophy. His administration raised six key objections to the proposed convention, which are interesting as they encapsulate a basic conflict between free market and welfare approaches to international organisation that is likely to reappear in many other contexts.

As set out in a detailed statement by Reagan's representative to UNCLOS III, Ambassador James L. Malone, the first objection was that the treaty had a protectionist bias in its provisions to safeguard the interests of existing producers. Secondly, in the Administration's view, the draft treaty discriminated against private sector mining companies in a number of ways, by not sufficiently providing for the rights of 'pioneer investors' who had already spent substantial sums on exploration and developing new technologies and by pushing them strongly towards joint venture operations with the Enterprise or developing countries. Thirdly, the Administration believed (somewhat unfairly) that US interests were not sufficiently protected in the decision-making system of the ISA. Fourthly, the review conference could, in theory, commit the US to treaty amendments against its wishes, and against the American constitutional requirement for Senate approval to international treaty obligations. Fifthly, Ambassador Malone stressed that neither the proposed treaty nor amendments to it should set 'undesirable precedents' for international organisations. Finally, Senate approval for the Treaty would be unlikely to be forthcoming if it continued to provide for mandatory transfer of private technology or participation by and funding for national liberation movements, such as the Palestine Liberation Organisation.[16]

The ten years since Reagan's bombshell saw a steady decline in the prices of nickel and copper, with improved technology and the development of substitutes for some of their uses, such as fibre optics. This made the controversy over Part XI of the convention, on deep seabed mining, somewhat academic, since it was clear that it might be several decades before it would be economic to commence seabed mining operations. However, the issue had assumed a symbolic importance and an initiative by the UN Secretary-General in 1990 was needed to break the deadlock and enable President Clinton to accept the convention in 1994, when it was due to become part of international law, having received the requisite 60 ratifications.[17] The real practical significance of the convention is to be found in those of its 446 articles that do not relate to deep seabed mining. However, for students of international organisation the ISA had many intriguing features, including its provisions for the Enterprise to be the first international organisation to have an income that was independent of governments and its acceptance of principles whose intention was in part to redistribute wealth in favour of the poorer countries.

Nuclear non-proliferation

The increasing destructiveness of weapons in the twentieth century has made their limitation a recurring theme of international organisation. Both the League and UN had frequent debates about the possibility of disarmament but the more successful regimes in this field have concerned measures to control the use of weapons, rather than eliminate them altogether. Since 1945 the most urgent issue has been the danger of a nuclear war, and many of the most important arms control agreements have concerned themselves with this question. Since the end of the Cold War, and the reduction in the threat of a nuclear war between the superpowers, attention has come to focus increasingly upon the risks associated with more countries availing themselves of nuclear technology, particularly in the case of unstable and aggressive dictatorships like Iraq or North Korea.

Several agreements have contributed to what may be seen as a non-proliferation regime. The most important of these is the Nuclear Non-Proliferation Treaty of 1968. This distinguishes between nuclear weapons states (NWS) and non-nuclear weapons states (NNWS), and commits the former:

> not to transfer to any recipient whatsoever nuclear weapons or other nuclear explosive devices directly, or indirectly; and not in any way to assist, encourage, or induce any non-nuclear weapon state to manufacture or otherwise acquire nuclear weapons or other nuclear explosive devices, or control over such weapons or explosive devices.[18]

There is a matching commitment by NNWS and a number of clauses relating to such matters as verification of compliance with the NPT in accordance with the International Atomic Energy Agency's safeguards system and with ensuring that the peaceful use of nuclear energy is not inhibited and that benefits flowing from this will not be restricted to NWS.

A recent study of non-proliferation suggests that, apart from their most basic function of setting norms, international regimes serve five other purposes: '(1) identifying and focusing on a problem; (2) generating and advancing reliable information and knowledge; (3) increasing trust and understanding among states; (4) facilitating bargaining and issue linkage among states; and (5) verifying and enforcing rules and guidelines.'[19] This is valuable in drawing our attention to the fact that regimes are more than structures of rules and norms: they are important aspects of the more basic political and cognitive processes through which progress is made in the international as well as the domestic sphere. However, in the non-proliferation context the author's fifth purpose remains crucial in any assessment of the NPT and it is here that some of the more worrying problems with the regime have surfaced in recent years.

The task of enforcing compliance with the NPT rests with the International Atomic Energy Authority (IAEA), formed in 1956, and to a lesser extent with the Nuclear Suppliers Group (NSG), set up in 1974 by exporters of materials for civil nuclear programmes. The IAEA has the right to inspect and monitor states' use of nuclear technology and the obligation to report on its findings to the Security Council, which has shown an increasing concern with the proliferation issue.[20] The NSG has undertaken a wider range of responsibilities over nuclear-related exports than the NPT and has a range of diplomatic and commercial sanctions at its disposal. However, as is frequently the case in an international society consisting of sovereign states, the regime ultimately depends upon a degree of self-restraint both by the suppliers of nuclear materials and by potential nuclear powers, especially the latter. Britain and France acquired nuclear weapons against the disapproval of the United States, clearly demonstrating their belief that such weapons imparted benefits. China, the fifth nuclear power, took a similar view when it exploded its first nuclear device in 1964. The original NPT was based, in effect, upon a bargain in which the NNWS agreed to refrain from developing nuclear weapons in return for a commitment from the nuclear powers to reduce their nuclear stockpiles and ensure access to peaceful nuclear technology. Complaints have frequently been heard, especially from the third world, that the NWS have not fulfilled their side of the bargain. These issues came to a head at the treaty renewal conference, held in New York in April 1995. Although agreement was reached on this occasion, the decisions of France and China to proceed with further nuclear testing caused much irritation among some of the signatories. Questions still surround the issues of a comprehensive ban on nuclear tests, a moratorium on the production of fissionable material for military purposes, the relaxation of restrictions on the export of peaceful nuclear technology, further reductions in nuclear weapons stockpiles, and the application of the treaty's rules to Israel, one of three suspected nuclear powers (the others being India and Pakistan) who are not signatories of the NPT.[21]

Unease about the non-proliferation regime has been heightened by problems arising out of the collapse of the Soviet Union, and the ability demonstrated by two NPT members, North Korea and Iraq, to disregard their treaty obligations. Two different kinds of issues have emerged in the former Soviet Union, both with potentially very serious implications. One concerns the fact that, on the collapse of the Soviet Union as a single sovereign state, three of the successor states apart from Russia found themselves in possession of nuclear weapons: Belarus, Kazakhstan and Ukraine. Although all eventually agreed to accede to the NPT, they did so only after a lengthy and sometimes acrimonious bargaining process. Their very clear apprehensions about their security against a nuclear-armed and unstable Russia raise the question whether they will, in fact, fully honour their NPT commitments.[22]

While the case of the former Soviet Union was perhaps unique and unpredictable and in the end may be accommodated within the non-proliferation regime, the Iraqi and North Korean cases are potentially more disturbing since they raise more general questions about the long-term prospects of non-proliferation. Iraq had been able to obtain a nuclear reactor and quantities of uranium from France in the 1970s, when France was not a member of the NPT (it acceded to the Treaty, along with China and South Africa, in 1992). Israel's bombing of Iraq's nuclear reactor in 1981 merely delayed Iraq's progress towards acquiring a significant nuclear capability through various subterfuges. Even after Iraq's defeat in the Gulf War of 1991, when the extent of its nuclear ambitions became fully apparent, it took two years – in what was, essentially, an occupied country – before the IAEA was able to declare that the situation was under control.[23] Similar difficulties were experienced, if on a lesser scale, when doubts began to emerge about North Korea's commitment to the NPT, which it had signed in 1985. Eventually, after two years of prevarications and threats to withdraw from it, North Korea agreed in 1994 to abide by the NPT.[24]

These three cases revealed many problems with the non-proliferation regime; the willingness of some companies to turn a blind eye to the implications of their exports to countries like Iraq (perhaps with governmental connivance), the ability of North Korea to use its apparent nuclear ambitions as a bargaining chip to gain concessions from the USA, the inadequacies of the IAEA's safeguards system, the ability of states to withdraw from the NPT, and the problems of any regime faced with entirely unique circumstances. The international community has taken numerous steps to strengthen the regime in recent years but, as of mid-1995, non-proliferation still seemed more troubled and uncertain than at any time since 1968.

Human rights

Traditionally international law is concerned solely with the rights and duties of states in their relations with each other. The sovereignty of states – the guiding doctrine of contemporary international society – has in particular precluded the international community from any responsibility for the rights of individuals or from any role with regard to a state's treatment of its own citizens. In a formal sense individuals were only accorded a personality in international law by virtue of their membership of a state. The UN's Article 2.7 enshrines the principle that states alone are responsible for matters falling within their domestic jurisdiction.

There have always been some exceptions to the general rule of no international involvement in human rights questions. Last century the practice of slavery was outlawed as a result of international pressure. Similarly, there were European interventions against Turkish mistreatment of Christian subjects of the Ottoman empire. Some even argued that 'humanitarian interventions' were in fact permitted under international law, an assertion that has been frequently reiterated in recent years in support of several such interventions by the UN or the United States.[25] But only since 1945 have much more extensive claims been advanced for the right of the international community to concern itself with the protection of human rights. This changed attitude was prompted most immediately by the atrocities committed by the fascist powers before and during the Second World War. Early evidence of a new international approach to human rights came with the UN Charter, which contained seven specific references to human rights.[26] To these could be added the Charter's anti-colonial principles, since colonialism was now increasingly seen as involving a more general violation of human rights. Since then several developments have contributed to the emergence of a multifaceted international human rights regime, comprising both global and regional arrangements and ranging in authority from documents with little more than declaratory significance to substantial and influential institutions.

The most universal and comprehensive, but probably the least effective part of the human rights regime is that deriving from the activities of the various bodies of the UN. The central UN body here is the Human Rights Commission, which operates under the auspices of the Economic and Social Council. Its first task was to draw up a Universal Declaration of Human Rights, which was passed by the General Assembly in 1948, with South Africa, Saudi Arabia and the Soviet bloc abstaining. This represented the first attempt to arrive at an agreed international definition of human rights, and contains 30 articles which are mainly concerned with setting out traditional civil and political rights such as equality before the law, freedom from arbitrary arrest and freedom of peaceful assembly. Article 28 is interesting in that it states the right of all to 'a social and international order in which the rights and freedoms set out in this Declaration can be fully realised'. This clearly articulates the principle that individual rights within states are to some extent dependent upon the nature of the system of relations between states. Apart from the Declaration, the Commission has also been responsible for drawing up several conventions on special aspects of human rights, such as racial discrimination, torture, the rights of women and the rights of the child. Each of these has its own supervisory committee. Two key legal documents are the two UN covenants, one on civil and political rights, the other on economic, social and cultural rights, the separate treatment of these two areas reflecting a divergence of opinion as to which was the more important. Although the Covenants were drawn up in the 1950s, they were not agreed by the General Assembly until 1966 and did not come into force until 1976.[27]

During its first 20 years, the UN contented itself primarily with laying down numerous norms in the human rights area, its relative inactivity largely a reflection of deep political divisions. In its second 20 years, it gradually acquired a greater assertiveness in relation to human rights, as in 1974 when a special sub-Commission was established to look into 'situations which reveal a consistent pattern of gross violations of human rights' and 1982 when a special rapporteur on summary or arbitrary executions was appointed.[28] Its last 10 years have been marked by even more determined efforts to strengthen the UN's human rights regime. In particular, a more extensive system for monitoring states' observance of their international human rights obligations has been developed, greater publicity has been given to serious violations of rights in a number of cases, more effective means of investigating and fact finding have been established, and human rights were a significant factor in several of the UN's peacekeeping missions.[29]

Yet none would claim that the UN operates anything remotely resembling an effective system for the international protection of human rights. Some of the reasons for this are to be found within the UN's human rights system itself, which has incurred charges of incompetence, bureaucratisation and corruption on various occasions. However, the more fundamental causes of the inadequacies of the UN's system relate to the inescapable constraints imposed by the nature of contemporary intenational society. At the most basic level there are profound differences of opinion as to how human rights should be defined and which category of rights should have priority in international deliberations. Even such a central principle as the right to life is defined differently in various UN and regional documents, in line with different points of view on capital punishment and abortion. However, the greatest divergence occurs between those who emphasise the traditional civil and political rights and those who would rather give priority to economic, social and collective rights. The problem is partly ideological: the traditional rights tend to concentrate upon the limits to the power of the state vis-à-vis individuals, a concern that runs counter to the values and interests of those societies where the state's requirements are seen as supreme. There is also an argument advanced by many developing countries that to stress the freedom of the individual and such rights as a free press and free elections is meaningless and may be counterproductive in societies where even the most basic standards of material well-being and literacy are yet to be attained.[30] This view is enshrined in the Covenant on Economic, Social and Cultural Rights, whose Preamble states that 'the ideal of free human beings enjoying freedom from fear and want can only be achieved if conditions are created whereby everyone may enjoy his economic, social and cultural rights as well as his civil and political rights'. Developing countries also frequently stress collective rather than individual rights, such as the right of national self-determination or the right of racial equality. This kind of thinking is behind Article 6 of the 1981 Banjul Charter, drawn up by the OAU, which asserts 'the right to liberty and the security of the person' but also states that 'no one may be deprived of his freedom except for reasons and conditions previously laid down by law'.[31]

Perhaps the greatest barrier to a universal human rights regime is the fact that in a world with many fierce interstate antagonisms, moves towards a system for the international protection of human rights will inevitably be exploited for diplomatic or propaganda purposes by one state against another. Such favourite targets of the third world as Israel and South Africa before the ending of apartheid have felt the full force, such as it is, of the UN's human rights machinery, while equally bad (or far worse) offenders have escaped relatively lightly. Similarly, in the early years of the UN, the then American-dominated General Assembly tended to focus its attention mainly on human rights violations in the Soviet bloc and Soviet spokesmen claimed that the concern shown by President Carter's administration in the 1970s had a similar anti-Soviet purpose.[32]

Finally, even if international relations were marked more than they are by good will and ideological consensus, the doctrine of state sovereignty would still prevent the development of an effective rights regime. Most states accused of human rights violations in the UN invariably respond by asserting their right to govern their internal affairs as they choose. Indeed there is some force to their argument. While states are sovereign in their responsibilities, in that they alone accept ultimate responsibility for their security or economic welfare, they will see little reason to surrender their sovereign rights and powers. In that sense, progress towards an effective universal human rights regime is dependent upon more fundamental changes in the nature of international relations from a sovereignty-based, pluralistic and decentralised community to the as yet unrealistic ideal of a world community.

This factor partly explains the relative success of some regionally-based human rights regimes, since they developed among states which already enjoyed some degree of economic or security integration. The work of many regional organisations often has implications for human rights, but only the American and Western European regions have extensive systems for the promotion and protection of human rights. In Africa, as already mentioned, the OAU adopted a 'Charter on Human and People's Rights' in 1981. This created a Commission with the task of investigating complaints but so far with little or no impact. A similar system in the Arab world was effectively stillborn. In Asia, there is as yet no regional human rights framework, indeed in recent years some Asian leaders, notably from Malaysia, Singapore and China, have embarked upon a counteroffensive against Western pressure over human rights, arguing that Western conceptions of human rights do not, in fact, embody genuinely universal principles but are opposed to traditional Asian ideas and a form of neo-colonialism.

The American system is based upon the 1948 American Declaration on the Rights and Duties of Man.[33] This was followed by the formation of an Inter-American Commission on Human Rights in 1959, whose powers were broadened in 1965 following several successful initiatives by the Commission, notably in promoting the rights of political prisoners and refugees in the Dominican Republic. In 1969 an American Convention on human rights was drawn up which by 1991 had been ratified by 19 out of the 33 OAS members.[34] There is also as Inter-American Court on Human Rights, with similar powers on paper to those of the European Court (considered shortly), although in practice only ten states, not including the United States, have accepted its jurisdiction.[35]

Given the notoriety of many Latin American countries in the human rights field, the American human rights system can hardly be acclaimed a great success. Indeed it should perhaps be remembered that no unrealistic expectations were held of the Commission from the outset, merely that it should promote an awareness of and respect for human rights in the region. It was given no powers to force states to adhere to the Declaration, nor were sanctions envisaged. Within these limitations it has performed its task with some success. It has gradually become bolder in its interpretation of its role, and has moved from its original function of preparing studies and reports to direct criticisms of original states, some of which have had a significant political impact.[36] But in all Latin American affairs much hangs on the attitude taken by the United States. Washington was not one of the early supporters of a strong regional human rights regime, partly because it did not wish racist practices in parts of the United States to come under international scrutiny and partly because of its preoccupation with communism, which led it to support some of the region's right-wing dictatorships as bastions against communism.[37] In the 1970s, when Congress and President Carter decided to make American aid dependent on recipient countries' human rights records, the worst Latin American cases came under considerable pressure. President Reagan reversed this emphasis in the 1980s but the increasing trend towards democratisaton in the region was accompanied by a steady growth in the willingness of many OAS members to use the human rights mechanisms, notwithstanding indifference and sometimes hostility from the US.

In Western Europe the regional human rights machinery has had a significant and growing impact. This was partly because the impetus given to the movement towards the international protection of human rights by the Second World War was naturally greatest in the region where the worst violations had taken place and partly because, for the first time in European history, all Western European nations found themselves with democratic governments devoted to the principle of the rule of law.

The parent body of the European human rights system is the Council of Europe, set up in 1949, with an original 18 members, including Turkey, Malta, Switzerland and Sweden. The Council gained a new lease of life after the collapse of communism in Europe in 1989, when it nearly doubled its membership to 34, as of early 1995.[38] The Council drew up a European Convention of Human Rights, which came into force in 1953. To date three separate organs have administered the system for implementing the protection of rights agreed to in the Convention: a Commission, a Court and a Committee of Ministers. The Commission receives petitions from both states and individuals, although in practice there have only been eight cases involving complaints by one government against another, compared to more than 20 000 cases originating in petitions from individuals. The first task of the Commission is to determine whether petitions are admissible for further consideration, with several grounds existing for rejecting a petition, including that 'local remedies' have not been exhausted and the rather sweeping powers of Article 27 (2) to reject any petition that is 'manifestly ill-founded'.[39] Most petitions fail at this first hurdle, and in the case of those deemed admissible, the Commission's first task is to seek to obtain a 'friendly settlement'. For instance, in several cases the offending state has amended a relevant law before a petition could progress further through the European system, thus enabling the Commission to drop the matter. At this stage the Commission is also empowered to undertake a fact-finding investigation, with member states required to provide it with all necessary facilities for this purpose. The Commission may then express its opinion on a petition and pass this on for consideration by a Committee or a Minister or, normally where some complex point of law is involved, it may request the European Human Rights Court to reach a judgement. All the Commission's decisions are arrived at by majority vote. At the Vienna Summit of October 1993, the decisions were taken to merge the Court and Commission and also to appoint full-time judges to the Court, the previous practice having been to use part-time jurists.

Democratic states with a free press are inevitably sensitive to accusations that they have violated human rights and the mere fact of a petition proceeding as far as the Court has often served to give an issue sufficient publicity to bring about a change in law or practice. The Court also has more direct powers, including its capacity under Article 50 to 'afford just satisfaction to the injured party'. The ultimate sanction is for a state to be expelled from the Council of Europe, as might have happened to Greece when it was under military government, had Greece not forestalled this by withdrawing from the Council.

The European human rights system has had an extraordinary success in redressing individual wrongs, causing the law of several countries to be amended, helping to bring the different legal systems of Western Europe into some harmony with each other, and generally increasing awareness of the many issues involved in human rights questions. Moreover its influence and prestige seem to be growing. Several explanations have been offered for this success, including the confidence of member states that the screening system will let through only a small minority of complaints, that proceedings will be private and that states will not abuse the system to score points off each other. But of central importance is the fact that the system operated – until 1989 – among states where there were already, for the most part, effective domestic safeguards of human rights. The Convention itself merely enshrined rights which had existed in law for many years in several member countries, and the primary role of the European system was to identify marginal areas where the domestic legal processes contained loopholes or had been bypassed. This raises questions about the European system's value as a model for the international protection of human rights elsewhere, and about its effectiveness in cases where states do not already have a high regard for human rights, as evidenced by the withdrawal of Greece's military regime. As is so often the case in the history of international organisation, changes in the attitudes of states are the crucial element which must precede the creation of effective international instruments. But once such changes have occurred, institutions like the European system may play an important part in safeguarding existing rights and lay the foundations for further progress. In the context of the new Europe, the Council of Europe also gave its 16 new members an invaluable framework for learning about, implementing and protecting the human rights systems they were anxious to adopt.

Appendix

The Specialised Agencies of the United Nations

Acronym	Name of Agency	Date established	Date approved/ estabished as UN agency
FAO	Food and Agriculture Organisation	1945	1946
UNESCO	UN Educational, Scientific and Cultural Organisation	1946	1946
ILO	International Labour Organisation	1919	1946
ICAO	International Civil Aviation Organisation	1947	1946
UPU	Universal Postal Union	1874	1947
ITU	International Telecommunication Union (Successor to International Telegraph Union – established 1865)	1932	1947
IMF	International Monetary Fund	1944 (Began operation 1947)	1947
IBRD	International Bank for Reconstruction and Development (The World Bank)	1945 (Began operation 1946)	1947
WHO	World Health Organisation	1948	1947
WMO	World Meteorological Organisation (Successor to International Meteorological Organisation, founded 1873)	1950 (Began operation 1951)	1951

IMO	International Maritime Organisation	1948 (Formally est. 1959)	1948
IFC	International Finance Corporation	1956	1957
IDA	International Development Association	1960	1961
WIPO	World Intellectual Property Organisation	1970	1974
IFAD	International Fund for Agricultural Development	1977	1977
UNIDO	UN Industrial Development Organisation	1966	1986
MIGA	Multilateral Investment Guarantee Agency	1988	1988

Other UN Agencies

Acronym	Name of Agency	Date established
GATT	General Agreement on Tariffs and Trade	1947
IAEA	International Atomic Energy Agency	1957

Note. Sources used: Martin Hill, *The United Nations System: coordinating its economic and social work* (Cambridge, London, New York, Melbourne, 1978), New Zealand Ministry of Foreign Affairs and Trade, *1993 United Nations Handbook* (Wellington, 1993).

Secretaries-General of the United Nations

Trygve Lie (Norway)	1 February 1946–10 April 1953
Dag Hammarskjöld (Sweden)	10 April 1953–18 September 1961
U Thant (Burma)	
Acting Secretary-General	3 November 1961–30 November 1962
Secretary-General	30 November 1962–31 December 1971

Secretaries-General of the United Nations (*Cont.*)

Kurt Waldheim (Austria)	1 January 1972–31 December 1981
Javier Pérez de Cuéllar (Peru)	1 January 1982–31 December 1991
Boutros Boutros-Ghali (Egypt)	1 January 1992–

Notes and References

INTRODUCTION

1. *Foreign Relations of the United States* (*FRUS*), vol. II (Washington, 1949) pp. 15–22.
2. Ibid., p. 17.
3. Ibid., p. 19.
4. *FRUS*, vol. 1 (1946) pp. 1136–7.
5. Ibid., pp. 1167–71.
6. D. P. Kommers and G. D. Loescher (eds), *Human Rights and American Foreign Policy* (Indiana, 1979) p. 154.

1. THE ORIGINS OF THE LEAGUE OF NATIONS

1. W. S. Churchill, *The World Crisis: The Aftermath* (London, 1929) p. 142.
2. About 200 disputes went to arbitration between 1815 and 1900.
3. P. S. Reinsch, *Public International Unions* (Boston, 1911) p. 21.
4. Ibid., p. 6 for an early use of the term 'interdependence'.
5. L. S. Woolf, *International Government* (London, 1916) pp. 102–4.
6. Ibid., p. 104.
7. *The Proceedings of the Hague Peace Conferences: The Conference of 1899*, Carnegie Endowment for International Peace (New York, 1920) pp. 18–19.
8. Ibid.
9. This was, in fact, little more than a list of arbitrators who were available to states which might wish to make use of their services.
10. F. Wilson, *The Origins of the League Covenant* (London, 1928) pp. 18, 58.
11. H. W. V. Temperley, *A History of the Peace Conference of Paris*, vol. IV, (London, 1924) p. 24.
12. Castlereagh, speaking on the proposed Protocol of the Congress of Troppau, quoted in Woolf, *International Government*, p. 24.
13. Viscount Grey, *Twenty Five Years* (New York, 1925) p. 256.
14. E. Bendiner, *A Time for Angels* (London, 1975) p. 12. See also F. P. Walters, *A History of the League of Nations* (London, 1952) p. 18.

15. D. F. Fleming, *The United States and the League of Nations, 1918–1920* (New York, 1932) pp. 3–8.

16. Ibid.

17. For a summary of the work of these groups, see A. Zimmern, *The League of Nations and the Rule of Law* (London, 1936) pp. 160–73; also A. J. Mayer, *Political Origins of the New Diplomacy, 1917–1918* (New Haven, Conn., 1959) pp. 46–155.

18. D. H. Miller, *The Drafting of the Covenant*, vol. I (New York, 1928) p. 4.

19. R. S. Baker, *Woodrow Wilson: Life and Letters* (London, 1939).

20. Bryan actually claimed that this idea originated in similar proposals that he had been advancing for some years as a means of resolving labour disputes. *The Memoirs of William Jennings Bryan* (Washington, 1925) pp. 384–5.

21. *Papers Relating to the Foreign Relations of the United States: The Paris Peace Conference (PPC)*, vol. I (Washington, 1943) p. 23.

22. The fourteenth point stated that 'a general association of nations must be formed under specific covenants for the purpose of affording mutual guarantees of political independence and territorial integrity to great and small states alike.'

23. C. Seymour (ed.), *The Intimate Papers of Colonel House*, vol. I (London, 1928) p. 209.

24. *PPC*, vol. I, pp. 22–5.

25. R. S. Baker and W. E. Dodd (eds), *The Public Papers of Woodrow Wilson*, vol. II (New York, 1927) pp. 184–8.

26. *PPC*, vol. I, p. 53.

27. Fleming, *The US and the League*, p. 12.

28. R. Lansing, *The Peace Negotiations: A Personal Narrative* (Boston, Mass., 1921) p. 34.

29. See his letter to House, dated 22 March 1918 in Baker, *Life and Letters*, vol. VIII, p. 43.

30. See House's letter to Wilson, 14 July 1918, ibid., p. 279.

31. Ibid., p. 43, also p. 74. See also S. F. Beamis (ed.), *The American Secretaries of State and their Diplomacy*, vol. X (New York, 1954) p. 154.

32. Baker, *Life and Letters*, vol. VIII, pp. 340, 343.

33. Baker and Dodd (eds), *Public Papers*, vol. 1, p. 330.

34. See his exposition of the League to the Senate Foreign Relations Committee, ibid.

35. Seymour (ed.), *Intimate Papers*, vol. IV (1928) p. 292.

36. Ibid., p. 161.

37. Zimmern, *The League of Nations*, pp. 196–208 for the full text of this memorandum. See also G. W. Egerton, *Great Britain and the Creation of the League of Nations* (London, 1979) pp. 94–7.

38. Seymour (ed.), *Intimate Papers*, vol. IV, p. 292.

39. Miller, *Drafting of the Covenant*, vol. II, p. 28. See also G. Curry, 'Woodrow Wilson, Jan Smuts and the Versailles Settlement', *American Historical Review*, LXVI, no. 4 (July 1961) 968–86.

40. *PPC*, vol. III (1928) p. 766.

41. Egerton, *Great Britain*, p. 114.

42. This is in fact too great a claim for any individual, if only because many important items in the Covenant were only arrived at in the course of the actual Paris negotiations.

43. Egerton, *Great Britain*, p. 83.

44. Beamis (ed.), *American Secretaries of State*, vol. X, p. 154.

45. Letter from Lansing to House, 8 April 1918, in *Papers Relating to the Foreign Relations of the United States: The Lansing Papers; 1914–1920* (Washington, 1940) pp. 118–20.

46. Lansing, *Peace Negotiations*, pp. 48–76.

47. Miller, *Drafting of the Covenant*, vol. II, pp. 7–15.

48. Hankey to Balfour, 25 May 1916, cited in Egerton, *Great Britain*, p. 35.

49. *Drafting of the Covenant*, vol. II, p. 56.

50. Ibid., pp. 106–16.

51. See Zimmern, *The League of Nations*, pp. 151–9.

52. See D. Mitrany, *The Functional Theory of Politics* (London, 1975), and the same author's seminal essay, *A Working Peace System: An Argument for the Functional Development of International Organisation* (London, 1943).

53. J. C. Smuts, 'A Practical Suggestion', in Miller, *Drafting of the Covenant*, vol. II, pp. 24–5.

54. Seymour (ed.), *Intimate Papers*, vol. IV, p. 296.

55. For the Italian draft see Miller, *Drafting of the Covenant*, vol. II, pp. 246–55.

56. Ibid., p. 300.

57. Seymour (ed.), *Intimate Papers*, vol. IV, p. 477.

58. *PPC*, vol. II, pp. 662–3.

59. Egerton, *Great Britain*, p. 85.

60. See Zimmern, *The League of Nations*, p. 207, and also Lloyd George's 'Fontainbleau Memorandum' in his *Memoirs of the Peace Conference* (New Haven, 1938) p. 269.

61. A. J. Mayer, *Politics and Diplomacy of Peacemaking* (London, 1968) pp. 9, 36 and 363. See also N. G. Levin, *Woodrow Wilson and World Politics* (New York, 1968) p. 6, and J. M. Thompson, *Russia, Bolshevism and the Versailles Peace* (New York, 1966) pp. 314, 385.

62. Egerton, *Great Britain*, p. 112.

63. Ibid., p. 120.

64. Miller, *Drafting of the Covenant*, vol. I, p. 63.

65. This was Wilson's so-called 'fourth draft'.

66. Egerton, *Great Britain*, pp. 121–5.

67. Miller, *Drafting of the Covenant*, vol. II, p. 237.

68. Ibid., vol. I, pp. 168–70, vol. II, p. 264.

69. Ibid., vol. II, p. 169.

70. Wilson, *Origins of the League Covenant*, p. 93.

71. Articles 11–17 in the Covenant.

72. Article 19 in the Hurst–Miller draft. Miller, *Drafting of the Covenant*, vol. II, p. 237.

73. Telegram to Lansing from American Ambassador in Tokyo, 15 November 1918, *PPC*, vol. I, p. 490.

74. Fleming, *The US and the League*, p. 184.

75. Miller, *Drafting of the Covenant*, vol. I, pp. 286–9 for the text of the memorandum.

76. Ibid., vol. II, pp. 580–91.

77. Wilson, *Origins of the League Covenant*, pp. 64–5.

78. Harold Nicholson writes of the atmosphere in Paris following the 'sinking of the vessel of Wilsonism' as follows: 'It was almost with a panic rush that we made for the boats, and when we reached them we found our colleagues of the Italian delegation already comfortably installed. They made us very welcome.' *Peacemaking 1919* (London, 1934) p. 70.

2. THE LEAGUE OF NATIONS

1. Cf. W. S. Schiffer, *The Legal Community of Mankind* (Columbia, 1954) pp. 199 and 205.

2. I. L. Claude, *Power and International Relations* (New York, 1962) pp. 196–7.

3. F. H. Hinsley, *Power and the Pursuit of Peace* (Cambridge, 1967) pp. 307–22.

4. A. Zimmern, *The League of Nations and the Rule of Law* (London, 1936) pp. 304–5.

5. 'Report to the 2nd Assembly of the League on the Work of the Council and on the Measures Taken to Execute the Decisions of the 1st Assembly', *League of Nations Document A.9.* (1921) p. 30.

6. 'Report to the 5th Assembly', *League of Nations Document A.8.* (1924) p. 18.

7. *Documents on British Foreign Policy (DBFP)* 1st ser. vol. XIII (London, 1963) p. 489.

8. Ibid., vol. VII (1958) pp. 134–5.

9. *DBFP*, ser. 1A, vol. I (London, 1966) p. 847.

10. Ibid., p. 848.

11. B. Dexter, *The Years of Opportunity: The League of Nations, 1920–1926* (New York, 1967) pp. 171–6.

12. *DBFP*, ser. 1A, vol. I, p. 7.

13. Notes of a conversation between Lloyd George and Briand, 5 January 1922, *DBFP*, vol. XIX (1974) p. 13.

14. *DBFP*, vol. XI (1961) pp. 337, 335–6, 372–3.

15. *League of Nations Document A.37.* (1920) p. 25.

16. For the text of Lloyd George's telegram to the League Secretary-General, see T. P. Conwell-Evans, *The League Council in Action* (London, 1929) p. 43.

17. 'Report to the 3rd Assembly', *League of Nations Document A.7.* (1922) p. 31.

18. *League of Nations Official Journal* (*LNOJ*) (February 1925) p. 146.

19. For a comprehensive account of this affair see J. Barros, *The Corfu Incident of 1923: Mussolini and the League of Nations* (Princeton, NJ, 1965).

20. 'Report to the 5th Assembly', *League of Nations Document A.8.* (1924) p. 19.

21. 'Report to the 7th Assembly', *League of Nations Document A.6* (1926).

22. Cited in E. Bendiner, *A Time for Angels* (London, 1975) p. 218.

23. Dexter, *The Years of Opportunity*, p. 135.

24. J. Barros, *Office without Power: Secretary-General Sir Eric Drummond, 1919–1933* (Oxford, 1979) p. 252.

25. Ibid., pp. 253–7.

26. See J. Barros, *Betrayal from Within: Joseph Avenol, Secretary-General of the League of Nations, 1933–1940* (New York, 1969) pp. 47–51 and Bendiner, *A Time for Angels*, pp. 317–19, Zimmern, *The League of Nations*, pp. 424–30.

27. The United States did however join a separate 'mediatory group', Zimmern, *The League of Nations*, p. 429.

28. The most comprehensive study of the Manchurian crisis is C. Thorne, *The Limits of Foreign Policy: The West, the League and the Far Eastern Crisis of 1931–1933* (London, 1972).

29. Japan's reasons for withdrawing from the League included an assertion of the 'just and equitable principle' that it was necessary for the operation of the Covenant to vary in accordance with the actual conditions prevailing in different regions of the world, *LNOJ* (May 1933) p. 657.

30. For one example out of many of this kind of thinking in the British Foreign Office, see *DBFP*, ser. 2, vol. VIII, pp. 681–2.

31. See F. P. Walters, *A History of the League of Nations*, vol. II (London, 1952) p. 474.

32. *DBFP*, ser. 2, vol. VIII, pp. 679–80.

33. Ibid., pp. 714–15.

34. For example, when China made a new appeal in January 1932, invoking Articles 10 and 15 for the first time, Japan insisted that this meant that the Chinese needed to supply the Council with a freshly documented

statement of their case. 6th meeting of the Council, *LNOJ* (January 1932) pp. 339–42.

35. Fifth meeting of the Council (28 January 1932) *LNOJ* (January 1932) pp. 327–8.

36. Telegram from the Tokyo Embassy, *DBFP*, ser. 2, vol. VIII, p. 700.

37. 'Foreign Office Memorandum', ibid., pp. 826–9.

38. For the text of the Ethiopian appeal, see *LNOJ* (May 1935).

39. Telegram to the French Ambassador in Rome, 19 July 1935, cited in G. Warner, *Pierre Laval and the Eclipse of France* (London, 1968) p. 96.

40. Laval had gone some way towards implying as much during a visit to Rome in January 1935, while another important indication came at the Stresa Conference of April 1935 between France, Britain and Italy, whose final communiqué opposed the unilateral repudiation of treaties but restricted this to cases which might endanger the peace 'of Europe'. See E. M. Robertson, *Mussolini as Empire Builder: Europe and Africa, 1923–1936* (London, 1977) pp. 114–16 and 129–31.

41. J. Barros maintains that part of the responsibility for the League's non-involvement in the early stages of the Ethiopian crisis rested with the Secretary-General, Avenol, whose consistent advice was that the affair should be settled informally between the major powers. This may be crediting him with rather more influence than he in fact possessed. See *Betrayal from Within*.

42. Warner, *Pierre Laval*, p. 106 and Robertson, *Mussolini*, pp. 172–3.

43. See *DBFP*, 2nd ser. vol. XV, *passim*, for details of these differences.

44. 'Minute by Sir R. Vansittart on the Position of Sanctions and the Possibility of Closing the Suez Canal to Italian Shipping', *DBFP*, 2nd ser. vol. XVI, pp. 358–60.

45. Memorandum dated 27 November 1935 by Sir S. Hoare and Mr A. Eden on a possible oil embargo, in *DBFP*, 2nd ser. vol. XV, pp. 332–40.

46. Telegram to British Ambassador in Washington, 4 December 1935, *DBFP*, 2nd ser., vol. XV, p. 377.

47. Hoare and Eden Memorandum, *DBFP*, 2nd ser., vol. XV, pp. 332–40.

48. See for example, telegram dated 26 November 1935 from Sir S. Hoare to the British Ambassador in Washington, *DBFP*, 2nd ser., vol. XV, pp. 324–5.

49. Memorandum dated 15 December 1935 from the British Ambassador in Paris to Sir S. Hoare, *DBFP*, 2nd ser., vol. XV, pp. 480–2.

50. Ibid.

51. *LNOJ* (June 1936).

52. For details of the Convention, see *LNOJ* (1930) Special Supplement no. 84.

53. *LNOJ* (January 1936) pp. 24–6.

54. *DBFP*, 2nd ser., vol. XV, pp. 269 and 274–5.

55. Robertson, *Mussolini*, p. 185.

56. *LNOJ* (June 1936) p. 660.

57. The problem of the 'sources' of international law is a controversial one. However, the dominant approach is probably the 'positivist' one, which argues that only treaties and the established customs of states create binding obligations.

58. M. O. Hudson, *The Permanent Court of International Justice, 1920–1942* (New York, 1943) pp. 92–112.

59. Article 9 of the Statute of the Court.

60. Sir Hersch Lauterpacht, *The Development of International Law by the International Court* (London, 1958) pp. 273–6.

61. Ibid., p. 4, and S. Rosenne, *The World Court* (New York, 1973) p. 25.

62. R. P. Dhakali, *The Codification of Public International Law* (Manchester, 1970) p. 115.

63. S. Rosenne (ed.), *The League of Nations Committee for the Progressive Codification of International Law (1925–1928)*, vol. I (Oceana Publications, 1972) introduction, pp. xxx–xxxi.

64. See ibid. for the history of this committee.

65. Sir Hersch Lauterpacht, however, disagrees with this verdict: *The Development of International Law*, p. 7.

66. The American Council on Public Affairs, *World Organisation* (Washington, 1942) p. 265.

67. Bendiner, *A Time for Angels*, pp. 328–32.

68. American Council on Public Affairs, *World Organisation*, p. 250.

69. *LNOJ* (February 1936) p. 203.

70. For further details on the regulations for each type of mandate, see the League of Nations, *The Mandates System* (Genega, 1945) pp. 24–32; F. White, *Mandates* (London, 1926) pp. 24–30, and Q. Wright, *Mandates under the League of Nations* (Chicago, 1930) pp. 24–63.

71. In its first report the Commission declared: 'We shall endeavour to exercise our authority less as a judge from whom critical pronouncements are expected than as collaborators who are resolved to devote their experience and their energies to a joint endeavour.' Cited in Wright, *Mandates*, p. 196.

72. *The Bruce Report on the Technical Work of the League*, Special Supplement to the Monthly Summary of the League of Nations (September 1939) p. 7.

73. Report to the 4th Assembly, *League of Nations Document A. 10* (1923) pp. 49–59.

74. Supplementary Report to the 8th Assembly, *League of Nations Document A.13 (a)* (1927) pp. 21–31.

75. League of Nations Secretariat, *Ten Years of World Co-operation* (Geneva, 1930) pp. 199–201.

76. Walters, *History of the League of Nations*, vol. II, pp. 518–23.

77. *LNOJ* (January 1932) pp. 152–4.

78. American Council on Public Affairs, *World Organisation*, p. 173.

79. See *The Bruce Report*, and League of Nations Secretariat, *Ten Years of World Co-operation*, pp. 232–60.

80. Report to the 2nd Assembly, *League of Nations Document A.9.* (1921) p. 64.

81. M. Burton, *The Assembly of the League of Nations* (New York, 1974) p. 45.

82. Ibid., pp. 73–5.

83. Ibid., pp. 175–205.

84. H. Butler, *The Lost Peace* (London, 1941) p. 31.

85. Burton, *The Assembly*, p. 382.

86. Barros, *Betrayal from Within*, p. 12.

87. Barros, *Office without Power*, p. 395.

88. Ibid., p. 291.

89. Ibid., p. 54.

3. THE AMERICAN-LED, COLD WAR UNITED NATIONS, 1945–1960

1. I am grateful to Dr David Armstrong for allowing me to make liberal use of the chapter on 'The United Nations in World Politics' in his book, *The Rise Of The International Organisation: A Short History* (London, 1982).

2. Sir Alexander Cadogan, 'The United Nations: a Balance Sheet', *The Year Book of World Affairs 1951* (London, 1951) p. 2. Cf. Charles Webster, 'The Making of the Charter of the United Nations', *History*, 32, March (1947) 17.

3. Smarting under recent insults to his pride, de Gaulle of France declined the invitation to be one of the four sponsoring powers. At America's insistence, China was included in the rank of great powers, but it did not really count.

4. Webster, 'The Making of the Charter', p. 16.

5. That is the 46 states that had declared war against Germany and another four admitted during the conference: Denmark, Argentina, Ukraine and Byelorussia.

6. *A Commentary on the Charter of the United Nations* Cmd 6666 (London, 1945) p. 4.

7. Articles 10, 13 and 14. Article 12, however, maintains the special position of the Security Council. The General Assembly can make recommendations on any matter unless the Security Council 'is exercising in respect of any dispute or situation the functions assigned to it in the present Charter'.

8. Security Council decisions required an affirmative vote of seven of the Council's then eleven members and (on other than procedural matters) had to include 'the concurring votes of the permanent members' (Article 27.3). Thus, if a permanent member voted against a resolution, it had cast a veto. After the 1965 enlargement of the Security Council, the number of affirmative votes needed rose to nine.

9. See Ruth B. Russell, *A History of the United Nations Charter. The Role of the United States 1940–1945* (Washington DC, 1958) p. 727.

10. HMSO Cmd. 6666, pp. 16–17. Cf. Inis Claude, 'The Security Council' in Evan Luard (ed.), *The Evolution of International Organizations* (London, 1966) pp. 71–2.

11. But they hoped to 'render [the American conception] more practical by an admixture of our own political sense'. *The Memoirs of Lord Gladwyn* (London, 1972) p. 114.

12. Thomas M. Franck, *Nation against Nation. What Happened to the UN Dream and What the US Can Do about It* (New York, 1985) pp. 20, 17.

13. See D. Yergin, *The Shattered Peace: the Origins of the Cold War and the National Security State* (London, 1978) pp. 47–8. Quoted in David Armstrong, *The Rise of the International Organisation* (London, 1982) p. 50.

14. T. M. Campbell, *Masquerade Peace: America's UN Policy, 1944–5* (Tallahassee, 1973) pp. 36–7. Quoted in Armstrong, *Rise of the International Organisation*, p. 51.

15. L. D. Weiler and A.P. Simons, *The United States and the United Nations* (New York, 1967) p. 40. Quoted in Armstrong, *Rise of the International Organisation*, p. 51.

16. Cadogan, 'The UN: a balance sheet', p. 3.

17. On important issues, however, a two-thirds vote is required in the General Assembly.

18. Article 22 of the Covenant, Article 76.b of the Charter.

19. Boutros Boutros-Ghali, *An Agenda for Peace. Preventive Diplomacy, Peacemaking and Peace-keeping* (New York, 1992) para. 14.

20. Sydney Bailey calculated that up to October 1967, in 68 matters out of 97, the use of the veto had not deadlocked the Council. In the remaining 29 cases, the Council was able to adopt resolutions in 17 cases but also encountered vetoes. Only on 12 matters was it unable to take substantive decisions because of the veto. Sydney Bailey, *Voting in the Security Council* (Bloomington, IN, 1969), p. 60.

21. According to Sydney Bailey, 'it might be claimed that 109 vetoes related to 66 separate proposals'. Ibid., p. 29.

22. See Alan Bullock, *Ernest Bevin. Foreign Secretary* (Oxford, New York, 1985) pp. 160–3. The threat was internal. When Britain withdrew in 1947 the Americans took over 'protecting' Greece, Iran and Turkey under the Truman Doctrine.

23. Alan James, *The Politics of Peacekeeping* (London, 1969), p. 212.

24. By early 1951 the number of contributing states had risen to 16.

25. The resolution also said that the General Assembly could be called into emergency session at the request of a majority of Security Council members.

26. On collective security, see Inis Claude, *Power in International Relations* (New York, 1962); Alan James, 'The Enforcement Provisions of the United Nations Charter' in United Nations Institute for Training and Research, *The United Nations and the Maintenance of International Peace and Security* (Dordrecht, Boston, Lancaster, 1987), pp. 213–35; Arnold Wolfers, *Discord and Collaboration* (Baltimore, MD, 1962); J. L. Brierly, *The Covenant and the Charter* (Cambridge, 1947); H. C. Johnson and G. Niemeyer, 'Collective Security: the Validity of an Ideal?', *International Organization*, 8, no. 1 (1954) 19–35; R. N. Stromberg, 'The Idea of Collective Security', *Journal of the History of Ideas*, 27, no. 2 (1956) 250–63.

27. US Secretary of State, Dean Acheson, in Department of State *Bulletin*, XXIII, no. 575 (10 July 1950) 46. Quoted in Leland M. Goodrich, 'Korea: Collective Measures against Aggression', *International Conciliation*, no. 494 (October 1953) 172–3.

28. In 1955–6 the Security Council considered only one substantive question. In 1956–7 it discussed six. In both sessions the General Assembly considered eleven substantive questions. In 1959 the Council met only five times.

29. On 27 September 1938, during the Munich crisis, the British Prime Minister, Neville Chamberlain, spoke of the lack of sense in going to war with Germany 'because of a quarrel in a far-away country between people of whom we know nothing'. Quoted in A. J. P. Taylor, *English History 1914–1945* (Harmondsworth, 1970 [first published 1965]) p. 528.

30. Cabinet meeting 6 February 1947. PRO, CP (47)49, CAB 129/16. Quoted in F. S. Northedge, 'Britain and the Middle East', in Ritchie Ovendale (ed.), *The Foreign Policy of the British Labour Governments, 1945–51* (Leicester, 1984), p. 158.

31. Ernest Bevin (Foreign Secretary), PRO CP(47) 259 CAB 129/21. Quoted in Northedge, 'Britain and the Middle East', p. 162.

32. As of October 1995, UNTSO is still present in the area.

33. The following discussion is heavily indebted to Alan James. See, for example, his *Peacekeeping in International Politics* (London, 1990).

34. Ibid., p. 1.

35. Interview with Francis D. Wilcox, 11 September 1960. CBS News, *The Collected Transcripts from the CBS Radio and Television Broadcasts*, vol. 6, *Face the Nation. 1960–1961* (New York, 1972), p. 299.

36. Max Jacobson, *The United Nations in the 1990s. A Second Chance?* (New York, 1993) p. 41.

37. At the time of Suez in 1956.

38. 'I have a responsibility to all those Member States for which the Organization is of decisive importance – a responsibility which over-rides all other considerations,' he said. 'It is not the Soviet Union or any of the other big Powers which need the United Nations for their protection. It is all the others. In this sense the Organization is first of all their Organization.' *GAOR*, 883rd plenary meeting, paragraphs 10–11. Quoted in Alan James, 'Neutral Men and Neutral Action', *International Relations*, 2, no. 4 (1961) 242.

39. See Alan James, 'The Congo Controversies', *International Peacekeeping*, 1, no. 1 (1994) 46–7.

40. See Brian Urquhart, *Hammarskjöld* (London, Sydney, Toronto, 1972) pp. 530–41.

41. See chart on the Specialised Agencies in the Appendix.

42. Martin D. Dubin, 'Toward the Bruce Report: the Economic and Social Programs of the League of Nations in the Avenol Era' in Proceedings of the symposium organised by the UN Library and the Graduate Institute of International Studies 1980, *The League in Retrospect* (Berlin & New York, 1980), p. 42.

43. H. G. Nicholas, *The United Nations as a Political Institution*, 5th edn (London, Oxford, New York, 1975) pp. 139–40.

44. Ibid., p. 148.

45. *United Nations Bulletin*, XV, 586–8. Quoted in Stephen S. Goodspeed, 'Political Considerations in the United Nations Economic and Social Council', *The Year Book of World Affairs, 1961* (London, 1961) p. 142.

46. It is worth noting, however, that advisory opinions are not binding.

47. Judge Shigeru Oda, 'Reservations in the Declarations of Acceptance of the Optional Clause and the Period of Validity of those Declarations: the Effect of the Shultz Letter', *The British Year Book of International Law, 1988* (Oxford, 1989) p. 20.

4. THIRD WORLD UN, 1960–1980

1. Even so, China vetoed Outer Mongolia and in retaliation the Soviet Union vetoed Japan (which was admitted in 1956). The states admitted between 1946 and 1955 were Burma, Indonesia, Israel, Pakistan, Sweden, Thailand, Yemen, Iceland and Afghanistan.

2. Lawrence S. Finkelstein, 'The United Nations: Then and Now', *International Organization*, 19, no. 3 (1965) 368–9. Cf. Leland M. Goodrich, 'San Francisco In Retrospect, *International Journal*, 25, no. 2 (1970) 239.

3. Between 1960 and 1980 the Assembly established the UN Conference on Trade and Development (UNCTAD), the UN Development Programme (UNDP), the World Food Programme (WFP) and World Food

Council (WFC), the UN Capital Development Fund (UNCDF), the UN Environment Programme (UNEP), the UN Population Fund (UNFPA) and the UN Industrial Development Organisation (UNIDO) which became a Specialised Agency in 1986.

4. Robert W. Gregg, 'The Politics of International Economic Cooperation and Development', in Lawrence S. Finkelstein, *Politics in the United Nations System* (Durham and London, 1988) pp. 109, 113.

5. For example, in 1958 he effectively appealed from the Council to the Assembly over the Lebanon–Jordan crisis and in 1959 he personally aired his disarmament proposals to the Assembly.

6. Minutes of US cabinet meeting, 7 October 1960, Ann Whitman file, Cabinet Series, Box 16, Dwight D. Eisenhower Library (DDEL), Abilene, Kansas.

7. Ibid.

8. Claire Clark, 'Soviet and Afro-Asian voting in the UN General Assembly 1946–65', *Australian Outlook*, 24 (1970) 303.

9. Whether and how democracy can apply to an interstate body is a large and controversial question.

10. One delegate's speech was annotated: 'Weak point. Shout!'. Geoffrey Goodwin, 'The General Assembly of the United Nations' in Evan Luard (ed.), *The Evolution of International Organizations* (London, 1966) p. 52.

11. In 1956 there was only one request to the Council for an oral hearing, but many to the General Assembly.

12. See Article 73.b of the Charter.

13. The voting was 89 to none, with nine abstentions. Abstainers included Britain, Belgian, France, Portugal and the USA – the latter apparently because of an appeal from Macmillan to Eisenhower. This was contrary to the advice of the entire US delegation and the only black member of the US delegation got up and applauded the adoption of the resolution.

14. In 1952 the word 'special' was dropped.

15. Belgium left in 1953, Portugal in 1956, Spain and France in 1958.

16. Originally composed of 17 members, the 'Special Committee on the Implementation of the Declaration on Decolonisation' gained its name from its 1962 membership figure. In 1994 it contained 25 members.

17. R. Emerson, 'Colonialism, Political Development and the UN', *International Organization*, 19, no. 3 (1965) 497–8.

18. Nauru became independent in 1968 and Papua New Guinea in 1975. The Northern Marianas came under US sovereignty in 1978. The Marshall Islands obtained self-government and entered into a compact of free association with the USA in 1986. In 1990 the Security Council terminated the trusteeship agreement for the Federated States of Micronesia, Marshall Islands and Northern Mariana Islands. The only remaining trust territory,

Palau, entered into a compact of free association with the United States in 1994 and joined the UN in 1995. The Trusteeship Council decided to meet thereafter on an ad hoc basis to deal with any outstanding business.

19. By 97 to 2, with one abstention.

20. South Africa ignored a 1950 ICJ advisory opinion that the former League mandate of South West Africa should be subject to UN supervision. After the ICJ had, in 1966, controversially decided Ethiopia and Liberia had insufficient legal interest to sue South Africa, the General Assembly terminated the mandate, declared illegal South Africa's occupation of Namibia and, through the UN Council for Namibia, constantly put pressure on South Africa.

21. Donald J. Puchala (ed.), *Issues before the 38th General Assembly of the United Nations, 1983–1984* (New York, 1983) p. 31. Cited in Robert E. Riggs and Jack C. Plano, *The United Nations. International Organization and World Politics* (Chicago, 1988) p. 200.

22. Under increasing internal and external pressure, but also greatly influenced by the ending of the Cold War, President de Klerk signalled capitulation in 1990 by repudiating apartheid and releasing Nelson Mandela from prison. The dismantling of apartheid led to sanctions being lifted and in April 1994 a multiracial government was elected under President Mandela.

23. Resolution 216 (1965).

24. Quoted in Susan Rice, 'The Commonwealth Initiative in Zimbabwe, 1979–80: Implications For International Peacekeeping', Unpublished DPhil thesis (Oxford University, 1990), p. 32.

25. Andrew Boyd, *Fifteen Men on a Powder Keg. A History of the UN Security Council* (London, 1971) pp. 261–2.

26. Michael Charlton, *The Last Colony in Africa. Diplomacy and the Independence of Rhodesia* (Oxford, Cambridge, MA, 1990), p. 5.

27. See ibid., pp. 9, 33, 155. That the UN was but a backdrop to the main drama is suggested by the scant references it receives in Antony Verrier, *The Road to Zimbabwe 1890–1980* (London, 1986) and M. Tamarkin, *The Making of Zimbabwe. Decolonisation in Regional and International Politics* (London, 1990).

28. Gregg, 'Politics of International Economic Cooperation', p. 109.

29. Ibid., p. 130.

30. U Thant, *View from the UN* (Newton Abbot, 1978) p. 441.

31. Ibid., p. 447.

32. By 1994 the Group numbered over 130 states.

33. Fred Hirsch, 'Is There a New International Economic Order?' *International Organization*, 31, no. 4 (1977) 524.

34. Gillian White, 'A New International Economic Order?', *Virginia Journal of International Law*, 16, no 2 (1976) 336.

35. Gregg, 'Politics of International Economic Cooperation', p. 141.

36. Ibid., p. 139.

37. Thant, *View from the UN*, 451, 453.

38. See A.H.M. Kirk-Greene (ed.), *Africa in the Colonial Period. III. The Transfer of Power: the Colonial Administrator in the Age of Decolonisation*, Proceedings of a Symposium held at St. Antony's College, Oxford, 15–16 March 1968 (Oxford: University of Oxford, Inter-Faculty Committee for African Studies, 1979), *passim.* Interviews with Sir John Moreton and Sir Duncan Watson, August 1994.

39. As late as 1984, *none* of South Africa's ten most important trading partners was prepared to support comprehensive economic sanctions. Newell M. Stultz, 'The Apartheid Issue at the General Assembly: Stalemate or Gathering Storm?', *African Affairs*, 86, no. 342 (1987) 42.

40. Quoted in Boyd, *Fifteen Men on a Powder Keg*, p. 226.

41. See Conor Cruise O'Brien and Feliks Topolski, *The United Nations: Sacred Drama* (London, 1968).

42. Thomas M. Franck, *Nation Against Nation. What Happened to the UN Dream and What the US Can Do About It* (New York, Oxford, 1985) p. 10.

43. The population of America's Pacific dependency of Guam had made clear they welcomed the presence of a US military base, but in 1982 the Committee proposed, and the Assembly overwhelmingly adopted, a resolution calling for the withdrawal of all military bases in colonial territories. Even though America's Pacific Trust territory – the Northern Marianas, the Marshall Islands, Micronesia and Palau – was not the Committee's responsibility, the Special Committee considered the territory and harassed the US. In 1953 the UN accepted that in 1948 Puerto Rico had voted freely in favour of a compact of association with the USA. However, in 1972 the Committee included Puerto Rico on its list of dependent territories and began demanding self-determination and independence in increasingly extreme and unwarranted terms. It also gave extremist Puerto Ricans a platform to broadcast often outrageous anti-US propaganda which generally went unanswered due to a US boycott of meetings. (See Franck, *Nation Against Nation*, pp. 187–204.)

44. Daniel Patrick Moynihan (with Suzanne Weaver), *A Dangerous Place* (London, 1979), pp. 36, 11.

45. Donald McHenry (Young's deputy and successor) quoted in Verrier, *Road to Zimbabwe*, p. 205. Young had to resign after getting in trouble for talking to the PLO representative, but McHenry served the US and the UN well.

46. After replacing Taiwan in the UN in 1971, the People's Republic of China neither participated in the ILO nor contributed to its budget.

47. Letter from Henry Kissinger to the Director General of the ILO, 6 November 1975. *Official Text*, United States Information Service, London.

48. Statement by President Carter, 1 November 1977. *Official Text*, USIS, London.

49. Mark Imber, *The USA, ILO, UNESCO and IAEA. Politicization and Withdrawal in the Specialized Agencies* (London, 1989), p. 65.

50. Sir Colin Crowe, 'Some observations on the operation of the Security Council including the use of the veto', in Davidson Nicol (ed.), *Paths to Peace: The UN Security Council and its Presidency* (New York, 1981), p. 96. Quoted in G. R. Berridge, *Return to the UN. UN Diplomacy In Regional Conflicts* (London, 1990) p. 5.

51. In December 1991 the Russian Federation replaced the USSR. Calculations of resort to the veto differ widely. Table 4.1 is derived from a Foreign and Commonwealth Office, Research and Analysis Department memorandum, 'Table of vetoed draft resolutions in the United Nations Security Council 1946–1991', London, January 1992. See Adam Roberts and Benedict Kingsbury, *United Nations, Divided World. The UN's Roles In International Relations*, 2nd edn (Oxford, 1993) p. 10.

52. Except where the Soviet Union was involved, the Chinese were less strident than expected and tended to register disapproval by abstention rather than the veto. Faithful to their Pakistani friend, they cast their first veto in 1972 against Bangladesh's admission. Bangladesh was admitted in 1974 without a vote being taken.

53. Thant, *View from the UN*, p. 382.

54. Boyd, *Fifteen Men on a Powder Keg*, p. 306.

55. Only Hungary sided with her Soviet master in the Security Council. The invasion was not debated in the Assembly because Czechoslovak delegates asked other states not to prejudice the prospect of further agreement with the Soviet Union by giving the issue prominence.

56. Thant, *View from the UN*, p. 424.

57. Ibid., p. 436. Cf. Brian Urquhart, *A Life In Peace and War* (London, 1987) pp. 223–4.

58. Until 1994 UNFICYP was the only peacekeeping operation not financed from assessed contributions by UN members. This resulted in considerable financial difficulties – in 1993 reimbursement claims from contributors had only been paid up to December 1981.

59. Following the withdrawal of troops in February 1966, UNMOGIP reverted to its original task and UNIPOM was disbanded.

60. Urquhart, *A Life in Peace and War*, p. 238.

61. Alan James, *Peacekeeping In International Politics* (London, 1990) p. 318; Urquhart, *A Life in Peace and War*, p. 240.

62. Boyd, *Fifteen Men on a Powder Keg*, p. 356.

63. Quoted in Thomas M. Franck, 'The Prerogative Powers of the Secretary-General', in M. S. Rajan, V. S. Mani and C. S. R. Murthy, *The Nonaligned and the United Nations* (New Delhi, 1987) pp. 280–1.

64. Thant, *View from the UN*, p. 80.

65. Urquhart, *A Life in Peace and War*, pp. 120–1.

66. The UN Security Force (UNSF) assisted UNTEA by maintaining public order during the process.

67. This, however, prompted Indonesia's three-year confrontation with Malaysia and, indirectly, her brief departure from the UN.

68. U Thant in 1962. Quoted in Boyd, *Fifteen Men on a Powder Keg*, p. 196.

69. H. G. Nicholas, *The United Nations as a Political Institution*, 5th edn (London, 1992), p. 73.

70. Urquhart, *A Life in Peace and War*, p. 228.

71. Alan James, 'Kurt Waldheim: Diplomats' Diplomat', *The Year Book of World Affairs 1983* (London, 1983) p. 92.

72. By a special allocation for this and subsequent peacekeeping operations, costs were allocated on a different basis from that which is operative for the UN's general budget: the permanent members paid proportionately more, the least well off proportionately less.

73. Franck, *Nation Against Nation*, p. 282.

74. Kurt Waldheim, *The Challenge of Peace* (London, 1980) p. 1.

75. See Kurt Waldheim, *In the Eye of the Storm* (London, 1985), pp. 1–11.

76. Urquhart, *A Life in Peace and War*, p. 324.

77. Nicholas, *United Nations*, p. 203.

5. THE UN IN CRISIS AND ITS REJUVENATION, 1980–1994

1. Kurt Waldheim, 'The United Nations: the Tarnished Image', *Foreign Affairs*, 63 (Fall 1984) 93.

2. G. R. Berridge, *Return to the UN, UN Diplomacy In Regional Conflicts* (London, 1990) pp. 34–5.

3. Thomas M. Franck, *Nation Against Nation. What Happened to the UN Dream and What the US Can Do About It* (New York, Oxford, 1985) p. 186.

4. Brian Urquhart, *A Life In Peace and War* (London, 1987) p. 327.

5. Burton Yale Pines (ed.), *A World Without a UN* (Washington DC, 1985) p. xix. Quoted in Robert C. Johansen, 'The Reagan Administration and the UN: the Costs of Unilateralism', *World Policy Journal*, 3 (1986) 603.

6. Urquhart, *A Life in Peace and War*, p. 327.

7. *The Independent*, 28 August 1993; Johansen, 'Reagan and the UN', p. 603.

8. Johansen, 'Reagan and the UN', p. 606.

9. They rose from $120.9 million in 1976 to $504 million in January 1986.

10. Berridge, *Return to the UN*, pp. 37–8. By 1992 both China and France had paid off their arrears.

11. Ibid., p. 35.

12. Elliot Abrams, Assistant Secretary of State for International Organization Affairs, addressing a meeting of the United Nations Association of the USA, 5 June 1981. Official text, USICA.

13. Ibid.

14. Professor Frederico Mayor (Director-General of UNESCO) in House of Commons, Foreign Affairs Committee, Fifth Report, *Membership of UNESCO* (London, 1993) p. 18. (Subsequently referred to as *Membership of UNESCO*.)

15. According to its constitution, 'real' peace rests 'upon the intellectual and moral solidarity of mankind'. And 'the wide diffusion of culture, and the education of humanity for justice and liberty and peace' are 'indispensable to the dignity of man and constitute a sacred duty.'

16. Richard Hoggart, *The Times*, 4 November 1977.

17. See letters from W. A. C. Mathieson (a member of the Executive Board), *The Times*, 4 January 1984 and John Gordon (Britain's last permanent representative to UNESCO), *The Independent*, 3 November 1993.

18. Richard Hoggart, *An Idea and its Servants. UNESCO from Within* (London, 1978) p. 81.

19. Quoted in Richard Hoggart, 'The Mass Media: a New Colonialism?', Eighth Standard Telephones & Cables Communication Lecture (1978) p. 1.

20. For example, in 1981 UNESCO launched the International Programme for the Development of Communication (IPDC) to help third world states set up projects for communication and the media. The IPDC helped form a Pan-African News Agency in 1983 and other recipients of assistance included the Asia-Pacific Institute for Broadcasting Development and the Latin American Special Information Agency.

21. UNESCO *What it Is, What it Does, How it Works* (Paris, 1980).

22. Elliot Abrams, cited in note 12 above.

23. *The Times*, 22 August 1983. The eight were the USA, Japan, West Germany, the Soviet Union, France, Britain, Denmark and New Zealand; 68 states paid 0.01 per cent of the budget.

24. Elliot Abrams, cited above. The 1964–5 budget was $48 million, the 1974–5 budget was $156 million, and the 1984–5 budget was $382 million (*The Times*, 7 December 1985).

25. 'World Information and Communication', Foreign and Commonwealth Office, Background Brief, May 1985.

26. *The Times*, 30 December 1983.

27. Quoted in ibid.

28. 'World Information and Communication'; *The Times*, 30 December 1983.

29. Lord Beloff to the author, November 1994.

30. Editorial, *The Times*, 30 December 1983.

31. 80 per cent of UNESCO's employees were at its headquarters in Paris and only 20 per cent of the budget was spent in the field.

32. Editorial, *The Times*, 20 October 1986.

33. *The Times Higher Education Supplement*, 7 November 1986.

34. *The Times*, 6 August 1981.

35. *The Times Higher Education Supplement*, 7 November 1986.

36. Letter from Professor Julius Gould, *The Times*, 10 November 1984. Cf. Nicholas A. Sims, 'Servants of an Idea: Hoggart's UNESCO and the Problem of International Loyalty', *Millennium: The Journal of International Studies*, 11, no. 1 (1982) 66.

37. Mark F. Imber, *The USA, ILO, UNESCO and IAEA. Politicization and Withdrawal in the Specialized Agencies* (London, 1989) p. 108.

38. *The Times*, 9 November 1987.

39. Frederico Mayor, in *Membership of UNESCO*, pp. viii, 31.

40. Ibid., p. viii.

41. Knut Hammarskjöld (Chairman of an independent commission which throughly and critically examined the reforms in 1989) quoted in letter from Malcolm Harper (Director) and Rashik Kareh (Secretary) of United Nations Association Working Committee on UNESCO, Appendix 2 to *Membership of UNESCO*, p. 49.

42. Miss Glynne Evans, Head of United Nations Department, Foreign and Commonwealth Office, in *Membership of UNESCO*, pp. ix, 40.

43. Douglas Hogg, Minister of State, Foreign and Commonwealth Office, in *Membership of UNESCO*, pp. xiii, 38.

44. See *Membership of UNESCO*, pp. xi–xii and Appendix 1, Memorandum by the Foreign and Commonwealth Office, p. 48.

45. UN *Press Release*, ILO/2194, 7 December 1984. Quoted in Imber, *USA, ILO, UNESCO and IAEA*, 68–9.

46. *The Times*, 28 February 1985.

47. Cited in Yves Beigbeder, 'The controversial re-election of the WHO Director-General and its consequences: reform proposals', Paper delivered to ISA convention, Washington DC, 28 March–1 April 1994, p. 7.

48. Ibid., p. 2. Twenty-three states did not participate in the election in which he obtained 93 votes to 58 with 6 abstentions.

49. Boutros Boutros-Ghali, 'Empowering the United Nations', *Foreign Affairs*, 75, no. 5 (1992) 100.

50. Sir Robert Jennings, 'An Expanding Court', *The World Today*, 48, no. 3 (March 1992), 44.

51. Keith Highet, 'The Peace Palace Heats Up: the World Court in Business Again?', *The American Journal of International Law*, 85, no. 4 (1991) 648.

52. Urquhart, *A Life in Peace and War*, p. 371.

53. See Sir Crispin Tickell in House of Commons, Foreign Affairs Committee, Third Report: *The Expanding Role of the United Nations and its Implications for United Kingdom Policy*, vol. 2, *Minutes of Evidence and Appendices*

(HCP 235–II) (London, 1993) p. 169. (Subsequently referred to as *The Expanding Role of the UN*, vol. 2.)

54. *Report of the Secretary-General on the Work of the Organization, 1991* (New York, Department for Public Information, 1991) (DPI/1168 4023).

55. Memorandum submitted by Paul Taylor in *The Expanding Role of the UN*, vol. 2, p. 184.

56. Berridge, *Return to the UN*, pp. 25–7.

57. Alan James, *Peacekeeping in International Politics* (London, 1990) p. 245.

58. One of those, cast in 1993, was, in effect, withdrawn.

59. The enforcement provisions of chapter 7 had previously only been used three times: to apply economic sanctions against Rhodesia in 1966, to prohibit arms sales to South Africa in 1977, and against Argentina when it invaded the Falklands in 1982. In 1951 the Security Council only *recommended* military action in Korea.

60. Despite close political, economic and military ties with Iraq, the USSR denounced the invasion and approved the use of force. China supported eleven of the Security Council resolutions, abstaining on one (Resolution 678), because it preferred not to be associated with the use of force to solve disputes.

61. Eighth Report of Committee on External Affairs and Trade, Canadian House of Commons (Ottawa, 1993). Quoted in House of Commons, Foreign Affairs Committee, Third Report: *The Expanding Role of the United Nations and its Implications for United Kingdom Policy*, vol. 1, *Report Together with Proceedings of the Committee* (HCP 235–1) (London, 1993) paragraph 238, p. lxii. (Subsequently referred to as *The Expanding Role of the UN*, vol. 1.)

62. *Report of the Secretary-General on the Work of the Organization, 1991* (New York, Department for Public Information, 1991) (DPI/1168 4023).

63. *Report of the Secretary-General on the Work of the Organization, 1992.* Quoted in memorandum by Adam Roberts in *The Expanding Role of the UN*, vol. 2, p. 306.

64. These were: 1990 Liechtenstein, Namibia; 1991 Democratic People's Republic of Korea, Estonia, Latvia, Lithuania, Marshall Islands, Micronesia, Republic of Korea; 1992 Armenia, Azerbaijan, Bosnia & Herzegovina, Croatia, Georgia, Kazakhstan, Kyrgyzstan, Moldova, San Marino, Slovenia, Tajikistan, Turkmenistan, Uzbekistan; 1993 Andorra, Monaco, the Former Yugoslav Republic of Macedonia, Eritrea; 1994 Palau. Two members were lost in 1990 when the two Yemens and Germanies merged. In 1993 Czechoslovakia was replaced by two members, the Czech and Slovak Republics. In 1992 the General Assembly decided that the Federal Republic of Yugoslavia (Serbia & Montenegro) could not automatically take Yugoslavia's seat but had to apply for membership.

65. Boutros Boutros-Ghali, '*An Agenda for Peace*: one year later', *Orbis*, 37, no. 3 (1993) 326.

66. Fourteen chapter 7 resolutions were on the former Yugoslavia, four on Somalia, four on Haiti, two on Iraq, one on Angola, one on Liberia and one on Libya. By contrast in 1987 the Security Council met 49 times, passed 13 resolutions and two draft resolutions were vetoed.

67. *Report of the Secretary-General on the Work of the Organization, 1992.* Quoted in memorandum by Adam Roberts in *The Expanding Role of the UN*, vol. 2, p. 306.

68. The exceptions were the frontier missions between Iraq and Kuwait (UNIKOM), Iran and Iraq (UNIIMOG), Uganda and Rwanda (UNOMUR), Serbia and Montenegro (UNPREDEP) and the UN Aouzou Strip Observer Group (UNASOG) between Chad and Libya.

69. Boutros Boutros-Ghali, '*An Agenda for Peace*: one year later', p. 329.

70. The appointment of a UN Commissioner for Human Rights in 1994 was seen as another important step towards creating more effective international human rights institutions.

71. *The Independent*, 29 October 1994.

72. Gareth Evans, 'The Comprehensive Political Settlement to the Cambodian Conflict: An Exercise in Cooperating for Peace', in Hugh Smith (ed.), *International Peacekeeping. Building on the Cambodian Experience* (Canberra, 1994) p. 12.

73. This paragraph and the next were written before NATO forces, under the authorisation of Security Council resolutions, began to engage in large-scale assaults on the Bosnian Serbs.

74. See UN Document S/1994/555 (9 May), paras 16 and 25. (The members of the Security Council did not like such plain speaking, and ignored the Secretary-General's request for his position to be endorsed.)

75. Private information.

76. Boutros Boutros-Ghali, 'Empowering the United Nations', p. 95.

77. Sir Anthony Parsons in *International Relations* (December 1992) 198. Cited in *The Expanding Role of the UN*, vol. 1, p. xlii; Erskine Childers, 'Old-boying', *London Review of Books*, 18 August 1994, p. 3.

78. *The Independent*, 27 January 1993.

79. Urquhart, *A Life in Peace and War*, pp. 230, 352. UN members had made a hefty contribution to the poor state of the secretariat by using intense political pressure to ensure the appointment of their nationals and making supplementary payments to them.

80. Berridge, *Return to the UN*, p. 19.

81. Thomas Franck, 'The Prerogative Powers of the Secretary-General' in M. S. Rajan, V. S. Mani and C. S. R. Murthy, *The Nonaligned and the United Nations* (New Delhi, 1987) p. 283.

82. See Thomas M. Franck and George Nolte, 'The Good Offices Function of the UN Secretary-General' in Adam Roberts and Benedict Kings-

bury, *United Nations, Divided World. The UN's Roles in International Relations*, 2nd edn (Oxford, 1993) p. 165.

83. Sir Crispin Tickell in *The Expanding Role of the UN*, vol. 2, pp. 360, 168.

84. 'Too blunt for his own good', Richard Dowden, *The Independent*, 31 October 1994.

85. Cited in Alan James, 'The Secretary-General as an Independent Political Actor' in Benjamin Rivlin and Leon Gordenker, *The Challenging Role of the UN Secretary-General. Making 'the most impossible job in the world' Possible* (New York, 1993) p. 37.

86. *Report of the Secretary-General on the Work of the Organization, 1991.*

87. Boutros Boutros-Ghali, '*An Agenda for Peace*: one year later', p. 325.

88. *The Independent*, 31 January 1994.

89. *The Independent*, 12 May 1994.

90. See Boutros Boutros-Ghali, *An Agenda for Peace*, Report of the Secretary-General pursuant to the statement adopted by the summit meeting of the Security Council on 31 January 1992, paras 20, 45. Peace enforcement units were impractical because quite apart from problems of soldiers being killed, even Britain and the US could not immediately provide inoculated troops, ready to go anywhere. However, two years' later Boutros-Ghali still clung to what had become a dead duck. (See Dowden, 'Too blunt for his own good'.)

91. *The Independent*, 20 January 1994.

92. Inis L. Claude Jr, 'Reflections on the Role of the UN Secretary-General' in Rivlin and Gordenker, *The Challenging Role*, p. 251.

6. THE EUROPEAN UNION, 1945–69: THE CREATION OF THE EUROPEAN COMMUNITY AND THE EARLY YEARS

1. D. W. Urwin, *The Community of Europe*, 2nd edn (Harlow, Essex, 1995) p. 2.

2. For an account of the Zollverein and other similar European developments in the nineteenth century see S. Pollard, *European Economic Integration, 1815–1970* (London 1974) pp. 112–20.

3. In particular, Konrad Adenauer, Georges Pompidou and Carlos Sforza were members of the Pan-European Union.

4. A. Briand, 'Memorandum on the Organisation of a Regime of Federal Union', *International Conciliation, Special Bulletin* (June, 1930) 327–53. This was actually the first formal proposal for European union made by a European government in the twentieth century. Similar ideas are also presented in a contemporary book by the former French Premier, E. Herriot, *The United States of Europe* (London, 1930).

5. R. Vaughan, *Postwar Integration in Europe* (London, 1976), pp. 94–106.

6. Ibid., pp. 16–20.

7. 'Winston Churchill's Speech at Zurich, 19 September 1946' in A. Boyd and F. Boyd (eds), *Western Union* (London, 1948).

8. Ibid., p. 18.

9. R. C. Mowatt, *Creating the European Community* (London, 1973) pp. 38–42.

10. United States Department of State, *Foreign Relations of the United States (FRUS)*, vol. III (Washington, 1949), p. 134.

11. M. Beloff, *The United States and the Unity of Europe* (London, 1963) p. 14.

12. See, for example, D. Mitrany, *A Working Peace System* (London, 1943).

13. D. Acheson, *Present at the Creation* (London, 1970) p. 339 and *FRUS*, vol. III (1950) pp. 697–701.

14. This was extended to become the Organisation for Economic Co-operation and Development (OECD) in 1961.

15. Mowatt, *Creating the European Community*, p. 28.

16. *FRUS*, vol. III (1950) pp. 646–52. Britain delayed agreement until it received assurances that it would retain sole control over the role of sterling as an international reserve currency. (Urwin, *Community of Europe*, p. 46.)

17. Robert Schuman, 'Declaration of 9 May 1950', reproduced in P. Fointaine, *Europe – A Fresh Start. The Schuman Declaration 1950–90* (Luxembourg 1990).

18. Ibid., p. 45.

19. Ibid., p. 46.

20. R. Pryce. *The Politics of the European Community* (London, 1973) p. 6.

21. For a brief discussion see Urwin, *Community of Europe*, pp. 58–9.

22. For a fuller account see Edward Fursdon, *The European Defense Community: A History* (New York, 1980).

23. See *FRUS*, vol. III (1950) pp. 167–8 and 273–8.

24. Technically the motion was not the ratification of the Treaty but whether or not its ratification should be discussed, but rejection of this obviously implied no ratification and hence the EDC failed and with it the EPC.

25. In addition Germany agreed never to produce atomic, chemical or biological weapons, and Britain stationed troops in mainland Europe and made a long-term commitment to European defence. All this paved the way for the eventual agreement to Germany's reinstatement as a full sovereign power and its membership of NATO in 1955.

26. In December 1952, in a letter from the Dutch Foreign Minister to the other five, a common market and further economic integration were proposed. This was endorsed at a meeting in February 1954 and sent for further examination to panels of experts.

27. Mowatt, *Creating the European Community*, pp. 128–30.

28. Text of the Messina Resolution in Keesings Research Report, *The European Communities: Establishment and Growth* (London, 1975) pp. 9–12.

29. M. Camps, *Britain and the European Community, 1955–63* (London, 1964), p. 49.

30. Common usage of the expression 'Treaty of Rome' refers to the treaty which created the EEC (and not the treaty creating Euratom); this practice will be continued here, although strictly speaking it is ambiguous.

31. For example, compare the structure of ASEAN, widely regarded as the second most successful attempt to develop regional integration, which is described in chapter 9.

32. France, Italy and Germany had 4 votes each, Belgium and Holland 2 each and Luxembourg 1; a qualified majority required 12 votes.

33. See, for example, W. Pickles, 'Political Power in the European Community' in C. A. Cosgrove and K. J. Twitchett (eds), *The New International Actors* (London, 1970) pp. 201–21.

34. See, for example, D. Coombes, *Politics and Bureaucracy in the European Community – a Portrait of the Commission* (London, 1970).

35. For example, see *Resolution and Joint Declaration of the Action Committee for the United States of Europe*, 18 January 1959, p. 1: 'the . . . [achievement] . . . that could and should be most rapidly carried out concerns atomic energy.'

36. See, for example, J. Pinder, 'Implications for the Firm', *Journal of Common Market Studies*, 1, no. 1 (1961), 41.

37. H. von der Groeben, *The European Community: The Formative Years* (Brussels, 1987) p. 61.

38. Ibid., p. 66

39. L. Lindberg, *The Political Dynamics of European Economic Integration* (Stanford, CA, 1963) p. 143.

40. The CAP financial arrangements would increase Community spending, which implied a need for more or 'own' resources, which, in turn, implied the need for democratic control, which logically should come from the Parliament.

41. Reproduced in J. Lambert, 'The Constitutional Crisis, 1965–66', *Journal of Common Market Studies*, 4, no. 3 (May 1966) 226.

42. Moreover, on the economic front, 1961 was the first year in which British exports to Europe were greater than those to the Commonwealth. (This compares dramatically to the situation at the end of the Second World War when the former were only between a quarter and a third of the latter.)

43. EFTA was created by the Stockholm Convention in 1960. In addition to the original seven members Liechtenstein, which had a customs union with Switzerland, was also covered: Finland became an associate member and then a full member in 1986 and Iceland joined in 1970. Of course, there was also a steady stream of departures to join the Community: Britain and Denmark in 1973, Portugal in 1986 and Austria, Sweden and Finland in 1995.

44. House of Commons Debates, 5th Series, vol. 645, Col. 928 ff.

45. The story of the first British application is told in S. George, *An Awkward Partner* (Oxford, 1990) pp. 28–35, S. George, *Britain and European Integration Since 1945* (Oxford, 1991) pp. 43–6, and J. W. Young, *Britain and European Unity, 1945–92* (London, 1993) pp. 76–85.

46. Young, *Britain and European Unity*, p. 84.

47. George, *Britain and European Integration*, p. 32.

48. The remaining members of EFTA had sought an associate status with the Community, being unwilling to seek full membership, for political reasons.

49. This was not to be the last change of mind. Labour Party ambivalence towards the Community was to continue for 15 years with a tendency towards grudging acceptance whilst in power and opposition when not. It was only in the early 1980s that the possibility of withdrawal from the Community was officially abandoned.

50. This practice has been adopted throughout this chapter. On many occasions the term 'Community' clearly refers specifically to one of the three Communities but, where necessary, it has also been used to refer implicitly to all three.

51. *Bulletin of the European Communities*, Supplement no. 1, January 1969.

52. Interestingly, after his retirement, Mansholt radically changed his views and became converted to the argument that, although inefficient in some respects, small farming units were preferable because they kept people in employment in situations where alternative work might not be available and also because they caused less ecological damage. See *The Common Agricultural Policy: Some New Thinking from Dr Sicco Mansholt*, pamphlet published by the Soil Association (August 1979).

53. See, for example, H. Simonian, *The Privileged Partnership: Franco-German Relations in the European Community, 1969–84* (Oxford, 1985) p. 35.

7. THE EUROPEAN UNION, 1970–1985: TURBULENCE, EUROPESSIMISM AND EUROSCELEROSIS

1. J. W. Young, *Britain and European Unity, 1945–1992* (London, 1993) pp. 107–8.

2. Heath's credentials in this respect are summarised in S. George, *An Awkward Partner* (Oxford, 1990) p. 49.

3. S. Z. Young, *Terms of Entry: Britain's Negotiations with the European Community, 1970–72* (London, 1973) p. 19.

4. For an account of this meeting, see U. Kitzinger, *Diplomacy and Persuasion: How Britain Joined the Common Market* (London, 1973) pp. 119–25.

5. The terms of entry are outlined in HMSO, *The United Kingdom and the European Communities* (Cmnd. 4715, July, 1971). For a detailed account of

both the outcome and the negotiations, see Kitzinger, *Diplomacy and Persuasion.*

6. The dire consequences of this for the net British position were well known from an early stage. See, for example, the *Economist,* 18 May 1974.

7. Article 108 of the Treaty of Rome (EEC) provides for mutual assistance from other member states to Community members experiencing balance of payments difficulties.

8. A flavour of this is provided by the extracts published in Section 5 'Growth and the British Economy', in J. Barber and B. Reed (eds), *European Community: Vision and Reality* (London, 1973).

9. The vote in the Commons was 356 in favour and 244 against. There were significant numbers of defectors on both sides with 39 Conservatives voting 'no' and 69 Labour MPs voting 'yes'. The vote in the House of Lords was much more decisive with 451 in favour and only 58 against.

10. 'The Dublin Amendment' is summarised in D. Swann, *The Economics of the Common Market* (Harmondsworth, 4th edn, 1978) ch. 1, Appendix I, pp. 53–4. A more detailed analysis is provided by J. R. Dodsworth, 'European Community Financing: An Analysis of the Dublin Amendment', *Journal of Common Market Studies* (1975/76). Essentially, the agreement set a number of conditions before repayments could be made that were so stringent that it was never to be triggered and, in any case, it related only to gross (i.e. rather than net) contributions and was subject to a maximum repayment of ECU 250 million.

11. The objectives and the outcome of the 'renegotiation' are outlined in HMSO, *Membership of the European Community: Report on Renegotiation* (Cmnd. 6003, March 1975).

12. Of course the 'government victory' was achieved because of the votes of the Conservative and Liberal opposition since more Labour MPs actually voted against membership (145) than in favour (137).

13. A number of Conservative MPs had the Party Whip withdrawn over the matter of the Party's European policy and this reduced the government's small majority to dangerous proportions.

14. This is described in F. Nicholson and R. East, *From Six to Twelve: the Enlargement of the European Communities* (Harlow, 1987) pp. 126–8.

15. This had been reduced from the standard IMF band of 2 (± 1) per cent around the dollar for participants in the European Monetary Agreement which replaced the European Payments Union in 1958.

16. At this time Britain and Ireland had a currency union. It was not until March 1979 when the Irish decided to join the European Monetary System and Britain did not that the British and Irish pounds became separate currencies.

17. It is true that the European Monetary Cooperation Fund (EMCOF) had been created in April 1973 but this had only a minimal role and in no way resembled even an embryonic European central bank.

18. This put upward pressure on the currencies of countries with relatively low inflation (like Germany) and corresponding downward pressure on those of high inflation countries (such as Britain and Italy).

19. For example, see P. Ludlow, *The Making of the European Monetary System* (London, 1982).

20. Most famously, see the speech reproduced as R. Jenkins, 'European Monetary Union', *Lloyds Bank Review*, no. 127 (1978) 1–14.

21. It also has a substantial unofficial role as a denominator of private transactions.

22. This is actually always less than 75 per cent and, in fact, varies depending on the currency. This is because national currencies also form part of the ECU but with differing weights and, consequently, as they fluctuate, they pull the ECU with them to some extent; the larger the weight of the currency, the more it pulls the ECU, and so an adjustment is made to compensate for this, otherwise the countries with larger weights would have an unfair advantage.

23. Wider bands of ± 6 per cent were offered to the 'weaker' economies of Britain, Ireland and Italy. Only Italy opted for these as Britain declined to join the ERM and Ireland chose the normal, narrower band.

24. The subsequent history of the EMS (after 1985) is taken up in the next chapter.

25. Commission of the ECs, 'European Union', *Bulletin of the European Communities*, Supplement 1/76 (January 1976). A useful summary and analysis is provided by M. Holland, *European Community Integration* (London, 1993) pp. 60–8.

26. This was also true of a subsequent report that was commissioned by the national leaders – the Report of the 'Three Wise Men' – which appeared in 1979 with conclusions along similar lines to those of Tindemans. For more detail see Commission of the ECs, *Thirteenth General Report on the Activities of the European Communities (1979)*, ch. 1, paragraph 8, p. 23.

27. Commission of the ECs, *Sixteenth General Report on the Activities of the European Communities (1982)*, ch. IV, paragraph 819, p. 299.

28. For a definitive analysis of the role and functions of summits, see S. Bulmer and W. Wessels, *The European Council* (London, 1987).

29. S. George, *Britain and European Integration since 1945* (Oxford, 1991) p. 25.

30. D. Swann, *The Economics of the Common Market* (Harmondsoorth, 7th edn, 1992) p. 69.

31. The EC's response is analysed in detail in J. Redmond, *The Next Mediterranean Enlargement of the European Community: Turkey, Cyprus and Malta* (Aldershot, 1993) pp. 74–7.

32. The Franco-German alliance in this period is comprehensively examined in H. Simonian, *The Privileged Partnership: Franco-German Relations and the European Community, 1969–1984* (Oxford, 1985).

33. The creation of the ERDF is described in George, *Britain and European Integration*, pp. 66–9 and, more fully, in R. B. Talbot, *The European Community's Regional Fund* (Oxford, 1977).

34. See, for example, J. Ravenhill, *Collective Clientism: the Lomé Convention and North–South Relations* (Columbia, 1985).

35. Commission of the ECs, *Memorandum on Industrial Policy in the Community* (1970).

36. These stemmed from the Treaty of Paris which established the ECSC.

37. The story of the creation of the CFP is told in M. Wise, *The Common Fisheries Policy of the EC* (London, 1984), M. Leigh, *European Integration and the CFP* (London, 1983) and J. Farnell and J. Elles, *In Search of a CFP* (Aldershot, 1984). A shorter, more recent account which also analyses some of the subsequent problems experienced with the policy is provided by J. Redmond, 'The CFP of the EC – A Genuine Crisis or Business as Usual?' *European Environment* (1/3, June 1991).

38. Commission of the ECs, 'Opinion on the Greek Application for Membership', *Bulletin of the ECs* (Supplement 2/76, 1976).

39. Greek demands were set out in the Greek Memorandum of March 1982 which is reproduced in Nicholson and East, *From Six to Twelve*, pp. 195–200.

40. This is not a percentage of the total VAT levied but a percentage of the total value of goods and services on which VAT is levied (that is, the common assessment base). Thus for example, a country with a VAT rate of 20 per cent retains 19 per cent and gives (up to) 1 per cent to the Community and, similarly, a country with a rate of 10 per cent retains 9 per cent and gives (up to) 1 per cent. Consequently, no member state can reduce its contribution to the EC's 'own resources' by reducing its VAT rate, since the 1 per cent is a percentage of the common assessment base and is not related to the actual amount of VAT collected or the rate at which it is levied.

41. For example, see any textbook on the economics of the EC and, for a more detailed analysis, see (amongst others) A. Buckwell, D. R. Harvey, K. J. Thomson and K. Parton, *The Costs of the CAP* (London, 1982), M. Franklin, *Rich Man's Farming: The Crisis in Agriculture* (London, 1988), and R. Fennell, *The Common Agricultural Policy* (Oxford, 2nd edn, 1987).

42. However there were some lesser problems on the revenue side: Britain tended to import more from outside the Community than other member states and consequently paid a larger proportion of customs duties and agricultural levies and also, as a country with high consumption and low investment and a tendency to import more than it exports, Britain had a relatively large VAT base (and hence paid more VAT).

8. THE EUROPEAN UNION, 1985–1995: THE RELANCE: FROM THE SINGLE EUROPEAN ACT TO THE MAASTRICHT TREATY AND EUROPEAN UNION

1. Tsoukalis, *The New European Economy* (Oxford, 2nd edn, 1993) pp. 47–55.

2. For example, see W. Dekker, *Europe–1990* (Eindhoven 1980). This was a report published by the President of Phillips calling for a programme to create a single market for Europe.

3. For a detailed analysis see M. Shackleton, 'The Delors II Budget Package', *Journal of Common Market Studies*, The European Community in 1992 – Annual Review of Activities, 31 (August 1993).

4. For further analysis of the IGC and the SEA see J. Lodge, 'The Single European Act: Towards a new Euro-Dynamism', *Journal of Common Market Studies*, 24, no. 3 (March 1986); J. W. De Zwann, 'The Single European Act: Conclusion of a Unique Document', *Common Market Law Review*, 23 (1986) and A. Moravcsik, 'Negotiating the SEA: National Interest and Conventional Statecraft in the European Community', *International Organisation*, 45 (Winter 1991).

5. Commission of the ECs, *Completing the Internal Market: White Paper from the Commission to the European Council* (Luxembourg, June 1985). This was produced under the auspices of Lord Cockfield, the then senior British Commissioner; consequently he is widely regarded as, in some sense, the architect of the SMP and so the White Paper often bears his name.

6. See for example, D. Swann, *The Economics of the Common Market* (Harmondsworth, 7th edn, 1992) and A. M. El-Agraa, *The Economics of the European Community* (London, 4th edn, 1994).

7. P. Cecchini, *The European Challenge, 1992: The Benefits of a Single Market* (Aldershot, 1988) is the popular version and is the one referred to here, as it is the most readily accessible. A more technical summary is provided by M. Emerson, 'The Economics of 1992', *European Economy*, no. 35 (1988). The full findings are summarised in 16 volumes as Commission of the ECs, *Research on the 'Cost of Non-Europe'* (Luxembourg, 1988). The Cecchini Report remains the only fully comprehensive study of the effects of the SMP with the partial exception of J. Pelkmans and L. A. Winters, *Europe's Domestic Market* (London 1988).

8. Cecchini, *The European Challenge*, p. 83.

9. Ibid., p. 97.

10. Ibid., Table 10.2, p. 101.

11. Ibid., pp. 104–6.

12. See A. B. Philip, *Implementing the European Internal Market: Problems and Prospects* (London: RIIA, Discussion Paper No. 5, 1988).

13. For example, see B. Burkitt and M. Baimbridge, *What 1992 Really Means: Single Market or Double Cross* (Bradford: British Anti-Common Market Campaign, 1988) and T. Cutler, C. Haslem, J. Williams and K. Williams, *1992 – The Struggle for Europe* (Oxford, 1988).

14. Commission of the ECs, *White Paper* . . . paragraph 19, p. 8, states that 'the commercial identity of the Community must be consolidated so that our trading partners will not be given the benefit of a wider market without themselves making similar concessions'.

15. R. E. Baldwin, 'The Growth Effects of 1992', *Economic Policy*, no. 9 (1989).

16. Jacques Delors, Speech at the College of Europe, Bruges, 20 October 1989.

17. A useful summary of the negotiations is provided by A. Duff, J. Pinder and R. Pryce (eds), *Maastricht and Beyond* (London, 1994), ch. 3.

18. Treaty of European Union, Title V, Article J.4.

19. Ibid., Agreement annexed to the Protocol on Social Policy, Article 1.

20. These are internal market rules, free circulation of workers, rights of establishment, general environment programmes, education and training, trans-European networks, health, consumer protection, the research and development framework programme and culture. In all but the last two categories decisions in the Council are taken by qualified majority.

21. Treaty of European Union, Title II, Articles 198a, 198b and 198c.

22. Ibid., Title XIV, Article 130d.

23. Ibid., Title II, Articles 8a to 8e inclusive.

24. Ibid., Title 2, Article 3b.

25. A comprehensive account of the problems is provided by Duff, Pinder and Pryce (eds), *Maastricht and Beyond*, ch. 4.

26. Changes were required to implement EU citizenship, transfer sovereignty from the Bundesbank to the European Central Bank and to safeguard the sovereign position of the Länder.

27. Mention should also be made of The Schengen Agreement which became effective, after much delay, in late March 1995. This allows free movement of people in a passport-free zone but only covers 7 of the 15 EU member states.

28. In principle, either of these will do since it is the ending of intra-union exchange rate fluctuations that is critical. In practice, however, there are important differences, particularly with regard to credibility and confidence.

29. Committee for the Study of Economic and Monetary Union, *Report on Economic and Monetary Union in the European Community* (Luxembourg: Office for the Official Publications of the ECs, 1989), Section 3, paragraph 25, p. 20.

30. See, for example, H. Ungerer, O. Evans and P. Nyberg, 'The European Monetary System – recent developments', *International Monetary Fund Occasional Paper*, no. 48 (1986) and A. A. Weber, 'EMU and asymmetrics and adjustment problems in the EMS – some empirical evidence', *European Economy*, special edition, no. 1 (1991).

31. Indeed, this view was encouraged by the Commission which produced what might almost be described as a 'Cecchini Report for EMU' in the shape of Commission of the ECs, 'One Market, One Money', *European Economy*, no. 44 (October 1990).

32. Committee for the Study of Economic and Monetary Union, *Report*.

33. Treaty of European Union, Protocol on the convergence criteria referred to in Article 109j of the Treaty establishing the European Community, Article 3. The ±2.25 per cent margins that prevailed at the time of the Maastricht summit were not specified and thus 'normal' can presumably be equally applied to the ±15 per cent bands that became applicable from August 1993.

34. In fact the widely held view that this is the latest date by which EMU must begin is not technically correct. The 1 January 1999 start date becomes applicable only if the Council fails to set a start date for EMU by the end of 1997 (Treaty of European Union, Title II, Article 109j, paragraph 4). There is nothing to stop the Council from deciding in 1997 to set a date later than the beginning of 1999. Indeed, given the performance of the ERM since 1992 this may begin to look like a desirable option.

35. D. M. Andrews, 'The Global Origins of the Maastricht Treaty on EMU: Closing the Window of Opportunity', in A. W. Cafruny and G. G. Rosenthal (eds), *The State of the European Community*, Vol. 2: *The Maastricht Debates and Beyond* (Boulder, CO, 1993) p. 117.

36. *Financial Times*, 7 March 1995, p. 2.

37. Commission of the ECs, *Growth, Competitiveness, Employment – the Challenges and Way Forward into the 21st Century* (COM(93) 700 final, 1993).

38. The stories of their accessions are told in F. Nicholson and R. East, *From the Six to the Twelve: the Enlargement of the European Communities* (Harlow, 1987) chs 10, 11.

39. The principal applicant countries are examined on an individual basis in J. Redmond (ed.), *Prospective Europeans: New Members for the European Community* (Hemel Hempstead, 1994).

40. For an overview of the motivations and attitudes of the EFTA countries see R. Schwok, 'The European Free Trade Association: Revival or Collapse?' in J. Redmond (ed.), *The External Relations of the European Community* (London, 1992).

41. For a detailed examination of the Swiss case see R. Schwok, *Switzerland and the European Common Market* (New York, 1991).

42. For a detailed survey see J. Redmond, *The Next Mediterranean Enlargement of the European Community: Turkey, Cyprus and Malta?* (Aldershot, 1993).

43. Commission of the ECs, *Opinion on Malta's Application for Membership* (Brussels: Bulletin of the ECs, Supplement 4/93, 1993) paragraph 44.

44. This summary is taken from the Federal Trust, *The State of the Union: The Intergovernmental Conference of the European Union 1996* (London: Federal Trust, Paper no. 1, 1995), p. 2, which is the first of a series of papers to be produced on the IGC by the Federal Trust (albeit from a federal perspective).

45. Ibid.

46. *Bulletin of the ECs*, no. 6 (1994), point 1.25.

47. Speech given by Mrs Thatcher at the College of Europe, Bruges, 20 September 1988.

48. W. Schäuble and K. Lamers, *Reflections on European Policy*, reproduced in K. Lamers, *A German Agenda for European Union* (London: Federal Trust and the Konrad Adenauer Stifung, 1994).

9. REGIONAL ORGANISATION OUTSIDE EUROPE

1. Membership currently comprises 35 member states from Northern, Central and Southern America. Cuba was suspended in 1962 but at the OAS Assembly in Brazil in June 1994, Costa Rica urged the opening of discussions on Cuba's readmittance, warning that the Organisation 'can no longer ignore the Cuban case'. Canada joined in January 1990 and Belize and Guyana in January 1991.

2. G. Pope Atkins, *Latin America in the International Political System* (New York, 1977) p. 308.

3. M. Margaret Ball, *The OAS in Transition* (Duke University Press, 1969) p. 5.

4. Cited ibid., p. 10.

5. G. Connell Smith, *The Inter-American System* (London, 1966) p. 15.

6. Pope Atkins, *Latin America*, pp. 322–5.

7. Bryce Wood, 'The Organisation of American States', in *The Yearbook of World Affairs, 1979* (London, 1979) p. 150.

8. G. Connell-Smith, 'The Organisation of American States', in A. Shlaim (ed.), *International Organisations in World Politics, Yearbook 1975* (London, 1976) p. 201.

9. In the amended Charter of 1967, which came into force in 1970, the relevant Articles are numbered 18 to 22.

10. Viron P. Vaky and Heraldo Munoz, *The Future of the Organization of American States* (New York, 1993) p. 10.

11. Cited in Connell-Smith, 'The Organisation of American States', p. 207.

12. I.L. Claude, 'The OAS, the UN and the United States', *International Conciliation* (March 1964).

13. Pope Atkins, *Latin America*, p. 332.

14. Ball, *The OAS in Transition*, pp. 471–2.

15. Ibid., pp. 479–80.

16. Pope Atkins, *Latin America*, pp. 330–1, Bryce Wood, 'Organisation of American States', pp. 157–9.

17. P. Calvert (ed.), *Political and Economic Encyclopaedia of South America and the Caribbean* (Longman, 1991).

18. Ibid., p. 12.

19. It is, however, fair to note as some observers have that the key to progress was not Charter reform but agreement among members on what should be done and commitment to do it. R. J. Bloomfield and A. F. Lowenthal, 'Inter-American Institutions in a Time of Change', *International Journal* (1990).

20. Declaration of Managua for the Promotion of Democracy and Development. Adopted at the fourth plenary session of the 23rd regular session of the OAS General Assembly, June 8 1993.

21. For a discussion of the work of the OAS in the field of technology transfer, see E. B. Haas, 'Technological Self-reliance for Latin America: the OAS Contribution', *International Organisation* (Autumn 1980) 541–70.

22. Vaky and Munoz, *The Future of the OAS*, p. 16.

23. Bloomfield and Lowenthal, 'Inter-American Institutions', p. 886.

24. Bryce Wood, 'Organisation of American States', p. 153.

25. Article 1 of the revised Charter. Text in A. J. Peaslee, *International Governmental Organisation*, vol. 1, part 1 (The Hague, 1974) pp. 1222–6.

26. F. Parkinson, 'International Economic Integration in Latin America and the Caribbean', *The Yearbook of World Affairs, 1977* (London, 1977) p. 255.

27. Pope Atkins, *Latin America*, p. 288.

28. Ibid.

29. Parkinson, 'International Economic Integration', p. 243.

30. P. Gunson, G. Chamberlain and A. Thompson, *The Dictionary of Contemporary Politics of Central America and the Caribbean* (London, 1991) p. 194.

31. Keesing's Record of World Events, vol. 36, p. 37502.

32. K. J. Middlebrook, 'Regional Organisations and Andean Economic Integration 1969–75', *Journal of Common Market Studies*, 17, no. 1 (September 1978) 78–80.

33. E. S. Milenky, 'The Cartagena Agreement in Transition', *The Yearbook of World Affairs, 1979* (London, 1979) p. 168.

34. Ibid.

35. Parkinson, 'International Economic Integration', p. 249.

36. R. Vargas-Hidalgo, 'The Crisis of the Andean Pact: Lessons for Integration among Developing Countries', *Journal of Common Market Studies*, 17, no. 3 (March 1979) 213–26.

37. Keesings Record of World Events, vol. 38, Reference Supplement, 1992.

38. G. C. Abbott, 'Integration and Viability in the Caribbean', *Journal of Commonwealth and Comparative Politics*, 29 (1991).

39. Ibid., p. 331.

40. Ibid., pp. 333–5.

41. I. Wallerstein, *Africa: the Politics of Unity* (New York, 1967).

42. I. Wallerstein, 'The Early Years of the OAU', *International Organisation* (Autumn 1966) 775.

43. N. J. Padelford, 'The Organisation of African Unity', *International Organisation* (Summer 1964) 526.

44. J. Mayall, 'African Unity and the OAU: The Place of a Political Myth in African Diplomacy', *The Yearbook of World Affairs 1973* (London, 1973) p. 120.

45. Cited in Peaslee, *International Governmental Organisation*, vol. 2 (1974) p. 1166.

46. S. Touval, 'The Organisation of African Unity and African Borders', *International Organisation* (Autumn 1967) 124.

47. M. Wolfers, *Politics in the Organisation of African Unity* (London, 1976) pp. 46–8.

48. On the history of this dispute and the OAU's role see P. B. Wild, 'The Organisation of African Unity and the Algeria–Morocco Border Conflict', *International Organisation* (1966) 18–36.

49. B. D. Meyers, 'Intraregional Conflict Management by the OAU', *International Organisation* (Summer 1974) 358–9.

50. Keesings Record of World Events, vol. 40 (1994) p. 39944.

51. Ibid. pp. 356–7.

52. For details of the OAU's response to the Biafran crisis, see Z. Cervenka, 'The OAU and the Nigerian Civil War', in Y. El-Ayouty (ed.), *The Organisation of African Unity After Ten Years* (New York, 1976) pp. 152–73.

53. Ibid.

54. Ibid., pp. 165–6.

55. L. T. Kapungu, 'The OAU's Support for the Liberation of Southern Africa', ibid, p. 136.

56. Wolfers, *Politics in the OAU*, p. 189.

57. Kapungu, 'The OAU's Support', p. 144.

58. Ibid., pp. 138–9.

59. C. Legum, 'The Organisation of African Unity: Success or Failure?', *International Affairs* (April 1975) 216.

60. Ibid., p. 217.

61. For a discussion of the work of the OAU's specialised commissions, see Wolfers, *Politics in the OAU*, pp. 91–119.

62. Meyers, 'Intraregional Conflict Management by the OAU', p. 369.

63. Adebayo Adedeji, 'Africa in the Nineties: A Decade for Socio-Economic Recovery and Transformation of Another Lost Decade?', 1989 Foundation Lecture to the Nigerian Institute of International Affairs, NIIA 1991, p. 7.

64. Ibid., p. 23.

65. O. J. B. Ojo, 'Nigeria and the Formation of ECOWAS', *International Organisation* (Autumn 1980) 571–604.

66. Cited in T.O. Elias, 'Economic Community of West Africa', in *The Yearbook of World Affairs, 1978* (London, 1978) p. 103.

67. Ibid., p. 104.

68. W. J. Feld and R. S. Jordan with L. Hurwitz, *International Organizations: A Comparative Approach*, 3rd edn (Westport, CT, 1994) pp. 97–8.

69. Ibid.

70. Ibid., p. 102

71. On the history of ASA, see B. K. Gordon, *The Dimensions of Conflict in South-east Asia* (New Jersey, 1966) pp. 162–87.

72. J. Wong, 'ASEAN's Experience in Regional Economic Cooperation', *Asian Development Review*, 3 (1985) 83.

73. H.C. Reichel, 'The European Community and ASEAN', *Aussenpolitik, English Edition*, 36, (1985) 193.

74. Catalogues of the reasons why non-European regional groupings have, in general, failed are provided by R. J. Langhammer, 'The Developing Countries and Regionalism', *Journal of Common Market Studies*, 30, no. 2 (June 1992) 214 and, particularly comprehensively, by A. Hazelwood, 'The East African Community' in A. M. El-Agraa (ed.), *International Economic Integration* (London, 1988) pp. 187–9.

75. For example, according to Reichel, 'The European Community and ASEAN', p. 193: 'ASEAN has essentially been a political community ... from the very beginning and has, in essence, remained so to this day'.

76. A. Broinowski (ed.), *ASEAN into the 1990s* (London, 1990) p. 18.

77. Ibid., p. 241.

78. Tan Sri M. Ghazali Shafie, 'Towards a Pacific Basin Community – a Malaysian Perception', Conference on New Foundations for Asian and Pacific Community, Pattaya, 12 December (1979).

79. These include, for example, the questions of the feasibility of integration of countries of different sizes and at different levels of development, the complementarity of ASEAN trade, the equitable distribution of benefits and investment and the potential clashes of political ideology.

80. 'Blood and Money', *Far Eastern Economic Review*, 147, no. 9 (1 March 1990) 8–9. The Malaysians also managed to upset the Thais by warning

Malaysian nationals not to visit the southern Thai 'red light' border areas because of the risk of AIDS.

81. 'Stormy Weather', *Far Eastern Economic Review*, 156, no. 30 (29 July 1993) 18–19.

82. 'Friction in the Club', *Far Eastern Economic Review*, 155, no. 42 (22 October 1992) 67.

83. Indonesian economist, Mohammad Sadli, quoted in ibid. For a security-focused discussion of intra-ASEAN tensions see T. Huxley, *Insecurity in the ASEAN Region* (London: RUSI, 1993) Whitehall Paper 23, pp. 11–14.

84. See, for example, 'ASEAN's Embrace', *Far Eastern Economic Review*, 154, no. 46, 14 (November 1991) 19.

85. Huxley, *Insecurity in the ASEAN Region*, pp. 74–5.

86. The principal disputes are outlined in ibid., pp. 11 and 29–30.

87. This involved not only ASEAN but also its seven dialogue partners together with China, Russia, Vietnam, Laos and Papua New Guinea.

10. INTERNATIONAL REGIMES

1. The literature on regimes is now vast, but the following are particularly useful: Oran Young, 'International Regimes: Problems of Concept Formation', *World Politics* (April 1978) 331–56; Oran Young, 'The Politics of International Regime Formation', *International Organization* (Summer 1989) 349–76; Stephen D. Krasner (ed.), *International Regimes* (Ithaca and London, 1983); Joseph M. Grieco, *Cooperation Among Nations. Europe, America and Non-tariff Barriers To Trade* (Ithaca and London, 1990); Oran Young, *International Cooperation. Building Regimes for Natural Resources and the Environment* (Ithaca and London, 1989); Jock A. Finlayson and Mark W. Zacher, *Managing International Markets. Developing Countries and the Commodity Trade Regime* (New York, 1988).

2. Stephen D. Krasner, 'Structural Causes and Regime Consequences: Regimes as Intervening Variables', in Krasner, *International Regimes*, p. 2.

3. See D. M. Leive, *International Regulatory Regimes* (Lexington, MA, 1976) especially Introduction and vol. 1, pp. 3–70 and, for details of the proposed regime for the moon, see *UN Chronicle*, XVII, no.2 (March 1980).

4. B. Tew, *International Monetary Cooperation 1945–70* (London, 1970).

5. D. T. Llewellyn, 'The International Monetary System Since 1972: Structural Change and Financial Innovation', in M. Posner (ed.) *Problems of International Money 1972–85* (International Monetary Fund, Washington DC, 1986).

6. See K. P. Sauvant and H. Hasenpflug (eds), *The New International Economic Order* (London, 1977), and L. Anell and B. Nygren, *The Developing Countries and World Economic Order* (London, 1980).

7. A. Oxley, *The Challenge of Free Trade* (New York, 1990).

8. J. J. Schott, assisted by J. W. Buurman, *The Uruguay Round: An Assessment* (Institute for International Economics, Washington DC, 1994).

9. Ibid.

10. *UN Conference on the Law of the Sea: Official Records* (New York, 1958).

11. B. Buzan, 'From the fire to the frying pan? Innovations in large-scale negotiating techniques at UNCLOS III', Paper at the British International Studies Association Conference, 1979.

12. *The Times*, 30 August 1980.

13. *Economic Implications of Seabed Mineral Development in the International Area*, Report of Secretary-General, May 1974.

14. *Third United Nations Conference on Law of Sea to Meet in New York*, United Nations Information Centre, BR/80/9, March 1980.

15. M. W. Zacher and J. G. McConnell, 'Down to the sea with stakes: the evolving law of the sea and the future of the deep seabed regime', *Ocean Development and International Law*, 21 (1990) 71–103.

16. 'Law of the Sea', *Current Policy*, no. 371 (Jan–Feb. 1982) United States Department of State, Bureau of Public Affairs, Washington DC.

17. D. H. Anderson, 'Efforts to Ensure Universal Participation in the United Nations Convention of the Law of the Sea', *International and Comparative Law Quarterly*, 15 (1993) 654, and B. H. Oxman, 'United States Interests in the Law of the Sea Convention', *American Journal of International Law*, 88, No. 1 (Jan. 1994) 167–78.

18. NPT in J. Simpson (ed.), *Nuclear Non-proliferation. An Agenda for the 1990s* (Cambridge 1987) pp. 215–21.

19. P. van Ham, *Managing Non-proliferation Regimes in the 1990s* (London, 1993) p. 38.

20. J. Simpson, 'The Nuclear Non-proliferation Regime – Options and Opportunities', *Disarmament*, XVI, No. 2 (1993).

21. J. Bone, 'Nuclear treaty under threat', *The Times*, London, 27 January 1995, p. 12.

22. J. Adams, 'Key Challenges to the Nuclear Non-proliferation Regime in the 1990s', unpublished dissertation, Graduate School of International Studies, University of Birmingham, 1995, pp. 23–7.

23. Ibid., pp. 14–18.

24. P. Bracken, 'Nuclear Weapons and State Survival in North Korea', *Survival*, 35, No. 3 (Autumn 1993), and *Financial Times*, 19 October 1994.

25. M. S. McDougal, *Human Rights and World Public Order* (New Haven and London, 1980) pp. 238–46.

26. In the Preamble and Articles 1, 13, 55, 62, 68 and 76. See also F. Newman, 'Interpreting the Human Rights Clause of the UN Charter', *Human Rights Journal*, V. No. 2 (1972).

27. For the text of the Covenants, see E. Luard (ed.), *The International Protection of Human Rights* (London, 1967) pp. 333–63.

28. General Assembly Document, A/10235, 7 October 1975, pp. 12–13, and J. Donnelly, *International Human Rights* (Boulder, CO, 1993) p. 62.

29. D.P. Forsythe, *The Internationalization of Human Rights* (Lexington, MA, 1991) pp. 55–86.

30. See, for example, E. Zvoodgo, 'A Third World View', in D. Kommers and G. Loesher (eds), *American Foreign Policy and Human Rights* (Indiana, 1979) ch. 5, and R. J. Vincent, *Human Rights and International Relations* (Cambridge, 1986) *passim.*

31. Donnelly, *International Human Rights*, p. 91.

32. See V. Chkhikvadze, 'Human Rights and Non-interference in the Internal Affairs of States', *International Affairs* (Moscow) No. 2 (1978).

33. For a detailed discussion of the American human rights system, see L. J. Le Blanc, *The OAS and the Promotion and Protection of Human Rights* (The Hague, 1977). See also Forsythe, *Internationalization of Human Rights*, pp. 87–118.

34. Forsythe, *Internationalization of Human Rights*, p. 88.

35. V. . Vaky and H. Munoz, *The Future of the Organization of American States* (New York, 1993) p. 10.

36. Forsythe, *Internationalization of Human Rights*, p. 106, credits a strongly critical Commission report on Nicaragua with a crucial role in Somoza's downfall.

37. J. G. Townsend, 'A Latin American Perspective', in F. E. Dowrick (ed.), *Human Rights* (Westmead, 1979) pp. 107–24.

38. The number would have been 35 but consideration of Russia's application to join was postponed because of the situation in Chechenia.

39. For a discussion of the Commission's procedure for examining admissibility, see F. G. Jacobs, *The European Convention on Human Rights* (Oxford, 1975) pp. 218–51.

Index